United States
Office of Personnel Management

Citizenship
Laws of the
World

Fredonia Books
Amsterdam, The Netherlands

Citizenship Laws of the World

by
United States Office of Personnel Management

ISBN: 1-4101-0807-4

Reprinted from the 2001 edition

Fredonia Books
Amsterdam, The Netherlands
http://www.fredoniabooks.com

CONTENTS

Introduction and
General Information

INTRODUCTION

This directory provides synopses of the citizenship laws for most of the world's countries. We obtained information for this directory from embassies, the Library of Congress, and the Department of State. The directory also provides the address, telephone number, and fax number of most countries' diplomatic representatives.

We have made this document as accurate and up-to-date as our resources have allowed. The information contained in this directory should not be considered formal legal advice. It is intended to serve as a quick reference document, summarizing the citizenship laws of foreign nations and providing contact information. You should direct detailed or specific questions to a nation's specific diplomatic representatives.

Readers should understand that citizenship laws are often amended to keep in step with political changes. A considerable time lapse between the enactment of new laws and their actual implementation is not uncommon. Moreover, it is not unusual to encounter differences between a nation's laws and its actual practices.

STRUCTURE OF DIRECTORY

This directory is an alphabetic listing of countries. The formal names of some countries are replaced by their more commonly known names. For example, the UNITED KINGDOM OF GREAT BRITAIN AND NORTHERN IRELAND is the formal name of England, Wales, Scotland, and Northern Ireland. In this directory it is listed as UNITED KINGDOM.

Most countries have changed their names at one time or another throughout history. For example, the country formerly known as Burma is now known as Myanmar, while the Ivory Coast is now Cote d'Ivoire. We have listed countries by their current names. In some instances, to avoid confusion, we have listed the most recent former names of nations next to their current names.

3

READING A COUNTRY ENTRY

STRUCTURE: Information in each country listing is presented as follows:

- CITIZENSHIP
- DUAL CITIZENSHIP
- LOSS OF CITIZENSHIP
- ADDRESS

CITIZENSHIP: This section lists the various methods by which a person may obtain the citizenship of a country.

1. **Citizenship by Birth:** Citizenship is granted due to birth within the country. The legal term for this is "*jus solis.*" In most cases, there are few stipulations on citizenship being granted. Birth in the country automatically confers citizenship regardless of the parents' citizenship or status.

> In the case of U.S. citizens born abroad in a country under the principle of *jus solis,* the question arises as to whether the other citizenship continues after the child has left the country of birth. For definitive answers to questions such as this, contact the proper embassy or the U.S. Immigration and Naturalization Service.

2. **Citizenship by Descent:** Citizenship of a nation is passed on to a child based upon at least one of the parents being a citizen of that nation, regardless of the child's actual country of birth. The term for this is "*jus sanguinis.*"

Though most countries adhere to the principle of citizenship by descent, they differ on some factors (father's vs. mother's rights, citizenship of one or both parents, the marital status of the parents, and others).

> As a person reaches an age of maturity, continuing the condition of citizenship by birth (*jus solis*) or citizenship by descent (*jus sanguinis*) may depend on factors unique to the nation of that citizenship.

3. **Citizenship by Naturalization:** This is a formal process by which persons may acquire the citizenship of a country. The process varies and citizenship is not guaranteed. Basic rules may include a period of residence, renunciation of other citizenship, and familiarity with the language and customs of the country.

4. **Citizenship by Marriage:** By some nations' laws, upon marriage, a person is entitled to become a naturalized citizen of their spouse's country without having to fulfill other naturalization requirements. These laws are often different for males than for females.

5. **Citizenship by Registration:** In some instances, A person may acquire citizenship by registration with the national government without meeting all

naturalization requirements for that nation. Usually these persons possess blood ties to the country through immediate relatives who are citizens, or by marriage to a citizen of that country.

DUAL CITIZENSHIP: Dual citizenship is the simultaneous possession of two citizenships. It arises because there is no common international law relating to citizenship. The most common reasons for dual citizenship are these:

- Marriage to a citizen of another country.
- Adoption by parents who are citizens of another country.
- Birth in a country that grants citizenship by birth, to parents who are citizens of a country that grants citizenship by descent.

Not all nations recognize that their citizens may possess simultaneous citizenship of another country. In this directory, dual citizenship is addressed in the individual country listings as either RECOGNIZED or NOT RECOGNIZED by that country. The EXCEPTION entries list any exceptions to recognition or non-recognition of dual citizenship.

LOSS OF CITIZENSHIP: This category is divided into two parts, the *voluntary* and the *involuntary* loss of citizenship.

1. **Voluntary Loss of Citizenship:** Most countries have laws which specify how a citizen may voluntarily renounce citizenship. Precise information on renouncing citizenship may be obtained from the country's embassy or consulate. In most cases, the person can do all the necessary paperwork through the embassy or consulate. Under the laws of some nations the person must return to the home country to complete the renunciation process.

> Voluntary renunciation of citizenship may be very difficult for citizens of some countries. The U.S. Department of State may be of assistance to citizens who wish to gather information concerning the voluntary renunciation of citizenship of a particular country.

2. **Involuntary Loss of Citizenship:** This entry lists the reasons a particular country may choose to withdraw the citizenship of one of its citizens.

Most countries' laws dictate the loss of citizenship upon a citizen's voluntary acquisition of another country's citizenship. The interpretation of what constitutes "voluntary" is not uniform, however. In certain countries it is not considered voluntary unless the person makes an explicit declaration of the citizenship of the other country. For example, in Austria a person automatically obtains Austrian citizenship when appointed as a professor at an Austrian university. Some countries interpret this as "involuntary" citizenship and, according to their laws, citizenship is not lost. Other countries state that if a citizen obtains another nationality, and makes no effort to renounce it, citizenship is lost.

Loss of naturalized citizenship usually occurs when the naturalized citizen:
- Resided for a specified time in another country.
- Obtained citizenship through fraud or false statements.
- Did not renounce previous citizenship.

Even if a nation's laws state that under certain circumstances citizenship is automatically removed, until officials of the government or embassy are informed, the embassy will probably still retain that person's name in its citizenship records.

ADDRESS OF THE EMBASSY: This entry gives the address, phone number, and fax number of the representatives of the country in the United States. Most nations have an embassy in Washington, DC; some countries have a United Nations Mission in New York City or a trade mission elsewhere.

There are some countries that either do not have a representative in the United States or which desire that their representatives not be contacted. They have provided us with no address or contact information. Two sources of information about these nations are the Library of Congress's International Law Library and the Department of State's Office of Consular Affairs. Although these are not primary sources of information, they can be helpful in resolving citizenship questions.

GENERAL INFORMATION ON DUAL CITIZENSHIP

PROBLEMS WITH DUAL CITIZENSHIP: Dual citizenship is not particularly desirable in many countries because a dual citizen is sometimes placed in a situation in which their obligation to the country is in conflict with the laws of the other country. An example is the problem of conflicting military obligations. In addition, a person's dual citizenship may hamper efforts to provide diplomatic or consular protection when the person is abroad.

The majority of countries do not recognize dual citizenship. That is, their governments do not recognize a person's prerogative to the rights, privileges, or immunities that may be the prerogatives of citizens of the other nation.

HOW DUAL CITIZENSHIP IS ACQUIRED:

1. **Dual Citizenship by Birth:** A child born abroad to United States citizens will acquire not only United States citizenship but perhaps the citizenship of the country in which the child was born (*jus solis*). Similarly, a child born in the United States to foreign parents may acquire both U.S. citizenship (*jus solis*) and the citizenship of the parents (*jus sanguinis*).

2. **Dual Citizenship by Marriage:** Dual citizenship can occur when a person automatically acquires their spouse's citizenship upon marriage.

Some countries provide that citizenship will be lost upon the voluntary acquisition of another citizenship. In the case of citizenship by marriage, some nations consider that, simply by marriage, their citizen did not voluntarily acquire the foreign citizenship and that, therefore, their original citizenship is not lost.

3. **Dual Citizenship by Naturalization:** A country may allow citizens who obtain foreign citizenship to retain their original citizenship. The country from which the person is obtaining their second citizenship may not require the person to renounce their former citizenship.

4. **Dual Citizenship by Treaty:** Some countries have agreements with certain other countries recognizing dual citizenships among their respective populations.

5. **Dual Citizenship by Default:** A person naturalized elsewhere without the approval of the country of origin might be considered to retain their original citizenship. If the original country is not notified that another citizenship has been acquired, it is possible for both citizenships to be officially documented.

RESOLVING DUAL CITIZENSHIP:

1. **Majority Divestiture:** This option allows a person with dual citizenship, upon reaching the age of majority (i.e., age of legal adulthood), to decide which citizenship to keep. Many countries have this provision in their constitution, charter, or in their citizenship laws. This is often used in cases of dual citizenship which arise due to adoption.

2. **Generational Requirement:** This consists of limiting the principle of citizenship by descent (*jus sanguinis*) to the first or second generations of individuals born and residing abroad.

3. **Registration:** In countries where non-native children must be registered at their parent's country's consular office shortly after birth, omitting this registration documentation can make it impossible or difficult for the child to later acquire the citizenship of either country.

4. **Delayed Conferment of Citizenship:** Persons, not born in the country where their parents are citizens, can be given the right to acquire their parents' citizenship upon renunciation of any other citizenship.

5. **Diplomatic Restrictions:** Children of diplomatic representatives are prevented by international law from acquiring the *jus solis* citizenship of the country in which their parents are serving.

6. **Restriction By Law:** A country may forbid its citizens to become naturalized in a foreign state, except with the original nation's permission When permission is granted, the person loses their former citizenship.

7. **Administrative Option:** A country may grant conditional freedom of expatriation and automatically release from its allegiance persons who become naturalized citizens of another country.

THE FOLLOWING PAGES USE THE UNITED STATES CITIZENSHIP LAWS ENTRY AS AN EXAMPLE TO ILLUSTRATE THE LAYOUT OF COUNTRY ENTRIES.

THE UNITED STATES ENTRY DOES NOT APPEAR LATER IN THE COUNTRY LISTINGS

UNITED STATES

CITIZENSHIP: Citizenship is based upon Title 8 of U.S. Code 1401 - 1409, dated 1986.

- **BY BIRTH:** Child born within the territory of the United States, regardless of the citizenship of the parents.

- **BY DESCENT:**
  - Child born abroad, both of whose parents are citizens of the United States, and one of whom resided in the United States before the birth of the child.
  - Child born abroad, one of whose parents is a citizen of the United States who resided in the United States for at least five years before the birth of the child.

- **BY NATURALIZATION:** United States citizenship may be acquired upon fulfillment of the following conditions:
  - Person must be 18 years old, have resided in the United States for at least five years as a lawful permanent resident, be able to speak, read, and write English, be of good moral character, be familiar with the history and culture of the country, be attached to the principles of the United States Constitution, and have renounced former citizenship.
  - Foreign citizens who marry citizens of the United States need only reside in the United States for three years, but must still fulfill the other conditions.

- **OTHER:** Certain provisions for granting citizenship have been extended to persons who have performed specific military service to this country. For more information, contact the U.S. Immigration and Naturalization Service.

DUAL CITIZENSHIP: RECOGNIZED

Based on the U.S. Department of State regulation on dual citizenship (7 FM 1162), the Supreme Court of the United States has stated that dual citizenship is a "status long recognized in the law" and that "a person may have and exercise rights of nationality in two countries and be subject to the responsibilities of both. The mere fact he asserts the rights of one citizenship does not without more mean that he renounces the other," (Kawakita v. U.S., 343 U.S. 717) (1952).

The Immigration and Nationality Act (INA) does not define dual citizenship or take a position for it or against it. There has been no prohibition against dual citizenship, but some provisions of the INA and earlier U.S. nationality laws were designed to reduce situations in which dual citizenship exists.

United States law does not contain any provisions requiring U.S. citizens who are born with dual citizenship or who acquire a second citizenship at an early age to choose one or the other when they become adults (Mandeli v. Acheson, 344 U.S. 133) (1952). The current citizenship laws of the United States do not specifically refer to dual citizenship.

While recognizing the existence of dual citizenship and permitting Americans to have other citizenships, the U.S. Government does not endorse dual citizenship as a matter of policy because of the problems that it may cause. Claims of other countries on dual-national U.S. citizens often place them in situations where their obligations to one country are in conflict with the laws of the other.

LOSS OF CITIZENSHIP:

- **VOLUNTARY:** Voluntary renunciation of United States citizenship is permitted by law. However, renunciation can only be made at a U.S. Consulate outside the United States.

- **INVOLUNTARY:** The following are grounds for involuntary loss of United States citizenship:
    - Person commits treason against the United States.
    - Person takes an oath of allegiance to a foreign state.
    - Person joins the armed forces of a country at war with the U.S.

ANY QUESTIONS concerning citizenship policy of the U.S. or its territories should be sent to the address below:

U.S. Department of State
Office of Consular Affairs
Washington, DC 20520

Telephone: 202-647-4000

Country Listings

IN THE COUNTRY LISTINGS THAT FOLLOW, THE WORDS
CITIZENSHIP and **NATIONALITY** ARE SYNONYMOUS,
AS ARE THE WORDS **CITIZEN** and **NATIONAL**.

THE INITIALS **SSR** REFER TO SOME STATES AS
"SOVIET SOCIALIST REPUBLIC," THAT IS, FORMER MEMBER
STATES OF THE FORMER SOVIET UNION.
SUCH USE IS ARCHAIC.

UKC-COMMONWEALTH NATIONS ARE, OR HAVE BEEN,
MEMBERS OF THE UNITED KINGDOM AND COLONIES OR THE
COMMONWEALTH OF NATIONS. CITIZENSHIP STATUS IN THESE
STATES IS OFTEN COMPLEX DUE TO THE VARIETY OF NATIONAL
STATUS A PERSON MAY HAVE.

An individual may be a citizen of the individual state itself,
a British Dependent Territory Citizen, a British Overseas Citizen, a
British Subject, a British Protected Person, a Commonwealth Citizen,
or have dual citizenship in combination with one of these.

A careful examination of the citizenship basis of UKC-Commonwealth
nationals may be necessary to determine their status with accuracy.

AFGHANISTAN

CITIZENSHIP: Citizenship laws are based upon the Official Gazette of the Ministry of Justice for the Republic of Afghanistan dated March 19, 1992.

- **BY BIRTH**: Birth within the territory of Afghanistan does not automatically confer citizenship. Exception is a child of unknown/stateless parents.

- **BY DESCENT**: Child whose mother or father is a citizen, regardless of the country of birth.

- **MARRIAGE**: Foreign national who marries a citizen of Afghanistan is granted citizenship upon application.

- **BY NATURALIZATION**: Afghan citizenship may be acquired upon fulfillment of the following conditions: Person was born in Afghanistan and has resided continually in country for at least five years.

DUAL CITIZENSHIP: NOT RECOGNIZED.
Exceptions: A former citizen of Afghanistan, who fled the country due to political instability or war and has acquired new citizenship, may still hold "unofficial" Afghan citizenship. This is recognition that those who fled the country might some day want to return as Afghan citizens without losing new citizenship.

The Afghani spouse of a foreign national is not required to renounce Afghan citizenship unless demanded by the spouse's country.

LOSS OF CITIZENSHIP:

- **VOLUNTARY**: Voluntary renunciation of Afghan citizenship is permitted by law. Contact the Embassy for details and required paperwork. The following persons are not allowed to renounce citizenship:
  - Person who has continuing financial obligations to the government or other institutions.
  - Person who has been convicted of a crime and sentenced to jail.
  - Persons involved in national security, whose loss to the country might endanger Afghan security.

- **INVOLUNTARY**: The following is grounds for involuntary loss of Afghan citizenship: Person voluntarily acquires foreign citizenship and does not fall under the exempted status described under "Dual Citizenship." Persons concerned with dual citizenship should not assume their Afghan citizenship was lost by default. Embassy should be contacted and citizenship formally renounced.

ANY QUESTIONS concerning citizenship, or requests for renunciation of citizenship, should be directed to the address below:

Embassy of the Republic of Afghanistan, Consular Section
2341 Wyoming Ave., NW
Washington, DC 20008

Embassy/Consular Section: 202-234-3770/71
Fax: 202-328-3516

www.afghan-web.com

ALBANIA

CITIZENSHIP: *Current Albanian policy toward citizenship is being debated in Parliament. According to the Albanian Consulate, the new Constitution will be the basis for all laws. Out of this Constitution will come the country's citizenship laws.*

ANY QUESTIONS concerning citizenship, or requests for renunciation of citizenship, should be directed to the address below:

Embassy of the Republic of Albania
1511 K Street, NW, Suite 1000
Washington, DC 20005

Embassy/Consular Telephone: 202-223-4942/8187 or 202-393-6255
Fax: 202-628-7342

www.undp.tirana.al
www.albanian.com

ALGERIA

CITIZENSHIP: Citizenship is based upon the Code of Algerian Nationality, dated December 15, 1978.

- **BY BIRTH**: Birth within the territory of Algeria does not automatically confer citizenship. The exception is a child born to unknown or stateless parents.

- **BY DESCENT**:
  - Child of an Algerian father, regardless of the country of birth.
  - Child of an Algerian mother and an unknown or stateless father, regardless of the country of birth.

- **BY NATURALIZATION**: Algerian citizenship may be acquired upon fulfillment of the following conditions: Person has resided in Algeria for at least seven years, (18 months if the person was born abroad to an Algerian mother or father), is of good morality, good health, has no criminal convictions, is at least 21 years of age, has assimilated into Algerian society and has a secure means of support.

DUAL CITIZENSHIP: NOT RECOGNIZED.

LOSS OF CITIZENSHIP:

- **VOLUNTARY**: Voluntary renunciation of Algerian citizenship is permitted by law. Contact the Embassy for details and required paperwork.

- **INVOLUNTARY**: The following are grounds for involuntary loss of Algerian citizenship:
  - Person voluntarily acquires a foreign citizenship.
  - Person's employment with a foreign nation or company is not in the interest of Algeria.
  - Naturalized citizen is convicted of a crime (abroad or in Algeria) and sentenced to five years or more.
  - Naturalized citizen is involved in acts incompatible with the interests of Algeria.

ANY QUESTIONS concerning citizenship, or requests for renunciation of citizenship, should be directed to the address below:

Embassy of the Democratic and Popular Republic of Algeria
Consular Section
2118 Kalorama Rd., NW
Washington, DC 20008

Embassy/Consular Telephone: 202-265-2800
Fax: 202-667-2174

ANDORRA

CITIZENSHIP: Per information provided by the U.S. Consulate General in Barcelona, Spain: the information provided does not include recent modifications approved by the Andorran Parliament on October 27, 1992, but never implemented.

- **BY BIRTH**: Birth within the principality of Andorra does not automatically confer citizenship. The exceptions are children of unknown parents or children born in Andorra if at least one parent was also born in Andorra.

- **BY DESCENT**: Child, at least one of whose parents is a citizen of Andorra, regardless of the country of birth.

- **BY NATURALIZATION**: Andorran citizenship is very difficult to obtain. The following are those most easily able to apply for citizenship:
  - Child born outside Andorra to an Andorran mother or father who was born outside Andorra.
  - Those married to an Andorran who has lived at least three years in the country.
  - Child age 14 and under, adopted by an Andorran.
  - Application by individuals who have 25 years of residence in Andorra.

DUAL CITIZENSHIP: NOT RECOGNIZED.
Exception: Due to the fact that the Andorran government has no way of knowing if a person has become a citizen of another country, dual citizenship can arise through default. For those who must be sure of no dual citizenship, it is best to contact the Andorran government and inform them of the change of citizenship.

LOSS OF CITIZENSHIP:

- **VOLUNTARY**: Voluntary renunciation of citizenship is permitted by law under the following conditions: Person has established residency abroad, has acquired another nationality, and has renounced citizenship in front of a notary. Given that Andorra has no representatives in the United States, it is assumed that renunciation must take place in Andorra.

- **INVOLUNTARY**: The following are grounds for involuntary loss of Andorran citizenship:
  - Person voluntarily acquires a foreign citizenship. (See "Dual Citizenship: Exception")
  - Person voluntarily enrolls in a foreign army.
  - Person holds a foreign political office.

ANY QUESTIONS concerning citizenship or information about Andorra should be directed to the address below:

Embassy of the Principality of Andorra to the United States
2 United Nations Plaza (25th Floor)
New York, NY 10017

Or

U.S. Embassy Madrid
Serrano 75
28006-Madrid

Telephone: 212-750-8064
Fax: 212-750-6630

Telephone: 34-91-587-2200

www.andorra.ad/cniavk.html

ANGOLA

CITIZENSHIP: Citizenship laws are based upon Law #13/91 dated May 13, 1991.

- **BY BIRTH**: Birth within the Republic of Angola does not automatically confer citizenship. The only exception is a child born in Angola to unknown or stateless parents.

- **BY DESCENT**: Child at least one of whose parents is a citizen of Angola, regardless of the country of birth.

- **MARRIAGE**: A foreign national who marries a citizen of Angola may apply for citizenship after marriage. A foreign spouse who obtains Angolan citizenship upon marriage may keep the citizenship in the event of a divorce or annulment if the marriage was entered into in good faith

- **BY NATURALIZATION**: Angolan citizenship may be acquired upon fulfillment of the following conditions: Person is of legal age (18), has resided in Angola for at least 10 years collectively, has an established means of support or livelihood, and is capable of integrating into Angolan society.

DUAL CITIZENSHIP: NOT RECOGNIZED.
Exception: Child born abroad of Angolan parents, who obtains the nationality of the country of birth, may retain dual citizenship until reaching the age of 18, when one citizenship must be chosen.

LOSS OF CITIZENSHIP:

- **VOLUNTARY**: Voluntary renunciation of Angolan citizenship is permitted by law. Contact the Embassy for details and required paperwork. Proof of new citizenship is required.

- **INVOLUNTARY**: The following are grounds for involuntary loss of Angolan citizenship:
    - Person voluntarily acquires foreign citizenship.
    - Naturalized citizen is convicted of crimes against the State.
    - Naturalized citizen serves in the military of a foreign State.
    - Naturalized citizenship was obtained by fraud or false statements.

ANY QUESTIONS concerning citizenship, or requests for renunciation of citizenship, should be directed to the address below:

Embassy of the Republic of Angola
Consular Section
1899 L St., NW STE 500
Washington, DC 20036

Embassy/Consular Telephone: 202-785-1156
Fax: 202-785-1258

www.angola.org

ANTIGUA AND BARBUDA

CITIZENSHIP: Citizenship is based upon the Citizenship Law of Antigua and Barbuda, dated November 1, 1981. (UKC-Commonwealth Nation). Automatic citizenship for:

> Persons Born On or Before October 31, 1981...
> - ...in Antigua and Barbuda.
> - ...outside the nation if either parent was a citizen of Antigua and Barbuda, and
> - Citizens of the UKC with particular ties to Antigua, other than those listed above. (Contact Embassy when questions arise.)

- **BY BIRTH**: Child born after October 31, 1981, in the territory of Antigua and Baruda, regardless of the nationality of the parents. The exceptions are the children born to diplomatic personnel.

- **BY DESCENT**: Child born abroad, after October 31, 1981, at least one of whose parents was a citizen of Antigua and Barbuda.

- **REGISTRATION**: The following persons are eligible to obtain citizenship through registration after October 31, 1981:
  - Person married to a citizen of Antigua and Barbuda at least three years and the marriage is still subsisting and such person is not living apart from the spouse.
  - Commonwealth citizen who resided in Antigua and Barbuda for more than seven years continuously.

- **BY NATURALIZATION**: *No information was provided.*

DUAL CITIZENSHIP: RECOGNIZED. A citizen shall not, solely on the ground that they are or become a citizen of another country, be deprived of citizenship, refused registration as a citizen; or required to renounce citizenship of the other country, by or under any law. The citizen shall not be refused a passport of Antigua and Barbuda or have such a passport withdrawn, cancelled, or impounded solely on the ground that the person is in possession of a passport issued by some other country of which they are a citizen or be required to surrender or be prohibited from acquiring a passport issued by some other country of which they are a citizen before being issued a passport of Antigua and Barbuda or as a condition of retaining such a passport.

LOSS OF CITIZENSHIP:

- **VOLUNTARY**: Voluntary renunciation of Antiguan and Barbudan citizenship is permitted by Parliament. Contact the Embassy for details and required paperwork.

- **INVOLUNTARY**: The following are grounds for involuntary loss of naturalized Antiguan and Barbudan citizenship:
  - Person obtains citizenship through fraud or false statement.
  - Person is convicted of sedition or treason against Antigua and Barbuda.

ANY QUESTIONS concerning citizenship should be directed to the address below:

Embassy of Antigua and Barbuda
Consular Section
3216 New Mexico Ave, NW
Washington, DC 20016
Embassy/Consular Telephone:
       202-362-5211/5166/5122

Fax: 202-362-5225
embantigua@aol.com
www.antigua-barbuda.com

ARGENTINA

CITIZENSHIP: Argentine citizenship is based upon Argentine Citizenship Law #346.

- **BY BIRTH**:
    - Child born in Argentina, except to accredited ministers of foreign powers.
    - Child born in Argentine legations or on Argentine warships.
    - Child born in neutral waters on ships flying the Argentine flag.

- **BY DESCENT**: Child born abroad, both of whose parents are Argentine citizens.

- **BY NATURALIZATION**: Argentine citizenship can be applied for in two ways:
    - Person must reside within the Republic for at least two years.
    - Person must have married an Argentine citizen. (This does not automatically confer citizenship, and spouse must still fulfill the two-year residency requirement.)

DUAL CITIZENSHIP: NOT RECOGNIZED.
Exception: Two groups are recognized as dual citizens. The first are children (18 and under), born abroad, who acquire citizenship of birth country. Upon reaching maturity at age 18, however, a declaration of allegiance must be made to one country. Citizens of Spain can hold dual citizenship per agreement with Argentina.

LOSS OF CITIZENSHIP:

- **VOLUNTARY**: Per Argentine consular office, citizenship can only be renounced in the capital, Buenos Aires. Papers must be signed at the police station and then the individual must appear before a judge where the renunciation must be accepted by the Argentine government.

- **INVOLUNTARY**: The following are grounds for involuntary loss of Argentine citizenship:
    - Person acquires foreign citizenship, but does not fall under "Dual Citizenship."
    - Person accepts employment or honors from a foreign government without permission.
    - Person commits fraudulent bankruptcy or has an infamous sentence.

ANY QUESTIONS concerning citizenship, or requests for renunciation of citizenship, should be directed to the address below:

The Embassy of the Argentine Republic
Consular Section
1600 New Hampshire Ave., NW
Washington, DC 20009

Embassy Telephone: 202-238-6400
Consular Telephone: 202-238-6460/63/64
Fax: 202-238-6471

ARMENIA

CITIZENSHIP: Citizenship laws are based upon the Constitution of Armenia dated July 5, 1995, and the Citizenship Law dated November 26, 1995.

- **BY RECOGNITION**:
  - Citizens of the former SSR-Armenia living permanently in the Republic of Armenia who have not acquired citizenship in another country.
  - People having no citizenship and living permanently in the Republic of Armenia during the 3 years before the present law came into effect, or citizens of the former USSR who apply for citizenship.
  - Citizens of the former SSR-Armenia who have lived abroad since September 21, 1991, have not acquired citizenship of another country, are who were registered in the Consulate before the present law came into effect.

- **BY BIRTH**:
  - A child, one of whose parents is a citizen and the other is unknown or a person having no citizenship, acquires citizenship of the Republic of Armenia.
  - The citizenship of a child, one of whose parents is an Armenian citizen and one a foreign citizen, will be decided by the written agreement of both parents. In the absence of agreement, the child acquires Armenian citizenship or no citizenship at all.

- **BY DESCENT**:
  - Child whose parents are both citizens of Armenia is a citizen regardless of birthplace.
  - A child under 14 years old, whose parents acquire the citizenship of Armenia, acquires citizenship as well.
  - A child adopted by citizens of the Republic of Armenia acquires Armenian citizenship.

- **BY NATURALIZATION**: Armenian citizenship may be acquired upon fulfillment of the following conditions:
  - Person must be 18 years old.
  - Person must have lived in Armenia for the last 3 years prior to application.
  - Person must be able to communicate in Armenian.
  - Person must be familiar with the Constitution of Armenia.

  - **Exceptions** to these conditions are granted for the following people:
    - A person who has married a citizen, or has a child, father, or mother who is a citizen of the Republic of Armenia.
    - A person whose parents are citizens, or was born in Armenia, and who within 3 years of their 18th birthday applies for Armenian citizenship.
    - A person who is Armenian by birth and has taken residence in the Republic of Armenia.
    - A person may resume their renounced citizenship through application.
    - Collective acquisition of citizenship is possible according to a decree of the President of the Republic.

ARMENIA (cont.)

DUAL CITIZENSHIP: NOT RECOGNIZED

LOSS OF CITIZENSHIP:

- **VOLUNTARY**:
    - A citizen may voluntarily change their citizenship except when under criminal investigation, if a court verdict will be issued concerning them, if giving up citizenship interferes with the interests of national security, or if the person has unfulfilled duties connected with the interests of the state, enterprises, organizations, or citizens.
    - A child under 14, whose parents' citizenship is renounced, loses citizenship if the child then acquires citizenship of another country.
    - In a case when parents have changed their citizenship, a child 14 to18 years old must consent to the same change in their own citizenship.

- **INVOLUNTARY**:
    - Citizen has lived abroad for the past seven years, has failed to register at the consulate.
    - Citizenship acquired citizenship by breaking the law, using false references, or false documents.

ANY QUESTIONS concerning citizenship, or requests for renunciation of citizenship, should be directed to the address below:

The Embassy of the Republic of Armenia
Consular Section
2225 R Street, NW
Washington, DC 20008

Embassy/Consular Telephone: 202-319-1976
Fax: 202-319-2982

AUSTRALIA

CITIZENSHIP: Based on the Australian Citizenship Act of 1948. Since 1948 there have been numerous legislative and administrative changes, but the critical factor is usually the date of birth of the applicant and the citizenship status of the parents. (UKC-Commonwealth)

Due to the numerous changes to criteria associated with citizenship status and eligibility, for further information it is essential that interested parties contact the Australian Department of Immigration and Multicultural Affairs (DIMA).

- **BY BIRTH**:
    - On January 26, 1949 Australian Law provided for acquisition of Australian citizenship by certain persons who were British subjects immediately before that date. Persons who were non-British residents at that time need to contact DIMA for further assistance.
    - From January 26, 1949, until August 19, 1986, with some exceptions, a person born in Australia acquires Australian citizenship automatically.
    - On or after August 20, 1986, a person born in Australia must have at least one parent who is either an Australian citizen or a permanent resident.
    - A person born in any external territory that has been, or still is, under Australian Government control should contact the nearest DIMA office for clarification of their status or eligibility for citizenship.

- **BY DESCENT**: (Based on date of birth and proper registration of birth.)
    - A child who is under 18 years of age at the time of the application may acquire citizenship by descent through registration at any Australian overseas post, provided: At least one parent is an Australian citizen at the time of the child's birth, and that person is the "responsible parent."
    - If the Australian parent is deceased, the person who normally has legal responsibility for the child may apply.
    - When a parent has acquired Australian citizenship by descent, they can only register their children if the parent has spent a period of time greater than 2 years legally residing in Australia.
    - An adult may register for citizenship by descent if they were born outside Australia between January 26, 1949, and January 15, 1974, have a natural parent who was an Australian citizen, and the applicant has an acceptable reason for not being registered under Section 10B as a child.

- **BY NATURALIZATION**: Persons who have fulfilled the following requirements may apply for grants of citizenship. (As a matter of policy, a certificate of Australian citizenship will not normally be granted to applicants overseas.)
    - Obtained permanent resident status and are 18 years of age or older. They are of good character, have a basic knowledge and grasp of the English language, are likely to reside permanently in Australia or, at least, maintain a close and continuing association.
    - Have spent 2 years out of the past 5 years in Australia with 12 months having been resident there within the last 2 years prior to submitting the application.
    - Children under the age of 18 years who are adopted from overseas may obtain Australian citizenship by application, provided at least one parent is an Australian citizen.

DUAL CITIZENSHIP: Current legislation does not favor dual or plural citizenship but does recognize it.

AUSTRALIA (cont.)

LOSS OF CITIZENSHIP:

- Australian citizenship can be lost by acquisition of another citizenship, by renunciation, or by deprivation (usually for false declarations and documents).
- A child will in most circumstances also lose their Australian citizenship if the "responsible parent" ceases to be an Australian citizen for any of the previously noted reasons.
- People who lose their Australian citizenship may in certain circumstances be able to apply to resume it.

ANY QUESTIONS concerning citizenship, or requests for renunciation of citizenship, should be directed to the address below:

Embassy of Australia
Immigration Department
1601 Massachusetts Ave., NW
Washington, DC 20036-2273

The Australian Consulate-Genera
Century Plaza Towers
19th Floor
2049 Century Park East
Los Angeles, CA 90067

Embassy/Immigration Telephone: 202-797-3000
Fax: 202-797-3100

www.austemb.org
www.abs.gov.au

AUSTRIA

CITIZENSHIP: Austrian citizenship is based upon the Citizenship law of 1965 as amended.

- **BY BIRTH**: Child born in the territory of Austria, with at least one parent being a citizen of Austria. However, a child born out of wedlock to a foreign mother and an Austrian father is not considered a citizen. Unless the couple marries, child obtains the citizenship of the mother.

- **BY DESCENT**: Child is born abroad, one of whose parents is an Austrian citizen. In case of a non-Austrian mother and an Austrian father, marriage law listed above applies.

- **BY NATURALIZATION**: Austrian citizenship can be applied for upon fulfillment of one of the following conditions:
    - Person has lived in Austria for at least 10 years.
    - Person has taken up a position as a professor at an Austrian University.
    - Person is the foreign spouse of an Austrian citizen and has resided in Austria for at least five years.

DUAL CITIZENSHIP: NOT RECOGNIZED.
Exception: Child of Austrian citizens who was born in a foreign country and acquired citizenship according to the other country's laws. Also, in exceptional cases, Austrian authorities may permit an Austrian citizen who obtains a new citizenship to retain their Austrian citizenship.

LOSS OF CITIZENSHIP:

- **VOLUNTARY**: Under certain conditions, Austrian citizenship may be voluntarily renounced:
    - Person possesses another citizenship.
    - Person has no criminal proceedings, or criminal penalties of more than six months, pending against them in Austria.
    - Person, if male, has fulfilled required military service.

- **INVOLUNTARY**: The following are grounds for loss of citizenship:
    - Person acquires citizenship of a foreign country.
    - Person performs voluntary military service for a foreign country.
    - Person has employment with a foreign government that is damaging to Austrian interests.

ANY QUESTIONS concerning citizenship, or requests for renunciation of citizenship, should be directed to the address below:

The Embassy of Austria
Consular Section
3524 International Court, NW
Washington, DC 20008-3035

Embassy Telephone: 202-895-6700
Consular Telephone: 202-895-6767/6709/6743
Fax: 202-895-6773

www.austria.org

AZERBAIJAN

CITIZENSHIP: A decree of citizenship is being drafted and will be submitted to the Parliament of the Republic of Azerbaijan. The information below represents current law.

- **BY BIRTH**: Birth within the territory of Azerbaijan does not automatically confer citizenship.

- **BY DESCENT**:
  - Child born in Azerbaijan, at least one of whose parents is a citizen of Azerbaijan.
  - Child born abroad of an Azerbaijani father is granted Azerbaijani citizenship if the mother does not object.

- **REGISTRATION**: A foreign woman who marries a citizen of Azerbaijan may register for citizenship after renouncing her previous citizenship.

- **BY NATURALIZATION**: No information available.

DUAL CITIZENSHIP: NOT RECOGNIZED.
Exception: the President of the Republic may grant dual citizenship.

LOSS OF CITIZENSHIP:

- **VOLUNTARY**: Voluntary renunciation of Azerbaijani citizenship is permitted by law. Contact the Embassy for details and required paperwork.

- **INVOLUNTARY**: The following are grounds for involuntary loss of Azerbaijani citizenship:
  - Person voluntarily acquires foreign citizenship.
  - Person commits an act that affronts the dignity of the Republic of Azerbaijan.

ANY QUESTIONS concerning citizenship, or requests for renunciation of citizenship, should be directed to the address below:

Embassy of the Republic of Azerbaijan
Consular Section
927 15th St., NW STE 700
Washington, DC 20005

Embassy/Consular Telephone: 202-842-0001
Fax: 202-842-0004

www.president.az/azerbaijan.htm

BAHAMAS

CITIZENSHIP: Citizenship is based upon the Constitution of The Bahamas, dated July 10, 1973. All persons who were citizens of The Bahamas before July 10, 1973, retain their citizenship.

- **BY BIRTH**: Birth within the territory of The Bahamas does not automatically confer citizenship

- **BY DESCENT**:
  - Child born legitimately in the territory of The Bahamas, at least one of whose parents is a citizen of The Bahamas.
  - Child born abroad legitimately, whose father is a citizen of The Bahamas.

- **REGISTRATION**: The following persons are eligible to obtain Bahamian citizenship through registration:
  - Foreign woman who marries a citizen of the Bahamas.
  - Person (18 years or older), born in the Bahamas, but whose parents were not citizens of the Bahamas.
  - Person (18 years or older), born in wedlock outside the Bahamas to a Bahamian mother.
  - Child adopted by Bahamian citizens.

- **BY NATURALIZATION**: Bahamian citizenship may be acquired upon fulfillment of the following conditions: Person has resided six to nine years in the country (12 months consecutively before applying), intends to reside permanently in the country, is of good character, and knows the language and customs.

DUAL CITIZENSHIP: NOT RECOGNIZED.
Exception: Dual citizenship obtained due to birth abroad may be retained up to 21 years of age. Person then has 12 months to renounce foreign citizenship; otherwise their Bahamian citizenship will be revoked.

LOSS OF CITIZENSHIP:

- **VOLUNTARY**: Voluntary renunciation of Bahamian citizenship is permitted by Parliament. Contact the Embassy for details and required paperwork.

- **INVOLUNTARY**: Parliament has the right to revoke the citizenship of any naturalized citizen. The following is grounds for involuntary loss of native-born citizenship: Person voluntarily acquires a foreign citizenship.

ANY QUESTIONS concerning citizenship, or requests for renunciation of citizenship, should be directed to the address below:

Embassy of the Commonwealth of The Bahamas   **bahemb@aol.com**
Consular Section   **www.bahamas.net.bs/government**
2220 Massachusetts Ave., NW   **www.bahamas.net**
Washington, DC 20008

Embassy/Consular Telephone: 202-319-2660
Fax: 202-319-2668

BAHRAIN

CITIZENSHIP: Citizenship laws are governed by the provisions of the Bahraini Nationality Law of September 16, 1963. For information on persons born before September 16, 1963, contact the Bahraini Embassy.

- **BY BIRTH**:
    - Child born in territory of Bahrain after September 16, 1963, whose father is a citizen of Bahrain (born and domiciled), provided the child does not have another nationality.
    - Child born in territory of Bahrain after September 16, 1963, of unknown parents.

- **BY DESCENT**: Child born after September 16, 1963, whose father or grandfather was a Bahraini citizen by birth.

- **BY NATURALIZATION**: Bahraini citizenship may be acquired upon fulfillment of the following conditions:
    - Person has lived continuously in Bahrain since September 16, 1963, for at least 25 years. (15 years for person of Arab descent)
    - Person must be of good character, have a good command of Arabic, and have an estate registered in his or her name in Bahrain.
    - Person must have acquired permission from the ruler of Bahrain.

DUAL CITIZENSHIP: NOT RECOGNIZED.

LOSS OF CITIZENSHIP: The ruler of Bahrain must approve loss of citizenship, either voluntary or involuntary. Citizenship lost through involuntary means extends to the person's minor children.

- **VOLUNTARY**: Bahraini law permits voluntary renunciation of citizenship. Contact Bahraini Embassy for details and proper paperwork.

- **INVOLUNTARY**: The following is grounds for involuntary loss of Bahraini citizenship: Person has voluntarily acquired foreign citizenship.

ANY QUESTIONS concerning citizenship, or requests for renunciation of citizenship, should be directed to the address below:

The Embassy of the State of Bahrain
Consular Section
3502 International Dr., NW
Washington, DC 20008

Embassy/Consular Telephone: 202-342-0741/42
Fax: 202-362-2192

BANGLADESH

CITIZENSHIP: Citizenship laws are based upon the Bangladesh Citizenship Order dated 1972. Questions concerning persons born before March 26, 1971, should be directed to the Bangladesh Embassy. (UKC-Commonwealth Nation)

- **BY BIRTH**: Birth within the territory of Bangladesh does not automatically confer citizenship. Only persons born before March 26, 1971 would be deemed Bangladesh citizens by birth.

- **BY DESCENT**: Rules stated below apply to persons born after March 26, 1971.
  - Child born of a Bangladesh father, regardless of the child's country of birth.
  - Child whose grandfather was a citizen of Bangladesh, regardless of the child's country of birth.
  - Child born of a Bangladesh mother and an unknown or stateless father, regardless of the child's country of birth.

- **OTHER**: Person who was a permanent resident of Bangladesh on March 26, 1971, is granted citizenship, unless disqualified by law at that time.

- **BY NATURALIZATION**:
  - A person may apply for citizenship upon investment of $5 million or its equivalent in an industrial or commercial project of Bangladesh or if the person transfers $1 million to any of the recognized financial institutions of Bangladesh (the funds may not be withdrawn).
  - Application for Permanent Residence may be made upon investment of $75,000 (may not be withdrawn).

DUAL CITIZENSHIP: NOT RECOGNIZED.
Exception: The government of Bangladesh reserves the right to recognize dual citizenship in certain cases. If questions arise, contact the Embassy.

LOSS OF CITIZENSHIP:

- **VOLUNTARY**: Law permits voluntary renunciation of Bangladesh citizenship. Contact the Embassy for details and appropriate paperwork.

- **INVOLUNTARY**: The following are grounds for involuntary loss of Bangladesh citizenship:
  - Person voluntarily acquires a foreign citizenship.
  - Naturalized citizen by investment in Bangladesh removes the investment from the country.

ANY QUESTIONS concerning citizenship, or requests for renunciation of citizenship, should be directed to the address below:

Embassy of the People's Republic of Bangladesh
Consular Section
2201 Wisconsin Ave., NW
Washington, DC 20007

Embassy/Consular Telephone: 202-342-8393
Fax: 202-333-4971

BARBADOS

CITIZENSHIP: Citizenship laws are based upon the Barbadian Constitution. (UKC-Commonwealth Nation)

- **BY BIRTH**: Child born in the territory of Barbados, regardless of the nationality of the parents.

- **BY DESCENT**:
  - Child born abroad, in wedlock, whose father is a citizen of Barbados. Child must be registered with the nearest Barbadian diplomatic representative.
  - Child born abroad, out of wedlock, whose mother is a citizen of Barbados. Child must be registered with the nearest Barbadian diplomatic representative.

- **REGISTRATION**: Foreign woman, who has married a citizen of Barbados, may apply for citizenship through registration.

- **BY NATURALIZATION**: Person may acquire Barbadian citizenship by having a longstanding residence of at least five years.

DUAL CITIZENSHIP: RECOGNIZED.

LOSS OF CITIZENSHIP:

- **VOLUNTARY**: Voluntary renunciation of citizenship is permitted under law. Letters of renunciation must be sent to:

  > Barbados Immigration Office
  > The Wharf
  > Bridgetown, Barbados,WI

  Person should request form REN 1, fill out the form, and return it to the Immigration Office along with their Barbadian passport. Person will receive form REN 2, a certificate of renunciation of Barbadian citizenship.

- **INVOLUNTARY**: Barbadian citizenship may be involuntarily removed by law. *No information is available on these laws.*

ANY QUESTIONS concerning citizenship should be directed to the address below:

The Embassy of Barbados
Consular Section
2144 Wyoming Ave., NW
Washington, DC 20008

Embassy/Consular Telephone: 202-939-9200/01/02
Fax: 202-332-7467

BELARUS

CITIZENSHIP: Citizenship law is based upon The Law of the Republic of Belarus, Laws of Citizenship, dated October 18, 1991. Persons who were permanent residents of Belarus during the adoption of the law remain citizens of Belarus.

- **BY BIRTH**: Birth within the territory of Belarus does not automatically confer citizenship. The exception is a child born in the territory of Belarus to stateless or unknown parents.

- **BY DESCENT**:
  - Child, both of whose parents are citizens of Belarus, regardless of the country of birth.
  - Child, one of whose parents is a citizen of Belarus and who (the parent) was born within the territory of Belarus.
  - Child, born abroad, at least one of whose parents was permanently residing in Belarus at the time of the child's birth.
  - Child, born abroad, one of whose parents is a citizen of Belarus and whose family is living permanently abroad, gains citizenship only upon the written request of the parents.

- **BY NATURALIZATION**: Belarusian citizenship may be applied for upon fulfillment of the following conditions: Person is capable of speaking the language, has resided in the territory for the last seven years, has a legitimate source of income, does not have citizenship of any other state, and assumes the obligation to follow the Constitution and laws of Belarus.

DUAL CITIZENSHIP: NOT RECOGNIZED.

LOSS OF CITIZENSHIP:

- **VOLUNTARY**: Permitted under Belarussian law, provided the person is not involved in any criminal proceedings and has no outstanding debts or obligations to Belarus. Contact nearest Belarussian Embassy for information on renouncing citizenship.

- **INVOLUNTARY**: The following are grounds for involuntary loss of Belarussian citizenship:
  - Person voluntarily acquires a foreign citizenship
  - Person enlists in the service (military, government, etc.) of another country.
  - Citizenship was acquired under false statements.

ANY QUESTIONS concerning citizenship, or requests for renunciation of citizenship, should be directed to the address below:

Embassy of the Republic of Belarus
Consular Section
1619 New Hampshire Ave., NW
Washington, DC 20009

Embassy Telephone: 202-986-1604
Consular Telephone: 202-986-1606
Fax: 202-986-1805

BELGIUM

CITIZENSHIP: Belgian citizenship is based upon the Code of Belgian Nationality, dated June 28, 1984, and amended January 1, 1992.

- **BY BIRTH**: Birth within the territory of Belgium does not automatically confer citizenship.

- **BY DESCENT**:
  - Child born in Belgium, at least one of whose parents is a citizen of Belgium. This same rule applies for an adopted child.
  - Child born abroad, at least one of whose parents was a native-born citizen of Belgium. Parents have up to five years to register child.

- **CHILDREN OF IMMIGRANTS**: Citizenship may be granted when:
  - Child is born in Belgium to non-citizens who were also born in Belgium.
  - Child is born to non-citizens who have lived in Belgium at least 10 years before the birth of the child and who have filed a citizenship claim for the child.
  - Child born in Belgium, who has resided there continuously since birth, may make a declaration of Belgian nationality between the ages of 18 and 30.

- **BY NATURALIZATION**: Belgian citizenship may be acquired upon fulfillment of the following conditions: Person is at least 18 years of age and has resided in country for at least 5 years.

DUAL CITIZENSHIP: NOT RECOGNIZED.
Exception: Belgian children born abroad, who received the citizenship of country of birth, may hold dual citizenship until age 18.

LOSS OF CITIZENSHIP:

- **VOLUNTARY**: Voluntary renunciation of citizenship can only be made if the person holds another citizenship or acquires it at the time of the declaration. Renunciations may be sent to the nearest Belgian Embassy.

- **INVOLUNTARY**: The following are grounds for involuntary loss of Belgian citizenship:
  - Person voluntarily acquires foreign citizenship.
  - Person, born abroad and not in the service of Belgium, who lives abroad from age 18 to 28, without making a declaration of citizenship.

ANY QUESTIONS concerning citizenship, or requests for renunciation of citizenship, should be directed to address below:

Embassy of Belgium
Consular Section
3330 Garfield St., NW
Washington, DC 20008

washington@diplobel.org
www.diplobel.org/usa/
www.belguim.fgov.be

Embassy/Consular Telephone: 202-333-6900
Fax: 202-333-3079

BELIZE

CITIZENSHIP: Citizenship is based upon the Belize Nationality Act, Chapter 127A of the Laws of Belize, R.E. 1980-1990. The following persons were granted citizenship at the date of independence (September 21, 1981):
- Person born in Belize, who was a citizen of the United Kingdom and Colonies (UKC).
- Citizen of the UKC, naturalized in Belize as a British Subject before September 21, 1981.
- Citizen of the UKC, born abroad, whose parents or grandparents were granted Belizean citizenship.
- Wife of citizen of the UKC who was granted Belizean citizenship.

- **BY BIRTH**: Birth within the territory of Belize, on or after September 21, 1981, regardless of the nationality of the parents. The exception is a child born to certain diplomatic personnel.

- **BY DESCENT**: Child born abroad, on or after September 21, 1981, at least one of whose parents is a citizen of Belize.

- **MARRIAGE**: Foreign national, who marries a citizen of Belize, is eligible to register for citizenship.

- **BY NATURALIZATION**: Belizean citizenship may be acquired upon fulfillment of the following conditions:
  - Person has resided in the country for at least five years and has renounced previous citizenship.
  - Person applies for economic citizenship by registration.

DUAL CITIZENSHIP: RECOGNIZED.
Exceptions: Dual citizenship is prohibited for:
- Belizean citizen by descent who has renounced such citizenship. However, such person may apply to resume Belizean citizenship but must renounce citizenship of any other country and demonstrate intent to continue to be an ordinarily resident in Belize.
- Belizean citizen, either by descent or registration, who has pledged allegiance to, or is a citizen of, a country which does not recognize the independence, sovereignty, or territorial integrity of Belize.

LOSS OF CITIZENSHIP: A person who acquired Belizean citizenship either by descent or registration and who makes an invalid or ineffective renunciation of foreign citizenship shall be deemed never to have acquired the status of citizen of Belize.

- **VOLUNTARY**: Voluntary renunciation of Belizean citizenship is permitted by law. Contact the Embassy for details and required paperwork.

- **INVOLUNTARY**: The following shall be grounds for involuntary loss of Belizean citizenship by a person who acquired such citizenship by registration:
  - Such Belizean citizen residing outside of Belize for five consecutive years or more.

The following may be grounds for involuntary loss of Belizean citizenship for a person who acquired Belizean citizenship by registration if such person:
- Has been convicted of an offence under the Belizean Nationality Act; or
- Has been convicted of any offence under Title XIV of the Criminal Code; or
- Was registered as a citizen of Belize by means of fraud, false representation, or the concealment of material circumstances, or by mistake; or
- Has, within five years after the date of registration as a citizen of Belize, been sentenced in any court to imprisonment for a term of twelve months or more; or

BELIZE (cont.)

- Has, since the date of his becoming a citizen of Belize by registration, been for a period of not less than two years ordinarily resident in a foreign country of which he was a national or citizen at any other time prior to that date, and has not maintained a substantial connection with Belize; or
- Has taken an oath or affirmation of, or made a declaration of, allegiance to a foreign country; or
- Has so conducted themself that their continuance as a citizen of Belize is detrimental to the interest of Belize.

ANY QUESTIONS concerning citizenship and requests for renunciation of citizenship, should be directed to the address below:

Embassy of Belize
Consular Section
2535 Massachusetts Ave., NW
Washington, DC 20008

Embassy/Consular Telephone: 202-332-9636
Fax: 202-332-6888

www.belizenet.com

BENIN

CITIZENSHIP: Citizenship is based upon the Law of Civil Rights.

- **BY BIRTH**: Birth within the territory of Benin does not automatically confer citizenship. The exception is a child born to stateless or unknown parents.

- **BY DESCENT**: Child of a Beninese mother or father, regardless of the country of birth.

- **BY NATURALIZATION**: Beninese citizenship may be acquired upon fulfillment of the following conditions: Person must have obtained the right to permanently reside in the country, and then have resided there for at least 10 years.

DUAL CITIZENSHIP: RECOGNIZED.

LOSS OF CITIZENSHIP:

- **VOLUNTARY**: Voluntary renunciation of Beninese citizenship is permitted by law. Person must be at least 21 years old. Contact the Embassy for details and required paperwork.

- **INVOLUNTARY**: The following are grounds for involuntary loss of naturalized Beninese citizenship:
    - Naturalized citizenship was obtained through fraud or false statement.
    - If naturalized citizen is convicted and jailed for a serious offense (and if the person will be deported after sentence is served).

ANY QUESTIONS concerning citizenship, or requests for renunciation of citizenship, should be directed to the address below:

Embassy of the Republic of Benin
Consular Section
2737 Cathedral Ave., NW
Washington, DC 20008

Embassy/Consular Telephone: 202-232-6656
Fax: 202-265-1996

BHUTAN

CITIZENSHIP: Citizenship is based upon the Nationality Law of Bhutan, dated 1958, and the Bhutan Citizenship Act, dated 1977 and 1985.

- **BY BIRTH**: Birth within the territory of Bhutan does not automatically confer citizenship.

- **BY DESCENT**:
  - Person born before June 10, 1985: Child of a Bhutanese father who was resident in Bhutan at the time, regardless of the country of birth.
  - Person born on or after June 10, 1985: Child of both a Bhutanese mother and father, regardless of the country of birth.

- **REGISTRATION**: On June 10, 1985, citizenship by registration was granted to persons who had legally resided in Bhutan since before December 31, 1958.

- **MARRIAGE**: When a Bhutanese woman marries a foreign man, husband and children must apply for citizenship through naturalization. When a Bhutanese man marries a foreign woman, the wife must apply for citizenship, while the children are granted Bhutanese citizenship by descent.

- **BY NATURALIZATION**: Bhutanese citizenship may be acquired upon fulfillment of the conditions listed below and upon obtaining permission of government:
  - Naturalized before June 10, 1985: Person had reached age 21, had resided in country for at least 10 years, owned agricultural land, and had the petition for naturalization accepted by government authority.
  - Naturalized after June 10, 1985: Person is 21 years old, has resided in country for 15 years if one or more parents is a citizen, (20 years for child of non-citizen), and knows the language and customs.

DUAL CITIZENSHIP: NOT RECOGNIZED.

LOSS OF CITIZENSHIP:

- **VOLUNTARY**: Voluntary renunciation of citizenship is permitted by law, but subject to final approval by the government. Contact the Mission for details and required paperwork.

- **INVOLUNTARY**: The following are grounds for involuntary loss of Bhutanese citizenship:
  - Person voluntarily acquires a foreign citizenship, has left the country, and is residing abroad or is working for a foreign state.
  - Naturalized citizenship was obtained through fraud or falsehoods.
  - Naturalized citizen is imprisoned within first 5 years in country.

ANY QUESTIONS concerning citizenship, or requests for renunciation of citizenship, should be directed to the address below:

Permanent Mission to the UN
Kingdom of Bhutan
Two United Nations Plaza, 27th floor
New York, NY 10017

Mission Telephone: 212-826-1919   **www.bhutan.org**
Fax: 212-826-2998

BOLIVIA

CITIZENSHIP: *Information about the basis for Bolivian citizenship laws was not provided.*

- **BY BIRTH**: Children born within the territory of Bolivia, regardless of the nationality of the parents. The only exception to this rule is children born to parents in the service of other governments.

- **BY DESCENT**: Child born abroad to either a Bolivian mother or father is granted citizenship either by returning to live in Bolivia, or by being registered at a consulate.

- **BY NATURALIZATION**: Bolivian citizenship may be acquired upon fulfillment of various conditions:
    - Persons with no ties to Bolivia may obtain citizenship after residing in the country for at least two years.
    - Foreign woman, married to a Bolivian citizen, acquires her husband's citizenship as long as she lives in the country and expresses her agreement. This nationality is not lost even through widowhood or divorce.
    - Persons who have Bolivian spouses or had children born in Bolivia need only to reside in country for one year.

DUAL CITIZENSHIP: NOT RECOGNIZED.
Exceptions:
- Bolivian woman, married to a foreigner, is not required to relinquish her Bolivian citizenship even if she acquires her husband's citizenship through their marriage.
- Former citizens of Spain and other Latin American countries, who become naturalized Bolivians, are not required to relinquish their previous citizenship as long as Bolivia has a reciprocal agreement with their former countries. *NO AGREEMENT WITH UNITED STATES.*

LOSS OF CITIZENSHIP:

- **VOLUNTARY**: Letters of voluntary renunciation of Bolivian citizenship may be sent to the nearest Bolivian embassy.

- **INVOLUNTARY**: The following are grounds for involuntary loss of Bolivian citizenship:
    - Person aids the enemy of Bolivia during time of war.
    - Person accepts a foreign government job without Senate approval.
    - Person acquires the citizenship of a foreign country that does not have a reciprocal dual citizenship agreement with Bolivia.

ANY QUESTIONS concerning citizenship, or requests for renunciation of citizenship, should be directed to the address below:

Embassy of Bolivia
Consular Section
3014 Massachusetts Ave., NW
Washington, DC 20008

Embassy Telephone: 202-483-4410/11/12
Consular Telephone: 202-232-4828
Fax: 202-328-3712
www.ine.gov.bo

BOSNIA AND HERZEGOVINA

CITIZENSHIP *Information concerning citizenship laws was not provided.*

ANY QUESTIONS concerning citizenship law should be directed to the address below

Embassy of the Republic of Bosnia and Herzegovina
Consular Section
2109 E St., NW
Washington, DC 20037

Embassy/Consular Telephone: 202-337-1500
Fax: 202-337-1502
info@bosniaembassy.org
www.bosnianembassy.org

BOTSWANA

CITIZENSHIP: Citizenship laws are based upon the Botswana Constitution and the Citizenship Act of Botswana dated December 31, 1982. Any person considered a citizen of Botswana born before December 31, 1982, is still considered a citizen of Botswana (UKC-Commonwealth Nation).

Specific questions concerning people born before December 31, 1982, should be directed to the Botswana embassy.

- **BY BIRTH**: Birth within the Republic of Botswana does not automatically confer citizenship.

- **BY DESCENT**:
    - Child, whose father is a citizen of Botswana, regardless of the country of birth.
    - Child born out of wedlock, whose mother is a citizen of Botswana.

- **BY NATURALIZATION**: Botswana citizenship is acquired upon fulfillment of the following conditions: Person is of good character, has sufficient knowledge of the Setswana language, has been a resident for a continuous period of 12 months prior to application, in the preceding 12 years has lived in country for an aggregate of 10 years, and intends to permanently reside in Botswana.

- **MARRIAGE**: Woman who marries a citizen may be immediately granted citizenship if preceding the date of application she has been a resident for a continuous period amounting to two and a half years.

DUAL CITIZENSHIP: NOT RECOGNIZED.
Exception: Children who acquire the citizenship of a foreign country may maintain their dual citizenship until the age of 21. Upon reaching the age of majority, the person must renounce the foreign citizenship, take an oath of allegiance, and make declarations concerning future residency.

LOSS OF CITIZENSHIP:

- **VOLUNTARY**: Voluntary renunciation of citizenship requires the citizen to make a declaration of renunciation to the Government. Upon confirmation that the person is not ordinarily a resident in Botswana the Minister of State shall register the declaration. Upon registration, citizenship is revoked, provided the person has proof of new citizenship.

- **INVOLUNTARY**: The following is grounds for involuntary loss of Botswana citizenship. Voluntary acquisition of a foreign citizenship.

ANY QUESTIONS concerning citizenship, or requests for renunciation of citizenship, should be directed to the address below:

Embassy of the Republic of Botswana
Consular Section
Intelsat Building
3400 International Dr., NW STE 7M
Washington, DC 20008

Embassy Telephone: 202-244-4990
Fax: 202-244-4164

BRAZIL

CITIZENSHIP: Brazilian citizenship is regulated by Law #818 of September 18, 1949, amended by Decree Law #961 of October 13, 1969, and Constitutional Amendment #3 of June 6, 1994.

- **BY BIRTH**: Child born in Brazil regardless of the nationality of the parents.

- **BY DESCENT**: Child born outside of the territory of Brazil, at least one of whose parents is a citizen of Brazil. All children born abroad to Brazilian parents are advised to be registered in the nearest Consular Office.

- **BY MARRIAGE**: Marriage to a Brazilian national does not automatically confer citizenship; the law does reduce the proof of residence in the country for foreigners married to Brazilian citizens.

- **BY NATURALIZATION**: Brazilian citizenship can be acquired by fulfillment of the following conditions: Person has lived within the country for at least 5 years

DUAL CITIZENSHIP: NOT RECOGNIZED.
Exception: In practice, children born abroad to Brazilian parents can hold dual citizenship at any time; when such a person resides in Brazil they are considered Brazilian citizens.

LOSS OF CITIZENSHIP:

- **VOLUNTARY**: Voluntary renunciation of Brazilian citizenship requires the presentation of the person's Brazilian birth certificate, and certificate of naturalization for new citizenship, to the local Brazilian consulate in that country, or the nearest one available. The process takes 6 to 12 months to be final.

- **INVOLUNTARY**: *No information was provided.*

ANY QUESTIONS concerning citizenship, or requests for renunciation of citizenship, should be directed to the address below:

The Embassy of Brazil
Consular Section
3009 Whitehaven Street, NW
Washington, DC 20008

Embassy Telephone: 202-238-2700
Consulate Telephone: 202-238-2828
Fax: 202-238-2818/2827

www.brasilemb.org
www.brasil.emb.nw.dc.us
www.ibge.gov.br

BRUNEI DARUSSALAM

CITIZENSHIP: The State of Brunei Darussalam became fully sovereign in January of 1984. The laws concerning citizenship were created to be in accordance with general Islamic law. (UKC-Commonwealth Nation)

- **BY BIRTH**: Birth within the territory of Brunei does not automatically confer citizenship.

- **BY DESCENT**:
  - Child born in wedlock of a Bruneian father, regardless of the country of birth.
  - Child born out of wedlock of a Bruneian mother and unknown or stateless father, regardless of the country of birth.

- **BY NATURALIZATION**: Acquisition of Bruneian citizenship is only possible through marriage or adoption.

- **MARRIAGE**:
  - Marriage of a Bruneian male and a foreign female. The foreign spouse may register for citizenship after 10 years residency.
  - Marriage of a Bruneian female and a foreign male. The foreign spouse must obtain permanent residency status, possess a means of support, and have resided in Brunei for 15 years.

DUAL CITIZENSHIP: NOT RECOGNIZED.
Exception: Child born abroad of Bruneian parents who obtains the citizenship of the country of birth, may retain dual citizenship until the age of majority (18). Upon reaching the age of majority, the person must choose which citizenship to retain.

LOSS OF CITIZENSHIP:

- **VOLUNTARY**: Voluntary renunciation of citizenship is permitted by law. Contact the Bruneian Embassy for details and proper paperwork.

- **INVOLUNTARY:** The following is grounds for involuntary loss of Bruneian citizenship: Person voluntarily acquires a foreign citizenship.

ANY QUESTIONS concerning citizenship, or requests for renunciation of citizenship, should be directed to the address below:

Embassy of the State of Brunei Darussalam
Consular Section
3520 International Court NW
Washington, DC 20008

Embassy/Consular Telephone: 202-342-0159
Fax: 202-342-0158

info@bruneiembassy.org
www.brunet.bn

BULGARIA

CITIZENSHIP: Citizenship is based upon the Law on Bulgarian Citizenship, dated November 1998.

- **BY BIRTH**: Birth within the territory of Bulgaria does not automatically confer citizenship. The exception is a child born in Bulgaria to unknown or stateless parents.

- **BY DESCENT**: Child, at least one of whose parents is a citizen of Bulgaria, regardless of the country of birth.

- **OTHER**: The following are eligible for Bulgarian citizenship through other than the normal naturalization process:
    - A stateless person, one of whose parents is of Bulgarian descent.
    - A child under 14, adopted by Bulgarian parents.
    - Refugees fleeing persecution.
    - Persons who have greatly contributed to Bulgarian society.

- **BY NATURALIZATION**: Bulgarian citizenship may be acquired upon fulfillment of the following condition: Person has resided legally in Bulgaria for at least five years.

DUAL CITIZENSHIP: RECOGNIZED.

LOSS OF CITIZENSHIP:

- **VOLUNTARY**: Voluntary renunciation of Bulgarian citizenship is permitted by law. Contact the Bulgarian Embassy for details and proper paperwork.

- **INVOLUNTARY**: The following are grounds for involuntary loss of naturalized citizenship:
    - Naturalized citizenship was obtained through fraud or false statement. This revocation only affects the person who made the false statements. The person's spouse and children may retain Bulgarian citizenship.
    - Person commits criminal acts against the security of the state outside of Bulgaria.

ANY QUESTIONS concerning citizenship, or requests for renunciation of citizenship, should be directed to the address below:

Embassy of the Republic of Bulgaria
Consular Office
1621 22nd St., NW
Washington, DC 20008

Embassy/Consular Telephone: 202-387-7969
Fax: 202-234-7973
www.embassy-bulgaria.org

BURKINA FASO (Upper Volta)

CITIZENSHIP: *Information on the basis for Burkinabe citizenship law was not provided.*

- **BY BIRTH**: Birth within the territory of Burkina Faso does not automatically confer citizenship the exception is a child born to unknown parents.

- **BY DESCENT**: Child, at least one of whose parents is a citizen, is granted citizenship regardless of the child's country of birth.

- **BY NATURALIZATION**: Burkinabe citizenship may be acquired upon fulfillment of the following conditions:
    - Person has resided in Burkina Faso for at least 10 years and is 18 years or older. There are some exceptions for the residency and age requirements.
    - Foreigners born in Burkina Faso and those who can be of service to the state need to fulfi a residency requirement of two years.

- **MARRIAGE**: Person who marries a citizen of Burkina Faso may register for citizenship six months after the marriage.

DUAL CITIZENSHIP: Dual Citizenship is not prohibited by law; therefore, it is accepted.

LOSS OF CITIZENSHIP:

- **VOLUNTARY**: Voluntary renunciation of citizenship is permitted by law. Contact Burkinabe Embassy for details and required paperwork.

- **INVOLUNTARY**: The following is grounds for involuntary loss of Burkinabe citizenship: Person has committed a crime against the institutions or the government of Burkina Faso.

ANY QUESTIONS concerning citizenship, or requests for renunciation of citizenship, should be directed to the address below:

Embassy of Burkina Faso
Consular Section
2340 Massachusetts Ave., NW
Washington, DC 20008

Embassy/Consular Telephone: 202-332-5577/6895
Fax: 202-667-1882

BURUNDI

CITIZENSHIP: Citizenship laws are based on the Burundian Nationality Code of August 10, 1971.

- **BY BIRTH**: Birth within the territory of Burundi does not automatically confer citizenship. The only exception is a person born in Burundi who is not a citizen of any state and who has resided there for 15 years.

- **BY DESCENT**:
  - Child born of a Burundian father, regardless of the country of birth.
  - Child born of a Burundian mother and an unknown or stateless father, regardless of the country of birth.

- **MARRIAGE**: A foreign woman who marries a Burundian citizen may acquire Burundi nationality two years after the marriage, provided she has renounced her previous citizenship.

- **OTHER**: A child, adopted before their twelfth birthday by a Burundian citizen.

- **BY NATURALIZATION**: Laws concerning the acquisition of Burundian citizenship are interpreted through the legislature.

DUAL CITIZENSHIP: NOT RECOGNIZED.

LOSS OF CITIZENSHIP: All renunciations, whether voluntary or involuntary, must be approved by a court finding.

- **VOLUNTARY**: Voluntary renunciation of citizenship is permitted by law, provided a court decree is granted. Contact Embassy for details and required paperwork.

- **INVOLUNTARY**: The following is grounds for involuntary loss of Burundian citizenship, provided a court decree is approved: Person voluntarily acquires a foreign citizenship.

ANY QUESTIONS concerning citizenship, or requests for renunciation of citizenship, should be directed to the address below:

Embassy of the Republic of Burundi
Consular Section
2233 Wisconsin Ave., NW STE 212
Washington, DC 20007

Embassy/Consular Telephone: 202-342-2574
Fax: 202-342-2578

CAMBODIA (Formerly Kampuchea)

CITIZENSHIP: Citizenship is based upon Decree No. 913-NS, of November 20, 1954, and Law No. 904-NS, dated September 27, 1954.

- **BY BIRTH**: Birth within the territory of Cambodia does not automatically confer citizenship. Two exceptions are these:
  - Child born in Cambodia, of non-citizen parents who were also born in Cambodia.
  - Child of unknown parents found in Cambodian territory.

- **BY DESCENT**: Legitimate child of a Cambodian mother or father, regardless of the country of birth. (According to Cambodian law, "legitimate" refers to the child being formally acknowledged by either of its parents.)

- **MARRIAGE**:
  - A foreign wife of a Cambodian citizen is eligible for citizenship upon the date of the marriage.
  - A foreign husband of a Cambodian citizen must fulfill all naturalization requirements, but need reside only for two years.

- **BY NATURALIZATION**: Cambodian citizenship may be acquired upon fulfillment of the following conditions: Person has resided for at least five years in the country, knows the language and culture, has a steady means of support, and is of good moral character.

DUAL CITIZENSHIP: NOT RECOGNIZED.
Exception: A Cambodian wife of a foreign national is permitted to retain her Cambodian citizenship unless required to renounce it by the laws of the husband's home country.

LOSS OF CITIZENSHIP:

- **VOLUNTARY**: *Voluntary renunciation of Cambodian citizenship was permitted under the old laws. Since the laws and government of Cambodia are in transition, it is unknown how official voluntary renunciation can presently be achieved.*

- **INVOLUNTARY**: The following have been traditional grounds for involuntary loss of Cambodian citizenship:
  - Person joins a foreign army or a foreign organization against the wishes of the Cambodian government.
  - Person acquires foreign citizenship.

ANY QUESTIONS concerning Cambodian Citizenship Law should be directed to the address below:

Royal Embassy of Cambodia
4500 16th Street NW
Washington, DC 20011

Telephone: 202-726-7742
Fax: 202-726-8381
cambodia@embassy.org
www.cambodia.org

CAMEROON

CITIZENSHIP: Citizenship is based upon Ordinance #2, dated 1959, and Ordinance #68 dated 1968.

- **BY BIRTH**: Birth within the territory of Cameroon does not automatically confer citizenship. The exceptions are as follows:
  - Child born of unknown or stateless parents.
  - Child born in Cameroon of foreign parents, at least one of whom was also born in Cameroon.

- **BY DESCENT**:
  - Child born in wedlock, whose father is a citizen of Cameroon, regardless of the country of birth.
  - Child born out of wedlock to a Cameroonian father and foreign mother, if paternity can be established.
  - Child born out of wedlock to a Cameroonian mother and an unknown or stateless father.

- **MARRIAGE**: A foreign woman who marries a citizen of Cameroon is permitted to acquire citizenship

- **BY NATURALIZATION**: Cameroonian citizenship may be acquired upon the fulfillment of certain strict qualifications concerning residency, age, health, and morality. *Details of these requirements are not available.*

DUAL CITIZENSHIP: NOT RECOGNIZED.
Exception: Child born abroad of Cameroonian parents, who obtains the citizenship of the country of birth. Upon reaching age 21, one citizenship must be chosen, or Cameroonian citizenship will be lost.

LOSS OF CITIZENSHIP:

- **VOLUNTARY**: Voluntary renunciation of Cameroonian citizenship is permitted by law. Proof of new citizenship must be presented. Contact the Embassy for details and required paperwork.

- **INVOLUNTARY**: The following are grounds for involuntary loss of Cameroonian citizenship:
  - Person voluntarily acquires foreign citizenship. (A Cameroonian woman who marries a foreign citizen is not required to renounce Cameroonian citizenship.)
  - Person is employed in the service of a foreign government.

ANY QUESTIONS concerning citizenship, or requests for renunciation of citizenship, should be directed to the address below:

Embassy of the Republic of Cameroon
Consular Section
2349 Massachusetts Ave., NW
Washington, DC 20008
Embassy/Consular Telephone: 202-265-8790 through 8794

Fax: 202-387-3826

www.camnet.cm

CANADA

CITIZENSHIP: Citizenship is based upon the Canadian Citizenship Act, dated 1947, the Citizenship Act, and the Citizenship Regulations dated 1977. All persons who were citizens of Canada before February 14, 1977 remained citizens of Canada.

Questions concerning persons born before January 1, 1947 (the date of independence), should be directed to the Embassy. (UKC-Commonwealth Nation)

- **BY BIRTH**: Person born on or after February 14, 1977, regardless of the nationalities of the parents. Exceptions to this law include children born to diplomatic personnel and children of parents who were not legal residents in Canada at the time of the birth.

- **BY DESCENT**: Person born abroad, on or after February 14, 1977, at least one of whose parents was a citizen of Canada. Upon reaching the age of 28, if the person has not returned to reside in Canada and applied to retain citizenship, Canadian citizenship will be revoked.

- **BY NATURALIZATION**: Canadian citizenship may be acquired upon fulfillment of the following conditions:
    - Person is 18 years or older.
    - Person has been a legal resident in Canada for three years out of the previous four years.
    - Person can communicate in English or French.
    - Person has knowledge of Canada, including the rights and responsibilities of citizenship.
    - Person is not under criminal sentence, order of deportation, or charged with or convicted of an indictable offence.

DUAL CITIZENSHIP: RECOGNIZED.
Before the Citizenship Act of February 15, 1977, Canadian law limited dual citizenship. Canadians who became citizens of another country before this date should check with the Embassy to see if they may still hold Canadian citizenship.

LOSS OF CITIZENSHIP:

- **VOLUNTARY**: Voluntary renunciation of Canadian citizenship is permitted by law. Contact the Embassy for details and required paperwork.

- **INVOLUNTARY**: The following are grounds for involuntary loss of naturalized Canadian citizenship:
    - Naturalized citizenship was obtained through fraud or false statement.
    - Naturalized citizen has spent more than 10 years living abroad.

ANY QUESTIONS concerning citizenship, or requests for renunciation of citizenship, should be directed to the address below:

Embassy of Canada, Consular Section
501 Pennsylvania Ave., NW
Washington, DC 20001

Embassy/Consular Telephone: 202-682-1740
Fax: 202-682-7726

www.canada.gc.ca/main_e.html
www.cic.gc.ca
www.statcan.ca

CAPE VERDE

CITIZENSHIP: *Data showing basis for citizenship regulations was not provided.*

- **BY BIRTH**: Birth within the territory of Cape Verde does not automatically confer citizenship The exception is a child born to unknown parents.

- **BY DESCENT**: Child, at least one of whose parents is a citizen of Cape Verde, is granted citizenship regardless of the country of birth.

- **BY NATURALIZATION**: Cape Verdean citizenship may be acquired upon fulfillment of the following conditions:
  - Person must have resided in the country for at least five years.
  - Person who makes a sizeable investment in Cape Verde may be granted citizenship without the residency requirement.

- **MARRIAGE**: Person who marries a citizen of Cape Verde is automatically eligible for citizenship upon request.

DUAL CITIZENSHIP: RECOGNIZED

LOSS OF CITIZENSHIP:

- **VOLUNTARY**: Voluntary renunciation of Cape Verdean citizenship is permitted under law. Contact Embassy for details and required paperwork.

- **INVOLUNTARY**: *No information was provided.*

ANY QUESTIONS concerning citizenship, or requests for renunciation of citizenship, should be directed to the address below:

Embassy of the Republic of Cape Verde
Consular Section
3415 Massachusetts Ave., NW
Washington, DC 20007

Embassy/Consular Telephone: 202-965-6820
Fax: 202- 965-1207

CENTRAL AFRICAN REPUBLIC

CITIZENSHIP: The basis for the laws on citizenship of the Central African Republic (CAR) is the Constitution adopted on January 7, 1995.

- **BY BIRTH**: Child born within the territory of the Republic regardless of the nationality of the parents. The exception is a child born to certain diplomatic personnel.

- **BY DESCENT**:
  - Child born abroad of a Central African Republic father.
  - Child born abroad of a foreign father and a CAR mother is eligible for CAR citizenship if desired by the parents. Child is also eligible to retain the citizenship of the father, due to CAR's recognition of Dual Citizenship.

- **MARRIAGE**: Foreign national who marries a citizen of the Central African Republic is automatically eligible for citizenship by registration upon marriage.

- **BY NATURALIZATION**: Central African Republic citizenship may be acquired upon fulfillment of the following condition: Person resides in the country five to seven years.

DUAL CITIZENSHIP: RECOGNIZED.

LOSS OF CITIZENSHIP:

- **VOLUNTARY**: Voluntary renunciation of Central African Republic citizenship is permitted by law. Contact the Embassy for details and required paperwork.

- **INVOLUNTARY**: The following are grounds for involuntary loss of naturalized Central African Republic citizenship:
  - Citizenship was obtained by fraud or false statement.
  - Person committed serious crimes after obtaining citizenship.
  - Person commits acts of disloyalty to the government.

ANY QUESTIONS concerning citizenship, or requests for renunciation of citizenship, should be directed to the address below:

Embassy of the Central African Republic
Consular Section
1618 22nd St., NW
Washington, DC 20008

Embassy/Consular Telephone: 202-483-7800/01
Fax: 202-332-9893

CHAD

CITIZENSHIP: Citizenship laws are based upon the Regulation of August 14, 1962.

- **BY BIRTH**: Birth within the territory of Chad does not automatically confer citizenship. The exception is a child born of unknown parents.

- **BY DESCENT**:
  - Child, both of whose parents are citizens of Chad, regardless of the country of birth.
  - Child, one of whose parents is a citizen of Chad, only when the results of non-recognition would leave the child stateless.

- **BY NATURALIZATION**: Chadian citizenship may be acquired upon fulfillment of the following conditions: Person has resided in country for at least 15 years and is of good health and morality.

DUAL CITIZENSHIP: Chadian law does not address dual citizenship. For all questions concerning dual citizenship, contact the Chadian Consul.

LOSS OF CITIZENSHIP:

- **VOLUNTARY**: Voluntary renunciation of citizenship is permitted by law. Contact the Embassy for details and proper paperwork.

- **INVOLUNTARY**: The President reserves the right to revoke the citizenship of any Chadian national if it is determined that acts were committed that were not in the interest of Chad.

ANY QUESTIONS concerning citizenship, or requests for renunciation of citizenship, should be directed to the address below:

The Embassy of the Republic of Chad
Consular Section
2002 R St., NW
Washington, DC 20009

Embassy/Consular Telephone: 202-462-4009
Fax: 202-265-1937

CHILE

CITIZENSHIP: *Information concerning the basis for Chilean citizenship law was not provided.*

- **BY BIRTH**: Child born in the territory of Chile, regardless of the nationality of the parents. The exceptions are children of foreign diplomats or of transient foreigners.

- **BY DESCENT**: Child born abroad, at least one of whose parents is a citizen of Chile, provided the person establishes a residence in Chile before the age of 21.

- **BY NATURALIZATION**: Chilean citizenship may be acquired upon fulfillment of the following conditions:
    - Person has resided in the country for at least five years.
    - Person has shown proof of renunciation of previous citizenship.

DUAL CITIZENSHIP: NOT RECOGNIZED.
Exceptions:
- Chile has a dual citizenship agreement with the country of Spain.
- Child born abroad to Chilean parents, who obtains citizenship of country of birth, may retain dual citizenship until the age of majority (21). Upon reaching the age of majority, person must choose which citizenship to retain.
- Persons, working or living abroad, who must acquire a foreign citizenship as a condition of remaining legally in that country.

LOSS OF CITIZENSHIP:

- **VOLUNTARY**: Voluntary renunciation of citizenship is permitted by law. No paperwork is necessary, but the person must notify the embassy, show proof of new citizenship, and turn in Chilean passport.

- **INVOLUNTARY**: The following are grounds for involuntary loss of Chilean citizenship:
    - Person voluntarily obtains foreign citizenship.
    - Person gives aid and comfort to wartime enemies of Chile.

ANY QUESTIONS concerning citizenship, or requests for renunciation of citizenship, should be directed to the address below:

Embassy of Chile
Consular Section
1732 Massachusetts Ave., NW
Washington, DC 20036

Embassy/Consular Telephone: 202-785-1746
Fax: 202-887-5579

www.segegob.cl/seg-ing/index2i.html

CHINA, People's Republic of China

CITIZENSHIP: Citizenship information is based upon The Nationality Law of the People's Republic of China (PRC), dated September 10, 1980. *On December 20, 1999, Macao became a Special Administrative Region of the People's Republic of China. The citizenship laws concerning Macao are based on the Interpretations of the Standing Committee of the National People's Congress on the Implementation of the Nationality Law of the People's Republic of China in the Macao Special Administrative Region, dated December 20, 1999.*

- **BY BIRTH**: Birth within the territory of the PRC does not automatically confer citizenship. The exception is a child born to unknown or stateless parents.

- **BY DESCENT**:
  - Child, at least one of whose parents is a Chinese citizen, regardless of the country of birth.
  - Child born abroad, whose parents have settled abroad and the child has acquired the nationality of the parents' new country, is not considered a citizen of the PRC.
  - Residents of Macao having a Chinese blood relationship, born on the territories of China (including Macao), as well as other persons of Chinese nationality, whether or not they hold Portuguese travel certificates or identity cards, are all Chinese citizens.
  - Residents of the Macao Special Administrative Region having both a Chinese blood relationship and a Portuguese blood relationship may, in accordance with their personal wishes, choose either the nationality of the People's Republic of China or the nationality of the Republic of Portugal. Selection of one of the nationalities shall mean the forgoing of the other nationality.

- **BY NATURALIZATION**:
  - PRC citizenship may be acquired upon fulfillment of one of the following conditions: Person has close relatives living in China; person has settled in China; or, the person has other legitimate reasons.
  - Foreign nationals who once held Chinese nationality may apply for restoration of Chinese nationality if they have legitimate reasons. Once the application is approved the person may not retain the foreign nationality.

DUAL CITIZENSHIP: NOT RECOGNIZED.

LOSS OF CITIZENSHIP:

- **VOLUNTARY**: Voluntary renunciation of PRC citizenship is permitted by law, upon fulfillment of at least one of certain requirements. The requirements are:
  - Person is a near relative of a foreign national.
  - Person has already settled abroad.
  - Person has other legitimate reasons.

  - State functionaries and military personnel are not permitted to renounce PRC citizenship.

Contact the PRC Embassy for details and required paperwork. Final approval for renunciation of PRC citizenship is granted by the Ministry of Public Security. *When dealing with the Embassy, Chinese speakers are preferred.*

- **INVOLUNTARY**: No information available.

CHINA, People's Republic of China (cont.)

ANY QUESTIONS concerning citizenship, or requests for renunciation of citizenship, should be directed to the address below:

If contact with the Chinese Embassy is difficult, some information may be obtained from either the State Department's Office of Citizen Consular Services or the Library of Congress's Far Eastern Law Library.

Embassy of the People's Republic of China
Consular Section
2300 Connecticut Ave., NW
Washington, DC 20008

Embassy Telephone: 202-328-2500/01/02
Consular Telephone: 202-328-2518
Fax: 202-328-2564
webmaster@china-embassy.org

COLOMBIA

CITIZENSHIP: Citizenship is based upon the Constitution of Colombia, dated July 1991, and Citizenship Law No.43, dated February 1, 1993.

- **BY BIRTH**: Birth within the territory of Colombia does not automatically confer citizenship.

- **BY DESCENT**:
    - Child born in Colombia, at least one of whose parents is a citizen of Colombia.
    - Child born in Colombia of foreign national parents, provided at least one of the parents is a legal resident of Colombia.
    - Child born abroad, at least one of whose parents is a citizen of Colombia, and the child later establishes residency in Colombia.

- **BY NATURALIZATION**: The following groups of persons may acquire Colombian citizenship under certain conditions:
    - Foreign nationals must legally reside in the country for at least five years.
    - Certain Latin American and Caribbean peoples need to reside in Colombia for one year.
    - Foreign citizens who marry a citizen of Colombia must reside for two years.

DUAL CITIZENSHIP: RECOGNIZED.

LOSS OF CITIZENSHIP:

- **VOLUNTARY**: Voluntary renunciation of Colombian citizenship is permitted by law. Contact the Embassy for details and required paperwork.

- **INVOLUNTARY**: The following is grounds for involuntary loss of Colombian citizenship: A naturalized citizen commits crimes against the existence and security of the State.

Note: A former citizen of Colombia, after having renounced Colombian citizenship, will be judged and sentenced as a traitor if the person acts against the interests of Colombia in a foreign war.

ANY QUESTIONS concerning citizenship, or requests for renunciation of citizenship, should be directed to the address below:

Embassy of Colombia
Consular Section
1825 Connecticut Ave., NW
Washington, DC 20009

Embassy Telephone: 202-387-8338
Consular Telephone: 202-332-7573
Fax: 202-232-7180

COMOROS

No information was provided concerning Comoran citizenship laws.

ANY QUESTIONS concerning citizenship, or requests for renunciation of citizenship, should be directed to one of the addresses below:

Permanent Mission to the UN
Federal and Islamic Republic of the Comoros
336 E 45th St., 2nd floor
New York, NY 10017

Mission Telephone: 212-972-8010
Fax: 212-983-4712

Law Library
Near Eastern and African Law Division
Madison Building RM LM 240
101 Independence Ave., NW
Washington, DC 20540-3060

Telephone: 202-707-5073
Fax: 202-707-1820

www.ksu.edu/sasw/comoros/comoros.html

CONGO (Formerly Zaire)

CITIZENSHIP: Citizenship is based upon the Congolese Civil Code and the Special Law on Congolese Nationality (date unknown).

- **BY BIRTH**: Birth within the territory of Congo does not automatically confer citizenship.

- **BY DESCENT**: Child of a Congolese parent, regardless of the child's country of birth.

- **REGISTRATION**: Citizenship may be granted by registration for the following persons:
    - Foreign woman who has been, or is, married to a citizen of Congo.
    - Foreign child adopted by citizens of Congo.

- **BY NATURALIZATION**: Congolese citizenship may be acquired upon fulfillment of the following condition: Person has legally resided in the country for at least five years.

DUAL CITIZENSHIP: NOT RECOGNIZED.
Exception: Child born abroad, who obtains the citizenship of the country of birth may retain dual citizenship until their 21st birthday. Person then has 12 months to renounce foreign citizenship or Congolese citizenship will be revoked.

LOSS OF CITIZENSHIP:

- **VOLUNTARY**: Voluntary renunciation of Congolese citizenship is permitted by law. Though the Embassy can provide information and assistance, the person seeking to renounce citizenship must return to Congo and present their case to a court of law. Due to this procedure, assume that renunciation is neither automatic nor guaranteed.

- **INVOLUNTARY**: The following is grounds for involuntary loss of Congolese citizenship: Person voluntarily acquires a foreign citizenship and is not covered by the dual citizenship exception listed above.

ANY QUESTIONS concerning citizenship, or requests for renunciation of citizenship, should be directed to the address below:

Embassy of the Democratic Republic of the Congo
Consular Section
1800 New Hampshire Ave. NW
Washington, DC 20009

Embassy/Consular Telephone: 202-234-7690/91
Fax: 202-234-2609

CONGO REPUBLIC

CITIZENSHIP: Citizenship is based upon the Congolese Nationality Code and the Regulation bringing it into effect on July 29, 1961.

- **BY BIRTH**: Birth within the territory of Congo does not automatically confer citizenship. The exceptions are as follows.
    - Child born of unknown or stateless parents.
    - Child born of foreign parents, at least one of whom was also born in Congo.

    The government of Congo reserves the right to repudiate citizenship claims that fall into the above categories.

- **BY DESCENT**:
    - Child of a Congolese mother and father, regardless of the country of birth.
    - Child, at least one of whose parents is a citizen of Congo and the other of whom was born in Congo, regardless of the child's country of birth.
    - Child born in Congo, at least one of whose parents is a citizen of Congo.

- **MARRIAGE**: A foreigner who marries a citizen of Congo is eligible for citizenship after five years communal living in the country.

- **BY NATURALIZATION**: Congolese citizenship may be acquired upon fulfillment of the following condition: Person has resided in country for at least 10 years.

DUAL CITIZENSHIP: NOT RECOGNIZED

LOSS OF CITIZENSHIP:

- **VOLUNTARY**: Voluntary renunciation of Congolese citizenship is permitted by law. Letter of renunciation must be sent to the Minister of Foreign Affairs in Brazzaville, Congo. Renunciation must be approved by the government and approval can take up to a year. Contact the Embassy for details and required paperwork.

- **INVOLUNTARY**: The following are grounds for involuntary loss of Congolese citizenship:
    - Person voluntarily acquires foreign citizenship.
    - Person enters into the service of a foreign state.
    - Naturalized citizen is convicted of certain crimes less than 10 years into naturalization.

ANY QUESTIONS concerning citizenship, or requests for renunciation of citizenship, should be directed to the address below:

Embassy of the Republic of the Congo
Consular Section
4891 Colorado Ave., NW
Washington, DC 20011

Embassy/Consular Telephone: 202-726-0825
Fax: 202-726-1860

www.gksoft.com/govt/en/cg.html

COSTA RICA

CITIZENSHIP: Citizenship law is based upon the Constitution of Costa Rica.

- **BY BIRTH**: Child born within the territory of Costa Rica, regardless of the nationality of the parents.

- **BY DESCENT**: Child born abroad, at least one of whose parents is a citizen of Costa Rica.

- **BY NATURALIZATION**: The following categories of people are eligible to become naturalized Costa Rican citizens:
  - Central Americans, Spaniards, and Latin Americans, (all categories by birth) who have resided in the country for at least five years.
  - Central Americans, Spaniards, and Latin Americans, other than by birth, as well as other foreign nationals, who have resided in the country for at least seven years.
  - Foreign woman who has married a citizen of Costa Rica and either has lost her own citizenship or simply seeks to apply for Costa Rican citizenship.

DUAL CITIZENSHIP: RECOGNIZED
A Costa Rican woman who marries a foreign national will not lose her citizenship even if such a loss is required by the husband's country.

LOSS OF CITIZENSHIP: NOT RECOGNIZED
As of June 6, 1995, Articles 16 and 17 of the Costa Rican Political Constitution were modified; as modified, the Constitution mandates that there are no grounds for loss of Costa Rican citizenship regardless of any voluntary or involuntary reason to renounce it. *(Such reasons would be those of another nation.)*

ANY QUESTIONS concerning citizenship, or requests for renunciation of citizenship, should be directed to the address below:

Embassy of Costa Rica
Consular Section
2112 S Street, NW
Washington, DC 20008

Embassy Telephone: 202-234-2945/46/47
Consular Telephone: 202-328-6628
Fax: 202-265-4795

www.costarica.com/embassy

COTE d'IVOIRE (Formerly Ivory Coast)

CITIZENSHIP: *Information about the basis for Cote d'Ivoire citizenship laws was not provided.*

- **BY BIRTH**: Birth within the territory of Cote d'Ivoire does not automatically confer citizenship. The only exception is a child born to unknown parents.

- **BY DESCENT**: Child, at least one of whose parents is a citizen of Cote d'Ivoire, regardless of the child's country of birth.

- **BY NATURALIZATION**: Citizenship of Cote d'Ivoire may be acquired upon fulfillment of either of these conditions:
    - Person has resided in the country for at least five years.
    - Person has made a significant investment in the country or rendered a special service.

DUAL CITIZENSHIP: RECOGNIZED.

LOSS OF CITIZENSHIP:

- **VOLUNTARY**: Voluntary renunciation of citizenship of Cote d'Ivoire is permitted by law. Contact the Embassy for details and required paperwork.

- **INVOLUNTARY**: There are no grounds for involuntary loss of citizenship.

ANY QUESTIONS concerning citizenship, or requests for renunciation of citizenship, should be directed to the address below:

Embassy of the Republic of Cote d'Ivoire
Consular Section
2424 Massachusetts Ave., NW
Washington, DC 20008

Embassy/Consular Telephone: 202-797-0300
Fax: 202-483-8482

www.lcweb2.loc.gov/frd/cs/citoc.html

CROATIA

CITIZENSHIP: Citizenship laws are specified in the Law of Croatian Citizenship of June 1991.

- **BY BIRTH**: Birth within the territory of Croatia does not automatically confer citizenship. The exception is a child born to unknown parents.

- **BY DESCENT**:
  - Child, both of whose parents are citizens of Croatia, regardless of the child's country of birth.
  - Child born in Croatia, at least one of whose parents is a citizen of Croatia.
  - Child born abroad, at least one of whose parents is a citizen of Croatia, the other either unknown or stateless.
    - Any child-citizen born abroad must be registered.

- **BY NATURALIZATION**: Croatian nationality may be acquired upon fulfillment of the following:
  - Person has resided in the country for at least five years.
  - Person is the legal age of 18.
  - Person has proved that former citizenship will be removed.
  - Person is proficient in the Croatian language.
  - Person's conduct indicates an attachment to the legal system and culture of Croatia.
  - Rules may be waived for individual cases where citizenship would be in the interest of the Republic of Croatia, or for foreigners who marry Croatian citizens.

DUAL CITIZENSHIP: NOT RECOGNIZED.

LOSS OF CITIZENSHIP: Croatian citizenship shall be terminated by revocation, renouncement, or in accordance with international treaties.

- **VOLUNTARY**: Voluntary renunciation of citizenship is permitted by law. Contact the Croatian Embassy for details and paperwork. Persons seeking to renounce citizenship must meet the following conditions:
  - Person is 18 years of age.
  - Person has fulfilled all military obligations.
  - Person has provided proof of future citizenship.
  - Person has settled all official, personal, and financial obligations to their family and the state.

- **INVOLUNTARY**: According to the Consulate, there are no reasons for the involuntary loss of Croatian citizenship. Persons who obtain a new citizenship do not lose their Croatian citizenship by default. In Croatian law, the persons are still citizens of Croatia until they have been formally released from their citizenship.

ANY QUESTIONS concerning citizenship should be directed to the address below:

Embassy of the Republic of Croatia
Consular Section
2343 Massachusetts Ave., NW
Washington, DC 20002

Embassy/Consular Telephone: 202-588-5899
Fax: 202-588-8936
Web Site: **www.croatia.emb.org**

CUBA

CITIZENSHIP: *The basis for Cuban citizenship laws was not provided.*

- **BY BIRTH**: Child born within the territory of Cuba, regardless of the nationality of the parents.

- **BY DESCENT**: Child born abroad, at least one of whose parents is a citizen of Cuba.

- **BY NATURALIZATION**: *Data not provided.*

DUAL CITIZENSHIP: NOT RECOGNIZED.

LOSS OF CITIZENSHIP:

Many countries automatically revoke citizenship upon a person's acquisition of a foreign citizenship, but this is known not to always be the case in Cuba. Former citizens of Cuba should not assume that acquisition of a new nationality has released them from obligations and responsibilities associated with Cuban citizenship.

- **VOLUNTARY**: Voluntary loss of citizenship is permitted by Cuban law; however, it is necessary to first acquire the permission of the Council of State.

- **INVOLUNTARY**: The following is grounds for involuntary loss of Cuban citizenship: Person serves in an enemy armed force during time of war.

ANY QUESTIONS concerning Cuban citizenship should be directed to the address below:

Cuban Interest Section
Embassy of Switzerland
2630 16th Street NW
Washington, DC 20007

Telephone: 202-797-8518 or 202-797-0748
Fax: 202-797-8521

[State Department Desk Officer for Cuba: 202-647-9272]

CYPRUS

CITIZENSHIP: Citizenship is based upon the Republic Law of 1967. The legal basis for citizenship is divided between those born before and those born after August 16, 1960, the date of independence. All questions regarding Turkish Cyprus should be directed to the Cypriot Embassy.

(UKC-Commonwealth Nation)

- **BY BIRTH**: All citizens of the United Kingdom and Colonies who were born in Cyprus between November 5, 1914, and August 16, 1960, and who were resident in Cyprus during the five years preceding independence (August 16, 1960).

- **BY DESCENT**: Person born in wedlock, after August 16, 1960, whose father is a citizen of Cyprus, regardless of the country of birth. In the event the father is unknown or stateless, Cypriot citizenship may be passed on by the mother.

- **BY NATURALIZATION**: *No information was provided.*

DUAL CITIZENSHIP: RECOGNIZED.

LOSS OF CITIZENSHIP:

- **VOLUNTARY**: Voluntary renunciation of Cypriot citizenship is permitted by law. Contact the Embassy for details and required paperwork. The following are not allowed to renounce citizenship:
  - Persons who have not fulfilled their military requirements.
  - Persons who are under sentence for criminal activities.

- **INVOLUNTARY**: The following reflect grounds for involuntary loss of naturalized Cypriot citizenship:
  - Citizenship was gained under fraud or false statements.
  - Person commits acts of disloyalty to the government of Cyprus.
  - Person, within five years of being naturalized, begins to live continually abroad without registering with the Cypriot Consul.

[**TURKISH CYPRUS**: According to the Cypriot Consul: "An exceptional situation was created in the part of the territory of the Republic of Cyprus which has remained outside the control of the Government of Cyprus since the invasion of Cyprus by Turkish troops in the summer of 1974. The Republic of Cyprus continues to recognize the citizenship and right to citizenship of all Turkish Cypriots and Cyprus Republic passports are issued to any persons who can provide proper documentation. However, the Republic of Cyprus does not consider those alien persons who have settled illegally and without its permission in the areas under control of the Turkish forces as legitimate claimants to Cypriot citizenship."]

ANY QUESTIONS concerning citizenship, should be directed to the address below:

Embassy of the Republic of Cyprus
Consular Section
2211 R St., NW
Washington, DC 20008

Embassy/Consular Telephone: 202-462-5772
Fax: 202-483-6710

CZECH REPUBLIC

CITIZENSHIP: Czech citizenship laws are based on an Act of January 1, 1993, of the Czech National Council on Acquisition and Loss of Citizenship, as amended by Law 272 dated October 12, 1993, on Law 140 dated June 28, 1995, and on Law 139 dated April 26, 1996. Any individual who was jointly a citizen (Czechoslovakian), or was a citizen of the Czech and Slovak Federal Republic on December 31, 1992, shall become a citizen of the Czech Republic.

- **BY BIRTH**:
  - Birth within the Czech Republic does not automatically confer citizenship.
  - Persons under 17 years old, found in the Czech Republic, shall acquire Czech citizenship, if such person does not have citizenship of another country.
  - Child born in the territory of the Czech Republic to stateless parents, one of whom has permanent residency in the Czech Republic.

- **BY DESCENT**:
  - Child, at least one of whose parents is a citizen of the Czech Republic.
  - Child born out of wedlock, whose mother is not a Czech citizen, is only granted citizenship if their father is a Czech citizen. Either of the parents must declare paternity or a court judgement assigns paternity.

- **OTHER**: Any person who was a Czechoslovakian citizen up to December 31, 1992, and has not specified whether they are a Czech or Slovak citizen can choose Czech citizenship. They may proclaim this either at local district offices in the Czech Republic or at the Czech Embassies abroad.

- **BY NATURALIZATION**: Czech citizenship can be applied for upon fulfillment of the following conditions: Person has resided within the Czech Republic for at least five years, possesses knowledge of the Czech language, has renounced previous citizenship, and has not been convicted of a crime in the previous five years. The five year residency requirement may be waived if the person has permanent residency and falls under any of the following categories:
  - Person was born in the territory of the Czech Republic.
  - Person was a citizen of the Czech Republic or Czechoslovakia.
  - Person is married to a Czech citizen.
  - An adopted child, one of whose parents is a Czech citizen, shall acquire Czech citizenship at the date of adoption.

DUAL CITIZENSHIP: NOT RECOGNIZED.
Exception: Person has been living in the Czech Republic for five years and the law of their home country does not allow them to be released from their citizenship. Person obtains dual citizenship (citizenship *ex-lege*).

LOSS OF CITIZENSHIP:

- **VOLUNTARY**: Voluntary renunciation of Czech citizenship is possible under the following conditions:
  - Person does not live permanently in the Czech Republic.
  - A Czech citizen shall lose Czech citizenship at the moment they acquire, at their own request, the citizenship of another country (unless it is acquired by marriage).
  - Person has been living abroad for at least 10 years.

- **INVOLUNTARY**: The involuntary loss of citizenship is constitutionally prohibited.

CZECH REPUBLIC (cont.)

ANY QUESTIONS concerning Czech citizenship, or requests for renunciation of citizenship, should be directed to the address below:

Embassy of the Czech Republic
3900 Spring of Freedom St., NW
Washington, DC 20008

Embassy/Consul Telephone: 202-363-6315 ext. 25
Fax: 202-966-8540

DENMARK

CITIZENSHIP: Citizenship is based on Danish Nationality Law. Embassy officials state that Danish Nationality law is very complicated; they recommend contacting the Danish Embassy with any questions, particularly concerning dual citizenship.

- **BY BIRTH**: Birth within the territory of Denmark does not automatically confer citizenship. The exception is a child born in Denmark to unknown parents.

- **BY DESCENT**: Child, at least one of whose parents is a citizen of Denmark, regardless of the child's country of birth. Restrictions apply if the child is born prior to January 1, 1979, and only the mother is a citizen of Denmark.

- **BY NATURALIZATION**: Danish citizenship may be acquired upon fulfillment of the following conditions:
  - Person has resided in Denmark for 7 consecutive years.
  - Person has proved, by presentation of evidence, that they no longer possesses former citizenship.

DUAL CITIZENSHIP: NOT RECOGNIZED.
Exceptions:
- Danish citizen who marries a foreign national and acquires spouse's citizenship is not required to renounce Danish citizenship.
- Child born abroad to Danish parents who acquires the nationality of the country of birth may keep dual citizenship until the age of 22. Before reaching the age of majority (22), the person must apply to retain citizenship. If person does not apply, their citizenship is lost.

LOSS OF CITIZENSHIP:

- **VOLUNTARY**: Person seeking to voluntarily renounce Danish citizenship must contact the nearest Danish Embassy, present proof of acquisition of new citizenship, and sign documents renouncing citizenship. These forms will be forwarded to Denmark by the Embassy for registration. The person will receive a confirmation of loss of citizenship from the Danish government.

- **INVOLUNTARY**: The following is grounds for involuntary loss of Danish citizenship: Voluntary acquisition of foreign citizenship.

ANY QUESTIONS concerning citizenship, or requests for renunciation of citizenship, should be directed to the address below:

Royal Danish Embassy
Consular Section
3200 Whitehaven St., NW
Washington, DC 20008-3683

Embassy/Consular Telephone: 202-234-4300
Fax: 328-1470

http://www.denmarkemb.org
wasmb@wasamb.um.dk
www.denmark.org

DJIBOUTI

CITIZENSHIP: Citizenship is based on Law No.200/AN/81 of October 24, 1981. Those who were citizens before June 27, 1977, retain their citizenship.

- **BY BIRTH**: Birth within the territory of Djibouti does not automatically confer citizenship. The exception is a child born to unknown parents.

- **BY DESCENT**:
  - Child whose father is a citizen of Djibouti, regardless of the child's country of birth.
  - Child born in Djibouti, of a Djibouti mother and an unknown father.

- **REGISTRATION**: Foreign national, who marries a citizen of Djibouti, may apply for citizenship after two years of marriage.

- **BY NATURALIZATION**: Djibouti citizenship may be acquired upon the fulfillment of the following condition: Person must have resided in the country for at least 10 years.

DUAL CITIZENSHIP: NOT RECOGNIZED.

LOSS OF CITIZENSHIP:

- **VOLUNTARY**: Voluntary renunciation of Djibouti citizenship is permitted by law. Contact the Embassy for details and required paperwork.

- **INVOLUNTARY**: The following are grounds for involuntary loss of Djibouti citizenship:
  - Person voluntarily acquires a foreign citizenship.
  - Person is condemned for an act against the national security of the country.
  - Person is a member of a foreign army or international organization and refuses to terminate employment or cease participation on orders from the government of Djibouti.

ANY QUESTIONS concerning citizenship, or requests for renunciation of citizenship, should be directed to the address below:

Embassy of the Republic of Djibouti
Consular Section
1156 15th St., NW STE 515
Washington, DC 20005

Embassy/Consular Telephone: 202-331-0270
Fax: 202-331-0302

DOMINICA

CITIZENSHIP: *No information was provided.*

ANY QUESTIONS concerning citizenship, or requests for renunciation of citizenship, should be directed to the address below:

Embassy of the Commonwealth of Dominica
3216 New Mexico Ave. NW
Washington, DC 20016

Telephone: 202-364-6781

DOMINICAN REPUBLIC

CITIZENSHIP: Citizenship laws are based upon Article 11 of the Dominican Constitution.

- **BY BIRTH**: Child born in the territory of the Dominican Republic, regardless of the nationality of the parents. The exception is a child of a diplomatic representative.

- **BY DESCENT**: Child born abroad, at least one of whose parents is a citizen.

- **BY NATURALIZATION**: Dominican citizenship may be acquired upon fulfillment of the following conditions: Person has legally resided in the country for at least five years and has renounced former citizenship.

DUAL CITIZENSHIP: NOT RECOGNIZED.
Exception: Child born abroad, who acquires the nationality of the country of birth, is allowed to maintain dual nationality until the age of 18. Upon reaching age 18, the person must renounce the other nationality or Dominican nationality will be revoked.

LOSS OF CITIZENSHIP:

- **VOLUNTARY**: Voluntary renunciation of Dominican nationality is permitted by law. Person must formally renounce citizenship in the Dominican Republic. Contact the Embassy for details and required paperwork.

- **INVOLUNTARY**: The following is grounds for involuntary loss of Dominican citizenship: Person voluntarily acquires a foreign citizenship.

ANY QUESTIONS concerning citizenship, or requests for renunciation of citizenship, should be directed to the address below:

Embassy of the Dominican Republic
Consular Section
1715 22nd St., NW
Washington, DC 20008

Embassy/Consular Telephone: 202-332-6280
Fax: 202-265-8057
embdomrepusa@msn.com

ECUADOR

CITIZENSHIP: Ecuadorian citizenship law is based on the Constitution of Ecuador of 1998.

- **BY BIRTH**: Child born within the territorial limits of the Republic of Ecuador, regardless of the nationality of the mother or father.

- **BY DESCENT**:
  - Child born abroad, of a native born Ecuadorian father or mother, who later becomes resident of the Republic or expresses the desire to be Ecuadorian.
  - Child born abroad, of a native born Ecuadorian father or mother, while either parent carried out an official appointment or was exiled for political reasons, unless he or she expresses a desire (regarding the child's citizenship) to the contrary.

- **BY NATURALIZATION**: Ecuadorian citizenship can be applied for upon fulfillment of certain (unspecified) conditions.
  - Person obtains naturalization according to the Laws (unspecified) of Ecuador.
  - Marriage to an Ecuadorian national does not automatically confer citizenship, but it does aid in expediting the naturalization process.
  - Congress can grant a person citizenship as a reward for important services to the country.

DUAL CITIZENSHIP: NOT RECOGNIZED.
Exception: Dual nationality is recognized between Ecuador and Spain by treaty between the two countries.

LOSS OF CITIZENSHIP:

- **VOLUNTARY**: Voluntary renunciation of citizenship can be accomplished through any Ecuadorian embassy abroad. The embassy will report the renunciation to the Ministry of Foreign Affairs in Ecuador, which will register the renunciation in the Civilian Registry. Once registered, the person will cease to be a citizen of Ecuador.

- **INVOLUNTARY**: The following is grounds for involuntary loss of Ecuadorian citizenship: Person voluntarily acquires foreign citizenship other than Spain.

ANY QUESTIONS concerning citizenship, or requests for renunciation of citizenship, should be directed to the address below:

The Embassy of Ecuador
Consular Section
2335 14th St., NW
Washington, DC 20009

Embassy Telephone: 202-234-7200
Consular Telephone: 202-234-7166
Fax: 202-265-9325
mecuawa@erols.com or **conecuwa@erols**

EGYPT

CITIZENSHIP: Egyptian citizenship laws are based on Law #17, promulgated on June 22, 1958. The law is based on the concept of legitimate descent.

- **BY BIRTH**: Birth within the country of Egypt does not automatically confer citizenship. Citizenship by birth is only granted under the following conditions:
    - Child born in Egypt, out of wedlock, to an Egyptian mother, when the father is unknown or stateless, is considered a citizen of Egypt.
    - Child born in Egypt of unknown parents is automatically granted Egyptian citizenship.

- **BY DESCENT**: Child, born in wedlock, whose father is an Egyptian citizen, is automatically a citizen of Egypt, regardless of the child's country of birth.

- **BY NATURALIZATION**: There is no standard law for naturalization. Different categories of people face varying requirements. Some groups include:
    - Persons born in Egypt, of a father who was born in Egypt, and who is a member of a racial minority, faces no residency requirements if their language is Arabic or religion is Islam.
    - Person, who was born in and has resided most of their life in Egypt, may opt for Egyptian nationality upon reaching the age of majority. However, a presidential decree is required.
    - Woman who marries an Egyptian national becomes a citizen of Egypt, providing that she declares her desire to acquire her husband's nationality to the Minister of the Interior. Upon making the declaration, two years of marriage must follow before citizenship is granted.
    - Most other persons face a residency requirement of 10 years, as well as the necessity of obtaining a presidential decree, for citizenship to be granted.

DUAL CITIZENSHIP: NOT RECOGNIZED.
Exceptions:
Voluntary renunciation of Egyptian citizenship is only valid when the person has obtained prior official authorization. Person must obtain presidential authorization to abandon their Egyptian nationality. In such cases where authorization is not obtained, dual citizenship can exist by default.

However, a woman who marries a foreign national and declares her intention to acquire her husband's nationality can lose her Egyptian citizenship without prior authorization and thus would not acquire this form of dual citizenship.

LOSS OF CITIZENSHIP: (See "Exceptions" to "Dual Citizenship" above for explanation of need for prior authorization in renunciation of citizenship.) In all cases of loss of citizenship, a presidential decree is required. Due to the uncertainty created by the emphasis on prior authorization, questions pertaining to loss of citizenship should be directed to the Egyptian embassy.

- **VOLUNTARY**: Voluntary renunciation of Egyptian citizenship is allowed, provided the person obtains prior authorization through a presidential decree. For aid in the process of properly renouncing Egyptian citizenship, contact the nearest Egyptian Embassy.

- **INVOLUNTARY**: The following are grounds for involuntary loss of Egyptian citizenship:
    - Person voluntarily obtains foreign citizenship.
    - Person commits certain offenses.
    - Person who takes permanent residency abroad will lose citizenship after six months.

EGYPT (cont.)

QUESTIONS concerning citizenship should be directed to the address below

Embassy of the Arab Republic of Egypt
Consular Section
3521 International Court, NW
Washington, DC 20009

Embassy Telephone: 202-895-5400
Consular Telephone: 202-966-6342
Fax: 202-244-4319/5131

www.sis.gov.eg
www.idsc.gov.eg

EL SALVADOR

CITIZENSHIP: Salvadoran citizenship law is based on the Salvadoran Constitution.

- **BY BIRTH**: Child born in El Salvador, regardless of the citizenship of the mother or father.

- **BY DESCENT**: Child born abroad of a Salvadoran mother or father.

- **BY NATURALIZATION**: Salvadoran citizenship can be acquired by fulfillment of the following conditions:
    - Persons of any origin who have maintained residency in El Salvador for at least five years. (Spaniards and native Hispano-Americans need only reside for 1 year; foreign spouses of Salvadoran citizens need to reside at least 2 years after the time of marriage.)
    - Persons can obtain citizenship from the legislative branch for noteworthy services rendered to the republic.

- **OTHER**: El Salvador recognizes a special citizenship designation for natives of other states that constituted the Federal Republic of Central America, who, having domicile in El Salvador, declare before a competent authority their desire to be Salvadoran.

DUAL CITIZENSHIP: RECOGNIZED. Salvadorans by birth have the right to enjoy double or multiple citizenship. This right is not extended to those whose citizenship was acquired through naturalization.

LOSS OF CITIZENSHIP: Salvadoran citizenship based on birth is lost only by an expressed renunciation before a competent authority and may be recovered by petition before the same authority. Naturalized citizenship that has been lost can not be regained.

- **VOLUNTARY**: Voluntary renunciation of citizenship can be requested through any Salvadoran embassy abroad.

- **INVOLUNTARY**: The following are grounds for involuntary loss of naturalized citizenship:
    - Residing more than two consecutive years in the country of birth.
    - Absence from the territory of the republic for more than five years, unless official permission is granted.
    - Final legal judgement, decree, or sentence by legitimate Salvadoran representative.

ANY QUESTIONS concerning citizenship, or requests for renunciation of citizenship, should be directed to the address below:

The Embassy of El Salvador
Office of Consular Affairs
1424 16th St., NW Suite 200
Washington, DC 20036

Embassy Telephone: 202-265-9671/72
Consular Telephone: 202-331-4032
Fax: 202-331-4036
74524.2306@compuserve.com

EQUATORIAL GUINEA

CITIZENSHIP: *Information on the basis for Equatorial Guinean citizenship laws was not provided.*

- **BY BIRTH**: Child born within the territory of Equatorial Guinea is granted citizenship, regardless of the nationality of the parents. The only exception is a child born to foreigners in the service of their country.

- **BY DESCENT**: Child born abroad, at least one of whose parents is a citizen of Equatorial Guinea.

- **BY NATURALIZATION**: Equatorial Guinean citizenship may be acquired upon fulfillment of the following conditions:
  - Person is of legal age (unspecified).
  - Person has resided in the country for at least 10 years.

DUAL CITIZENSHIP: NOT RECOGNIZED.

LOSS OF CITIZENSHIP:

- **VOLUNTARY**: Voluntary renunciation of Equatorial Guinean citizenship is permitted under law. Contact Equatorial Guinean Embassy for details and required paperwork.

- **INVOLUNTARY**: The following is grounds for involuntary loss of Equatorial Guinean citizenship: Person voluntarily acquires a foreign citizenship.

ANY QUESTIONS concerning citizenship, or requests for renunciation of citizenship, should be directed to the address below:

Embassy of Equatorial Guinea
Consular Section
2020 16th Street NW
Washington, DC 20009

Embassy/Consular Telephone: 202-518-5700
Fax: 202-518-5252
info@equatorialguinea.org

ERITREA

CITIZENSHIP: Citizenship laws are based upon the Eritrean Nationality Proclamation.

- **BY BIRTH**: Birth within the territory of Eritrea does not automatically confer citizenship. The exception is a child born of unknown parents.

- **BY DESCENT**: Child, at least one of whose parents is a citizen of Eritrea, regardless of the child's country of birth.

- **ORIGIN**: Person who was a resident of Eritrea prior to 1934 is considered to have "Eritrean origin" and is granted citizenship.

- **BY NATURALIZATION**: Naturalization laws for Eritrea are divided into two time periods: 1934 to 1951, and 1951 to the present.
    1934 to 1951:
    - Eritrean nationality is granted to non-citizens who had entered and resided in Eritrea during the period of 1934 to 1951.
    1951 to Present:
    - Person has entered Eritrea legally and resided continually for 10 years before 1974 or 20 years if many trips abroad were made.
    - Person has renounced previous citizenship, speaks one of the languages of Eritrea, plans to permanently reside in the country, has adequate financial support, and has never been convicted of a crime.

- **MARRIAGE**: Non-citizens who marry Eritrean nationals may be granted citizenship if the non-citizen has lived in the country at least three years after marriage and has renounced previous nationality. Citizenship may be revoked upon an attempted readoption of the previous citizenship or a divorce from the citizen spouse.

DUAL CITIZENSHIP: NOT RECOGNIZED.
Exception: Special arrangements may be made for Eritrean citizens by birth who wish to retain a foreign citizenship they have since acquired.

LOSS OF CITIZENSHIP:

- **VOLUNTARY**: Permitted under Eritrean law. Contact embassy representatives of the Eritrean government for guidelines on renunciation.

- **INVOLUNTARY**: The following are grounds for involuntary loss of Eritrean citizenship:
    - Person voluntarily acquires another citizenship.
    - Person voluntarily serves the interests of another country.
    - Naturalized citizen has been sentenced to more than five years in prison or gained citizenship under false pretenses.

ANY QUESTIONS concerning citizenship, should be directed to the address below:

Embassy of the State of Eritrea
1708 New Hampshire Ave., NW
Washington, DC 20009

Embassy Telephone: 202-319-1991
Fax: 202-319-1304/1308
www.netafrica.org/eritrea

ESTONIA

CITIZENSHIP: Citizenship is based upon the Estonian Law passed by the Riigikogu (the Parliament) on January 19, 1995, with an effective date of April 1, 1995.

- **BY BIRTH**: Birth within the territory of Estonia does not automatically confer citizenship. The exception is a child born to unknown parents.

- **BY DESCENT**: Child of a recognized Estonian mother or father, regardless of the child's country of birth, even if the father dies before birth.

- **OTHER**: The following are eligible to acquire Estonian citizenship:
  - Foreign woman who married a citizen of Estonia before February 26, 1992.
  - Child under 18 years of age, of a foreign mother who marries a citizen of Estonia and establishes permanent residency.
  - Child born out of wedlock, who is legitimized (recognized) by the Estonian father.

- **BY NATURALIZATION**: Estonian citizenship may be acquired upon fulfillment of the following conditions: Person is at least 15 years old, is familiar with the Estonian language, and has permanently resided in Estonia for at least five years. (Permanent residency time is calculated after March 30, 1990, but may be waived in certain situations.)

  Persons Not Eligible For Naturalized Citizenship:
  - Person convicted of a serious crime.
  - Foreign military personnel on active duty.

DUAL CITIZENSHIP: NOT RECOGNIZED.

LOSS OF CITIZENSHIP:

- **VOLUNTARY**: Voluntary renunciation of Estonian citizenship is permitted by law. Persons who have not completed compulsory military service may not renounce citizenship. Contact Embassy for details and required paperwork.

- **INVOLUNTARY**: The following are grounds for involuntary loss of Estonian citizenship:
  - Person voluntarily acquires a foreign citizenship.
  - Person has entered into the military or civilian service of a foreign state.

ANY QUESTIONS concerning citizenship, or requests for renunciation of citizenship, should be directed to the address below:

Embassy of Estonia
Consular Section
2131 Massachusetts Ave., NW
Washington, DC 20008

Consulate General of the Republic of Estonia
600 Third Avenue, 26th Floor
New York, NY 10016

Embassy/Consular Telephone: 202-588-0101
Fax: 202-588-0108
www.ciesin.ee/undp/nhdr97/eng/index.html
www.vm.ee

info@estemb.org

ETHIOPIA

CITIZENSHIP: *Data was not provided.*

ANY QUESTIONS concerning citizenship, or requests for renunciation of citizenship, should be directed to the address below:

Embassy of Ethiopia
Consular Section
2134 Kalorama Rd., NW
Washington, DC 20008

Embassy/Consular Telephone: 202-234-2281/82
Fax: 202-328-7950

[Department of State Desk Officer for Ethiopia: 202-647-9742]

FIJI

CITIZENSHIP: Citizenship law for the Republic of Fiji is based on the 1997 Federal Constitution. All those who were citizens before October 1987 retain their citizenship.

- **BY BIRTH**: Child born within the territory of Fiji, with at least one parent being a citizen of Fiji.

- **BY DESCENT**: Child born outside the territory of Fiji, with the father being a citizen of Fiji.

- **BY REGISTRATION**: Citizenship may be granted by registration for the following persons:
    - Any woman who has been married to a citizen of Fiji.
    - Every person (age 21 or older) who was born outside Fiji, one of whose grandparents was a citizen of Fiji.
    - Children adopted by citizens of Fiji.

- **BY NATURALIZATION**: Fijian citizenship can be applied for upon fulfillment of one of the following conditions:
    - Person must have resided in Fiji for a continuous period of five years.
    - Person must have resided in Fiji for a continuous period of 12 months, and over a 10 year period, have resided in Fiji for an aggregate of at least five years.

DUAL CITIZENSHIP: NOT RECOGNIZED.
Exception: Dual citizenship obtained due to birth abroad may be retained up to 21 years of age. Upon reaching age of majority, foreign citizenship must be renounced within 12 months. If other citizenship is not renounced, Fijian citizenship is revoked at the end of 12 months.

LOSS OF CITIZENSHIP:

- **VOLUNTARY**: Right to voluntarily renounce citizenship has been granted by parliament.

- **INVOLUNTARY**: Parliament has the right to revoke the citizenship of any naturalized citizen. In the case of native-born Fijians, citizenship can be involuntarily revoked for the following reasons:
    - Person voluntarily acquires foreign citizenship.
    - For the dual citizenship exception, when foreign citizenship is not renounced before 22nd birthday.

ANY QUESTIONS concerning citizenship, or requests for renunciation of citizenship, should be directed to the address below:

Embassy of the Republic of Fiji
2233 Wisconsin Ave., NW STE 240
Washington, DC 20007

Embassy Telephone: 202-337-8320
Fax: 202-337-1996

FINLAND

CITIZENSHIP: Citizenship laws are based upon the Finnish Citizenship Act of June 28, 1968, amended in 1984.

- **BY BIRTH**: Birth within the territory of Finland does not automatically confer citizenship. The exception is a child who is stateless or whose parents are unknown.

- **BY DESCENT**:
  - Child born in wedlock of a Finnish father, regardless of the child's country of birth.
  - Child born out of wedlock of a Finnish mother, regardless of the child's country of birth.

- **BY NATURALIZATION**: Finnish citizenship may be acquired upon fulfillment of the following conditions: Person has renounced, or will renounce, former citizenship, is over 18 years of age, has continually resided in Finland for five years, has not committed any offenses, and has a means of support. (This does not apply to foreigners who marry Finnish nationals.)

DUAL CITIZENSHIP: NOT RECOGNIZED.
Exceptions: Dual citizenship is accepted under these circumstances:
- Child acquires Finnish citizenship from one parent and another citizenship from the other parent.
- Finnish citizen who marries a foreigner and automatically acquires the nationality of the foreign spouse without formal request.
- Child born to Finnish parents who becomes a foreign citizen by birth in another country.
    A child born abroad (as dual citizen) must return to live in Finland before the age of 22 and upon reaching 22 must choose one nationality in order to retain Finnish citizenship.

LOSS OF CITIZENSHIP: Laws concerning automatic revocation of citizenship upon acquiring a new citizenship are conflicting. Finnish citizenship may not be lost by default. Person concerned with dual citizenship should formally make renunciation request.

- **VOLUNTARY**: Voluntary renunciation of Finnish citizenship is permitted by law. Contact the Embassy for details and required paperwork.

- **INVOLUNTARY**: The following are grounds for involuntary loss of Finnish citizenship: Person who acquires a foreign citizenship by enlisting in the service of another country.

ANY QUESTIONS concerning citizenship, or requests for renunciation of citizenship, should be directed to the address below:

Embassy of Finland
3301 Massachusetts Ave., NW
Washington, DC 20008

Embassy/Consular Telephone: 202-298-5800
Fax: 202-298-6030
info@finland.org

FRANCE

CITIZENSHIP: Citizenship laws are based upon the French Nationality Code.

- **BY BIRTH**: Child born within the territory of France, regardless of the nationality of the parents.

- **BY DESCENT**: Child born abroad, at least one of whose parents is a citizen of France.

- **MARRIAGE**: The spouse of a French citizen can apply for French citizenship after one year of marriage with no residency requirement.

- **BY NATURALIZATION**: Persons seeking naturalization as French citizens face varying conditions. Residence circumstances are significant. These persons may seek naturalization:
  - Person who has been a resident of France for five years.
  - Person who has resided in France for two years and has a degree from a French University or has rendered important service to France.

  The following persons have no residency requirement and may seek naturalization:
  - Person who has rendered exceptional service to France.
  - Person who has served in a combat unit of the French Army.
  - Person who is the spouse or minor child of a person acquiring French citizenship.

DUAL CITIZENSHIP: RECOGNIZED.

LOSS OF CITIZENSHIP: Final authority for loss of citizenship lies with the French government.

- **VOLUNTARY**: Contact the French Embassy for details and proper paperwork.

- **INVOLUNTARY**: The following is grounds for involuntary loss of French citizenship: Person serves in a foreign military or civil service and has not complied with French orders to leave such service.

ANY QUESTIONS concerning citizenship, or requests for renunciation of citizenship, should be directed to the address below:

Embassy of France
Consular Office
4101 Reservoir Rd., NW
Washington, DC 20007-2185

Embassy Telephone: 202-944-6000
Consular Telephone: 202-944-6195
Fax: 202-944-6148

www.france-consulat.org
www.info-france-usa.org
www.france.org

GABON

CITIZENSHIP: *Basis for citizenship law was not provided.*

- **BY BIRTH**: Birth within the territory of Gabon does not automatically confer citizenship. The exception is a child born to unknown parents within Gabon.

- **BY DESCENT**: Child, at least one of whose parents is a citizen of Gabon, is considered a citizen regardless of the child's country of birth.

- **BY NATURALIZATION**: Gabonese citizenship may be acquired upon fulfillment of the following conditions: Person must prove relinquishment of former citizenship and have resided within the country for at least 10 years.

DUAL CITIZENSHIP: NOT RECOGNIZED.

LOSS OF CITIZENSHIP:

- **VOLUNTARY**: Voluntary renunciation of citizenship is permitted by law. Contact Gabonese Embassy for details and required paperwork.

- **INVOLUNTARY**: The following is grounds for involuntary loss of Gabonese citizenship: Person voluntarily acquires foreign citizenship.

ANY QUESTIONS concerning citizenship, or requests for renunciation of citizenship, should be directed to the address below:

Embassy of the Gabonese Republic
Consular Section
2233 Wisconsin Avenue, NW
Washington, DC 20007

Embassy/Consular Section: 202-797-1000
Fax: 202-332-0668

GAMBIA, THE GAMBIA

CITIZENSHIP: Based upon the Constitution of the Republic of The Gambia. (UKC-Commonwealth Nation) As a former British colony, Gambian citizenship laws are divided to accommodate people born before and after independence. The division date is February 18, 1965 Unless otherwise stated, laws listed are general in nature and apply both to those born before and after independence. Specific questions dealing with persons born before February 18, 1965, should be directed to the Gambian Embassy.

- **BY BIRTH**: Child born within the territory of The Gambia, regardless of the nationality of the parents. The only exception is children born to non-citizens when the father is an accredited representative of a foreign power.

- **BY DESCENT**: Child born abroad whose father is a citizen of The Gambia.

- **REGISTRATION**: Woman married to a citizen of The Gambia is entitled, upon making the proper application, to be registered as a citizen of The Gambia.

- **BY NATURALIZATION**: *Information was not provided.*

DUAL CITIZENSHIP: NOT RECOGNIZED.
Exception: Gambian citizen, who acquires new citizenship through marriage, is not required to renounce Gambian citizenship.

The Gambian government is debating changes to Gambian laws concerning dual citizenship. Questions concerning this issue should be directed to the Gambian Embassy.

LOSS OF CITIZENSHIP:

- **VOLUNTARY**: Permitted. Voluntary letters of renunciation should be directed to the nearest Gambian Embassy.

- **INVOLUNTARY**: The following are grounds for involuntary loss of Gambian citizenship:
    - Person voluntarily acquires foreign citizenship.
    - Person voluntarily claims or exercises any rights accorded to citizens of a foreign country.

ANY QUESTIONS concerning citizenship, or requests for renunciation of citizenship, should be directed to the address below:

Embassy of The Gambia
Consular Section
1155 15th St., NW STE 1000
Washington, DC 20005-2076

Embassy/Consular Telephone: 202-785-1399/1379/1425
Fax: 202-785-1430
www.gambia.com

GEORGIA

CITIZENSHIP: *Information was not provided.*

ANY QUESTIONS concerning citizenship, or requests for renunciation of citizenship, should be directed to the addresses below:

Permanent Mission to the United Nations
Republic of Georgia
136 E 67th St
New York, NY 10021

Mission Telephone: 212-288-8319
Fax: 212-288-8319

Embassy of the Republic of Georgia
Consular Section
1511 K St., NW STE NW424
Washington, DC 20005

Embassy/Consular Telephone: 202-393-6060
Fax: 202-393-6060

State Department Desk Officer for Georgia
202-647-6795

www.parliament.ge

GERMANY

CITIZENSHIP: Based upon German citizenship law, the principle of descent from the parents (*jus sanguinis*), and, after January 1, 2000, *jus soli.*

- **BY BIRTH**: Birth within the Federal Republic of Germany does not automatically confer citizenship. However, from January 1, 2000, citizenship will be acquired by birth in Germany if one parent has lived in the country for eight years.

- **BY DESCENT**:
    - Child born in wedlock whose father or mother is a citizen of Germany.
    - Child born out of wedlock whose father is stateless or unknown and whose mother is a citizen of Germany.
    - Child born out of wedlock to a foreign woman and a German father will be granted German citizenship upon the legitimization (recognition) of the child by the German father.

- **BY NATURALIZATION**: At the discretion of the German naturalization authority; 8 years residence in Germany is a requirement.

DUAL CITIZENSHIP: In principle, not recognized.
Exceptions:
- German citizens abroad who acquire another citizenship can forego the automatic forfeiture of their German citizenship by obtaining a decree from the German authorities permitting them to retain their German citizenship.
- After January 1, 2000, dual citizenship is allowed until age 23.

LOSS OF CITIZENSHIP:

- **VOLUNTARY**: The law allows Germans to petition for a release from German citizenship if they have applied for the acquisition of foreign citizenship and the authorities of the foreign state have stated that they will be naturalized. Petitions may be directed to the federal government in Germany or the nearest German Embassy.

- **INVOLUNTARY**: Voluntary acquisition of foreign citizenship without having received a decree from the German authorities permitting concurrent retention of German citizenship.

ANY QUESTIONS concerning citizenship, or requests for renunciation of citizenship, should be directed to the address below:

Embassy of the Federal Republic of Germany
Consular Section
4645 Reservoir Dr., NW
Washington, DC 20007

Embassy Telephone: 202-298-4360
Fax: 202-471-5558

www.germany-info.org
www.undp.org/missions/germany
www.government.de/english/01/newsf.html

GHANA

CITIZENSHIP: Citizenship law is based upon the Constitution of Ghana of April 1992. Every person who was a citizen of Ghana before the date of the Constitution remains a citizen of Ghana. (UKC-Commonwealth Nation)

- **BY BIRTH**: Birth within the territory of Ghana does not automatically confer citizenship. The exception is a child, born since the constitution, of unknown parents.

- **BY DESCENT**: Child, at least one of whose parents or grandparents is a citizen of Ghana, regardless of the child's country of birth.

- **MARRIAGE**: Foreign national who marries a citizen of Ghana is eligible to apply for citizenship by registration. If the marriage ends in divorce, death, or annulment, both may retain Ghanian citizenship, however, a registered male will be asked to prove the marriage was entered into in good faith.

- **BY NATURALIZATION**: Ghana does not encourage naturalization of foreigners with no blood or marital ties to Ghana. Decisions to grant citizenship to foreign nationals may be made by Parliament, providing the person is able to speak and understand the native language.

DUAL CITIZENSHIP: NOT RECOGNIZED.
Exceptions:
- A child born abroad, who obtains the citizenship of the country of birth, may retain dual citizenship until the age of 21, when one citizenship must be chosen or Ghanian citizenship will be lost.
- A Ghanian citizen who marries a foreign national and is required to renounce Ghanian citizenship may regain it upon the dissolution of the marriage. Thus, a form of dual citizenship exists.

LOSS OF CITIZENSHIP:

- **VOLUNTARY**: Voluntary renunciation of Ghanian citizenship is permitted by law. Contact the Embassy for details and required paperwork.

- **INVOLUNTARY**: The following are grounds for involuntary loss of naturalized Ghanian citizenship:
    - Person is shown to be a threat to Ghanian security, interests, or morality.
    - Citizenship was obtained through fraud, or false statement.

ANY QUESTIONS concerning citizenship, or requests for renunciation of citizenship, should be directed to the address below:

Embassy of Ghana
Consular Section
3512 International Dr., NW
Washington, DC 20008

Embassy/Consular Telephone: 202-686-4520
Fax: 202-686-4527

GREECE

CITIZENSHIP: Citizenship laws are based upon the Code of Greek Citizenship, amended in 1968 and 1984.

- **BY BIRTH**: Birth within the territory of Greece does not automatically confer citizenship. The only exceptions are abandoned children or children of stateless parents.

- **BY DESCENT**:
  - Child born in wedlock, of a Greek father, regardless of the child's country of birth.
  - Child born out of wedlock, of a Greek mother and an unknown or stateless father, regardless of the child's country of birth.

- **BY NATURALIZATION**: *No information provided.*

DUAL CITIZENSHIP: NOT RECOGNIZED.
Exception: Greek law does not automatically remove citizenship upon a person acquiring a foreign citizenship. When a Greek citizen acquires another nationality, they are technically a dual citizen until the Greek government has given permission for the removal of Greek citizenship.

LOSS OF CITIZENSHIP: A person may not acquire a foreign citizenship until they have received permission from the Ministry of the Interior to renounce Greek citizenship. One cannot assume Greek citizenship to be lost by default.

- **VOLUNTARY**: Voluntary renunciation of Greek citizenship is permitted by law, after receiving permission from the Ministry of the Interior. Those who have not fulfilled required military service or have been prosecuted for a felony are not granted permission to renounce Greek citizenship. Contact Embassy for details and required paperwork.

- **INVOLUNTARY**: The following are grounds for involuntary loss of Greek citizenship:
  - Person voluntarily acquires a foreign citizenship.
  - Person undertakes service with a foreign country.
  - Person has committed acts contrary to the national interest of Greece.

ANY QUESTIONS concerning citizenship, or requests for renunciation of citizenship, should be directed to the address below:

Embassy of Greece
Consular Section
2221 Massachusetts Ave., NW
Washington, DC 20008

Embassy Telephone: 202-939-5800
Consular Telephone: 202-939-5818
Embassy Fax: 202-939-5824
Consular Fax: 202-234-2803

www.hiway.gr/gi

GRENADA

CITIZENSHIP: Citizenship is based upon the Grenada Constitution Order, dated December 19, 1973. (UKC-Commonwealth Nation) The following persons were granted citizenship on February 7, 1974:

- Person born in Grenada, on or before February 6, 1974, who was a citizen of the United Kingdom and Colonies.
- Citizen of the UKC who, on or before February 6, 1974, was naturalized in Grenada as a British Subject.
- Person born abroad, on or before February 6, 1974, whose mother or father was granted Grenadian citizenship.
- Spouse of a person who was granted Grenadian citizenship, if married before February 6, 1974, is entitled to register for Grenadian citizenship.

- **BY BIRTH**: Child born within the territory of Grenada, on or after February 6, 1974, regardless of the nationality of their parents. The exception is a child born to certain diplomatic personnel.

- **BY DESCENT**: Person born abroad, on or after February 6, 1974, at least one of whose parents is a citizen of Grenada.

- **MARRIAGE**: Foreign person who marries a citizen of Grenada, on or after February 6, 1974, is able to register for Grenadian citizenship.

- **BY NATURALIZATION**: A Certificate of Naturalization may be issued to any alien or British protected person of full age (over 18) who makes application, provided:
  - The person has resided in Grenada for 12 continuous months immediately preceding the date of application.
  - Before the 12 months, that person resided in Grenada for 7 years (citizens from non-Caribbean countries), or 4 years (citizens from Caribbean countries).

- **BY REGISTRATION**: Persons born abroad after February 7, 1974, of at least one Grenadian parent, may be registered as a Grenadian citizen.

DUAL CITIZENSHIP: RECOGNIZED.
Grenadian law does not specify any prohibitions or requirements concerning dual citizenship for persons either emigrating to the island or seeking to obtain another citizenship.

LOSS OF CITIZENSHIP:

- **VOLUNTARY**: Voluntary renunciation of Grenadian citizenship is permitted. Contact the Embassy for details and required paperwork.

- **INVOLUNTARY**: There is no specificity about on the grounds for involuntary loss of Grenadian citizenship. However, the constitution states that only citizenship gained by registration or naturalization may be revoked.

ANY QUESTIONS concerning citizenship, should be directed to the address below:

Embassy of Grenada
1701 New Hampshire Ave, NW
Washington DC 20009

Telephone: 202-265-2561
www.grenada.org

GUATEMALA

CITIZENSHIP: Citizenship laws are based upon the Constitution of Guatemala.

- **BY BIRTH**: Child born within the territory of Guatemala, regardless of the nationality of the parents, including birth on any Guatemalan ship or aircraft.

- **BY DESCENT**: Child born abroad, at least one of whose parents is a citizen of Guatemala.

- **BY NATURALIZATION**: Guatemalan citizenship may be acquired upon fulfillment of the following conditions:
    - Person has renounced previous citizenship.
    - Person has legally resided in the country for one of the following time periods:
        - Five years collectively without being out of the country for more than one year.
        - Periods of time that total ten years.
        - Two years continuously.

    Other persons eligible for citizenship include:
    - Person who has rendered service to Guatemala.
    - Person who has lived in another Central American country.
    - Person who is stateless.
    - Person who is accomplished in science, art, or philanthropic efforts.

DUAL CITIZENSHIP: NOT RECOGNIZED.
Exception: Guatemala maintains dual citizenship agreements with some countries of Central and South America. If questions arise, contact the Embassy.

LOSS OF CITIZENSHIP:

- **VOLUNTARY**: Voluntary renunciation of Guatemalan citizenship is permitted by law. Contact the Embassy for details and required paperwork.

- **INVOLUNTARY**: The following are grounds for involuntary loss of Guatemalan citizenship: Person voluntarily acquires the citizenship of a foreign country (other than those nations with which dual citizenship agreements exist).

ANY QUESTIONS concerning citizenship, or requests for renunciation of citizenship, should be directed to the address below:

Embassy of Guatemala
Consular Section
2220 R St., NW
Washington, DC 20008

Embassy/Consular Telephone: 202-745-4952/53/54
Fax: 202-745-1908

GUINEA

CITIZENSHIP: *Information was not provided.*

- **BY BIRTH**: Birth within the territory of Guinea does not automatically confer citizenship. The exception is a child born to unknown or stateless parents.

- **BY DESCENT**:
  - Child of a Guinean father, regardless of the child's country of birth.
  - Child of a Guinean mother and an unknown father, regardless of the child's country of birth.

- **MARRIAGE**: A foreign woman who marries a citizen of Guinea is eligible for citizenship.

- **BY NATURALIZATION**: *No information was provided.*

DUAL CITIZENSHIP: NOT RECOGNIZED.

LOSS OF CITIZENSHIP:

- **VOLUNTARY**: Voluntary renunciation of Guinean citizenship is permitted by law. Contact the Embassy for details and required paperwork.

- **INVOLUNTARY**: The following is grounds for involuntary loss of Guinean citizenship: The person voluntarily acquires a foreign citizenship.

ANY QUESTIONS concerning citizenship, or requests for renunciation of citizenship, should be directed to the address below:

Embassy of the Republic of Guinea
Consular Section
2112 Leroy Place, NW
Washington, DC 20008

Embassy/Consular Telephone: 202-483-9420
Fax: 202-483-8688

GUINEA-BISSAU

CITIZENSHIP: Citizenship is based upon the Law of Nationality, dated 1973.

- **BY BIRTH**: Child born within the territory of Guinea-Bissau, regardless of the nationality of the parents.

- **BY DESCENT**: Child born abroad, at least one of whose parents is a citizen of Guinea-Bissau

- **BY REGISTRATION**: The following persons are eligible for citizenship through registration:
  - Foreign person whose grandparents were citizens of Guinea-Bissau.
  - Foreign person who marries a citizen of Guinea-Bissau.

- **BY NATURALIZATION**: Guinea-Bissauain citizenship may be acquired upon fulfillment of the following conditions: Person has legally resided in the country for at least five years, has renounced former citizenship, has a job or means of support, and does not have a criminal record.

DUAL CITIZENSHIP: NOT RECOGNIZED.
Exception: Child born abroad who obtains the citizenship of the country of birth, can retain dual citizen until the age of 18. Then the person must renounce the foreign citizenship or Guinea-Bissauain citizenship will be revoked.

LOSS OF CITIZENSHIP:

- **VOLUNTARY**: Voluntary renunciation of Guinea-Bissauain citizenship by birth is permitted. Contact the Embassy for details and required paperwork.

- **INVOLUNTARY**: The following are grounds for involuntary loss of Guinea- Bissauain citizenship:
  - Person obtains new citizenship.
  - Person is employed by a foreign government or armed force without permission of the Guinean-Bissauain government.
  - Naturalized citizenship was obtained through fraud or false statement.
  - Naturalized citizen lives more than a year abroad without registering with the local consulate.

ANY QUESTIONS concerning citizenship, or requests for renunciation of citizenship, should be directed to the address below:

Embassy of the Republic of Guinea-Bissau
Consular Section
918 16th Street NW, Mezzanine Suite
Washington, DC 20006

Embassy/Consular Telephone: 202-872-4222
Fax: 202-872-4226

GUYANA

CITIZENSHIP: Citizenship is based upon the Constitution of Guyana, dated 1980. Persons who were citizens of Guyana before the date of the Constitution remain citizens of Guyana. Persons who were already spouses of these people are entitled to register as citizens of Guyana. (UKC-Commonwealth Nation)

- **BY BIRTH**: Child born after 1980 in the territory of Guyana, regardless of the nationality of the parents. The exception is a child born to parents who are diplomatic personnel, neither of whom is a citizen of Guyana.

- **BY DESCENT**: Child born abroad after 1980, either of whose parents is a native-born citizen of Guyana.

- **MARRIAGE**: Foreign citizen who marries a citizen of Guyana after 1980 is eligible to register for citizenship.

- **BY NATURALIZATION**: *No information was provided.*

DUAL CITIZENSHIP: NOT RECOGNIZED.
Exception: The Constitution of 1980 states that any person who obtains the citizenship of another country after May 25, 1966 (except through marriage), shall lose their Guyanese citizenship. Questions concerning activities before this date should be directed to the Embassy.

LOSS OF CITIZENSHIP:

- **VOLUNTARY**: Voluntary renunciation of Guyanese citizenship is permitted by law. Contact the Embassy for details and required paperwork.

- **INVOLUNTARY**: The following is grounds for involuntary loss of Guyanese citizenship: Person voluntarily acquires a foreign citizenship (except through marriage).

ANY QUESTIONS concerning citizenship, or requests for renunciation of citizenship, should be directed to the address below:

Embassy of Guyana
Consular Section
2490 Tracy Pl. NW
Washington, DC 20008

Embassy/Consular Telephone: 202-265-6900/03
Fax: 202-232-1297

HAITI

CITIZENSHIP: Citizenship laws are based upon the Constitution of Haiti.

- **BY BIRTH**: Birth within the Republic of Haiti does not automatically confer citizenship.

- **BY DESCENT**: Child, at least one of whose parents is a native-born citizen of Haiti, regardless of the child's country of birth. Child born abroad must be registered at the nearest Haitian consulate or embassy for the citizenship to be recognized.

- **BY NATURALIZATION**: Haitian citizenship may be acquired upon fulfillment of the following condition: Person has resided within Haiti for a continuous period of five years.

DUAL CITIZENSHIP: NOT RECOGNIZED.
Exception: Child, born abroad to Haitian parents, who acquires the citizenship of the country of birth. This dual citizenship is allowed until the child reaches the age of majority (18). Upon reaching 18, one of the nationalities must be renounced.

LOSS OF CITIZENSHIP: Citizenship involuntarily lost may not be regained.

- **VOLUNTARY**: Voluntary renunciation of citizenship must take place in the country, before the Justice Department, Port-au-Prince, Haiti.

- **INVOLUNTARY**: The following are grounds for involuntary loss of Haitian citizenship:
  - Person voluntarily acquires foreign citizenship.
  - Person holds a political post in the service of a foreign government.
  - Naturalized Haitian citizen maintains continuous residence abroad without authorization by Haitian authority.

ANY QUESTIONS concerning citizenship, or requests for renunciation of citizenship, should be directed to the address below:

Embassy of the Republic of Haiti
Consular Section
2311 Massachusetts Ave., NW
Washington, DC 20008

Embassy/Consular Telephone: 202-332-4090/91/92
Fax: 202-745-7215

www.haiti.org/embassy/

HONDURAS

CITIZENSHIP: Citizenship laws are based upon the Honduran Constitution.

- **BY BIRTH**:
    - Child born within the territory of Honduras, regardless of the nationality of the parents. Children of diplomats are excluded.
    - Child born on a Honduran vessel or aircraft of war or on a merchant vessel located in Honduran territorial waters, regardless of the nationality of the parents.

- **BY DESCENT**: Child born abroad, at least one of whose parents is a citizen of Honduras.

- **BY NATURALIZATION**: Honduran nationality may be acquired by:
    - Central American by birth who has resided one year in Honduras.
    - Spaniards and Spanish-Americans by birth who have resided two years in Honduras.
    - Any person who has resided in Honduras for at least three years.
    - Person who has married a Honduran citizen (by birth).
    - Person granted citizenship by the Honduran National Congress.
    - Person admitted to Honduras for economic reasons, who has resided in Honduras for at least one year.

DUAL CITIZENSHIP: Permitted. The following may possess dual citizenship:
- Child of Honduran citizens born abroad.
- Honduran who acquires foreign citizenship by marriage.
- Person granted citizenship by act of the National Congress.
- Citizens of countries with which Honduras has dual nationality treaties.
- Hondurans seeking citizenship of countries with which Honduras has dual nationality treaty.

LOSS OF CITIZENSHIP: The citizenship of those whose citizenship was acquired through marriage, and that of their children, is not revoked upon dissolution of that marriage.

- **VOLUNTARY**: Permitted under Honduran law. Send letters of renunciation to Honduran Embassy.

- **INVOLUNTARY**: The following is grounds for involuntary loss of Honduran citizenship: Person voluntarily acquires foreign citizenship and does not fall under the dual citizenship exceptions.

ANY QUESTIONS concerning citizenship, should be directed to the address below:

Embassy of Honduras
Consular Section
1528 K Street NW (First Floor)
Washington, DC 20005

Embassy/Consular Telephone: 202-737-2972/2978
Fax: 202-737-2907

hondconswash@earthlink.net
www.hondorus.com

HUNGARY

CITIZENSHIP: Citizenship laws are based upon Law #55 dated June 1, 1993.

- **BY BIRTH**: Birth within the territory of Hungary does not automatically confer citizenship. The exception is a child born to unknown or stateless parents.

- **BY DESCENT**: Child, at least one of whose parents is a citizen of Hungary, regardless of the child's country of birth.

- **BY NATURALIZATION**: Hungarian citizenship may be acquired upon fulfillment of the following conditions:
    - Persons with no ethnic ties to Hungary must reside in the country for eight years.
    - Foreigners who marry Hungarian nationals, or who are parents of Hungarian citizen minors, or who have been adopted by Hungarian nationals, or who have been recognized as refugees by Hungarian authorities, need only reside in the country for three years.
    - Members of an ethnic Hungarian minority of another country need only reside in the country for one year.

DUAL CITIZENSHIP: RECOGNIZED.

LOSS OF CITIZENSHIP:

- **VOLUNTARY**: Voluntary renunciation of Hungarian citizenship is permitted. Persons seeking to renounce citizenship must address a written statement to the President of the Republic. The Embassy can provide information and assistance, but is not able to act for the person.

- **INVOLUNTARY**: The following is grounds for involuntary loss of Hungarian citizenship: Naturalized citizenship was gained by false statements.

ANY QUESTIONS concerning citizenship, or requests for renunciation of citizenship, should be directed to the Hungarian Embassy or Consulate whose consulate district extends to the person's permanent or usual residence. The consular districts are as follows:

Embassy in Washington covers the following states: Alabama, Arkansas, Florida, Georgia, Kentucky, Louisiana, Maryland, Mississippi, North Carolina, Ohio, Pennsylvania, South Carolina, Tennessee, Virginia, Washington DC, and West Virginia.

> Contact the Embassy of the Republic of Hungary, Consular Section, 3910 Shoemaker St., NW, Washington, DC 20008, Embassy/Consular Telephone: 202-362-6730, Fax: 202-966-8135. Office hours: Monday to Friday 9:00 - 3:00.

Consulate General in New York covers the following states: Connecticut, Delaware, Illinois, Indiana, Iowa, Maine, Massachusetts, Michigan, Minnesota, New Hampshire, New Jersey, New York, Rhode Island, Vermont, and Wisconsin.

> Contact the Consulate General of the Republic of Hungary, Consular Section, 223 52nd Street, New York, NY 10022, Consular Telephone 212-752-0661. Office hours: Monday to Friday 9:30 - 12:30.

Consulate General in Los Angeles covers the following states: Alaska, Arizona, California, Colorado, Hawaii, Idaho, Kansas, Montana, Nebraska, Nevada, New Mexico, North Dakota, South Dakota, Oklahoma, Oregon, Texas, Utah, Washington, and Wyoming.

> Contact the Consulate General of the Republic of Hungary, Consular Section, 11766 Wilshire Blvd. Suite 410, Los Angeles, CA 90025, Consular Telephone 310-473-9344. Office hours: Monday to Friday 9:30 - 13:00

www.hungaryemb.org

ICELAND

CITIZENSHIP: Citizenship laws are based upon the Icelandic Nationality Act, dated December 23 1952, amended May 11, 1982, and June 12, 1998. Iceland maintains agreements with the Nordic Contracting States (Denmark, Finland, Norway and Sweden). Questions concerning these countries should bedirected to the appropriate Embassy.

- **BY DESCENT**:
    - Child born in wedlock of an Icelandic mother or father, regardless of the child's country of birth.
    - Child born out of wedlock to an Icelandic woman, regardless of the child's country of birth.
    - Child born out of wedlock by an unmarried mother who is a foreign national and the father is an Icelandic national and the paternity is established in accordance with Icelandic law.

- **BY NATURALIZATION**: Icelandic Citizenship is granted by Parliament and the Ministry of Justice with various rules applied to people of different situations. For requirements, contact Icelandic Embassy. Some basic principles are these:
    - Residency of three to seven years depending on the person and their relationship to an Icelandic national.
    - Person must have either a job or some means of support.
    - Some who qualify for special consideration include members of the Nordic Contracting States, foreigners who marry Icelandic nationals, and former citizens of Iceland who have taken up domicile again.

DUAL CITIZENSHIP: NOT RECOGNIZED.
Exceptions:
- Child born to married parents of different nationalities, one being Icelandic and the other a foreigner.
- A naturalized person is not required to renounce their former citizenship.

LOSS OF CITIZENSHIP: *Information was not provided.*

ANY QUESTIONS concerning citizenship, or requests for renunciation of citizenship, should be directed to the address below:

The Embassy of Iceland
Consular Section
2022 Connecticut Ave., NW
Washington, DC 20008

Embassy/Consular Telephone: 202-265-6653/54/55
Fax: 202-265-6656

www.iceland.org

INDIA

CITIZENSHIP: Citizenship is based upon the Citizenship Act of 1955. Despite the variety of states, peoples, and languages in India, the law recognizes only Indian citizenship. (UKC-Commonwealth Nation)

- **BY BIRTH**: Child born within the territory of India, regardless of the nationality of the parents. Though the law of India does recognize citizenship through birth in the country, unless the citizenship is actively applied for, the Indian government does not consider the child a citizen of India. The person has the right to return to India upon reaching the age of 18 and applying for Indian citizenship.

- **BY DESCENT:**
    - Child born of an Indian father, regardless of the child's country of birth.
    - Child of an Indian mother and a foreign father is considered an Indian citizen if the mother and child continue to live in India and the father does not give the child his country's citizenship.
    - Child born out of wedlock to an Indian mother, regardless of the child's country of birth.
    - Children born abroad must be registered at an Indian Consulate.

- **BY NATURALIZATION**: Indian citizenship may be acquired upon fulfillment of the following conditions: Person has resided in the country for the last five years and has renounced previous citizenship.

DUAL CITIZENSHIP: NOT RECOGNIZED.

LOSS OF CITIZENSHIP:

- **VOLUNTARY**: Voluntary renunciation of Indian citizenship is permitted by law. Contact the Embassy for details and required paperwork.

- **INVOLUNTARY**: The following are grounds for involuntary loss of Indian citizenship:
    - Person voluntarily acquires a foreign citizenship.
    - Naturalized citizenship was acquired through false statements.
    - Naturalized citizen commits acts against the state of India before the end of a five-year grace period.

ANY QUESTIONS concerning citizenship, or requests for renunciation of citizenship, should be directed to the address below:

Embassy of India
Consular Section
2107 Massachusetts Ave., NW
Washington, DC 20008

Embassy Telephone: 202-939-7000
Consular Telephone: 202-939-9839/9845
Fax: 202-797-4693

www.nic.in
www.indianembassy.org
www.tourindia.com/

INDONESIA

CITIZENSHIP: Citizenship is based upon the Nationality Laws of Indonesia, dated January 1, 1946, and amended on August 1, 1958. Questions concerning persons born before January 1, 1946, should be directed to the Embassy.

- **BY BIRTH**:
  - Child born in the territory of Indonesia, between January 1, 1946, and August 1, 1958, regardless of the nationality of the parents.
  - Birth in the territory of Indonesia, on or after August 1, 1958, does not automatically confer citizenship. The exception is a child born to unknown parents.

- **BY DESCENT**:
  - Child born abroad, between January 1, 1946, and August 1, 1958, of an Indonesian father or of an Indonesian mother and an unknown father.
  - Child born on or after August 1, 1958, of an Indonesian father, regardless of the child's country of birth.
  - Child born on or after August 1, 1958, of an Indonesian mother and an unknown father, regardless of the country of birth.

- **MARRIAGE**: A foreign woman who marries a citizen of Indonesia may obtain Indonesian citizenship upon revocation of previous citizenship.

- **BY NATURALIZATION**: Indonesian citizenship may be acquired upon fulfillment of the following conditions: Person provides proof of loss or renunciation of former nationality, is at least age 21, was either born in Indonesia or has resided continuously for five years or not continuously for ten years, knows the Indonesian language, has knowledge of Indonesian history, has no criminal record, is of good mental and physical health, has a regular means of support, and, if applicable, has obtained their spouse's permission.

DUAL CITIZENSHIP: NOT RECOGNIZED.

LOSS OF CITIZENSHIP:

- **VOLUNTARY**: Voluntary renunciation of Indonesian citizenship is permitted by law. Contact the Embassy for details and required paperwork.

- **INVOLUNTARY**: The following are grounds for involuntary loss of Indonesian citizenship:
  - Person voluntarily acquires foreign citizenship; without permission from Indonesian Minister of Justice.
  - Person joins official military of a foreign country; without permission from Indonesian Minister of Justice.
  - Person conducts official tasks of an organization the Indonesian Government is not a member of and, according to Indonesian rules, the tasks are normally carried out only by a citizen of the country and requires him to take an oath to be devoted to the foreign country.
  - Person has a valid passport or other documents, in lieu of a passport, of foreign country on their behalf.
  - Person freely takes part in the official election of a foreign country, without any obligation.
  - Because of other than official tasks, lives in foreign country continuously for five years without declaring intention to still be an Indonesian citizen and fails to declare citizenship for two years consecutively.

INDONESIA (cont.)

ANY QUESTIONS concerning citizenship, or requests for renunciation of citizenship, should be directed to the address below:

Embassy of the Republic of Indonesia
Consular Section
2020 Massachusetts Ave., NW
Washington, DC 20036

Embassy/Consular Telephone: 202-775-5200
Fax: 202-775-5365

IRAN

CITIZENSHIP: Based upon the Iranian Civil Code.

- **BY BIRTH**: In general, birth within the territory of Iran does not automatically confer citizenship. The following are instances where birth within the territory of Iran does confer citizenship:
  - Child born to unknown parents.
  - Child born to non-citizens, one of whom was born within Iran.
  - Child born to non-citizens, who, after reaching the age of 18, continues to reside within Iran for at least one year.

- **BY DESCENT**: Child born to an Iranian father regardless of the child's country of birth.

- **MARRIAGE**: Foreign woman who marries an Iranian man is entitled to citizenship.

- **BY NATURALIZATION**: Iranian citizenship may be acquired upon fulfillment of the following conditions: Person must be at least 18 years of age, have resided in Iran for five years, not be a military service escapee, and not have been convicted of a major crime in any country.

  The wives and minor children (under 18) of naturalized Iranian citizens are also considered Iranian citizens.

DUAL CITIZENSHIP: NOT RECOGNIZED.
Exceptions:
- Child of an Iranian father, who acquires citizenship due to birth in a foreign country.
- A foreign woman who marries an Iranian is automatically granted Iranian citizenship, whether it is requested or not.

LOSS OF CITIZENSHIP:

- **VOLUNTARY**: Person seeking to voluntarily renounce Iranian citizenship must have reached the age of 25, have performed military service, have settled all affairs in the country, and acquired the permission of the Council of Ministers. Though the rules for renunciation of citizenship are stated in Iranian Law, practical experiences have shown that Council permission is difficult to obtain, thus hindering legal renunciation of Iranian citizenship.

- **INVOLUNTARY**: Voluntary acquisition of a foreign citizenship does not lead to automatic loss of Iranian citizenship. According to Iranian law, any Iranian national who acquires foreign citizenship without due observance of legal procedures will not have a renunciation of citizenship recognized by the government of Iran. In the eyes of the government, a male (and, in some cases, his wife and children) is still considered a citizen of Iran, regardless of the individual's status in the new country of citizenship.

ANY QUESTIONS concerning citizenship, should be directed to the address below:

Iranian Interest Section
2209 Wisconsin Ave., NW
Washington, DC 20007

Telephone: 202-965-4990/1/2/3/4/9
Fax: 202-965-1073/2050

IRAQ

CITIZENSHIP: *Information was not provided.*

ANY QUESTIONS concerning citizenship, and requests for renunciation of citizenship, should be directed to the address below:

Iraqi Interest Section
1801 P St., NW
Washington, DC 20036

Telephone: 202-483-7500
Fax: 202-462-5066

[State Department Desk Officer for Iraq: 202-647-5692]

www.iragi-mission.org

IRELAND

CITIZENSHIP: Citizenship is based upon the Irish Nationality and Citizenship Act of 1956.

- **BY BIRTH**: Child born within the territory of Ireland, regardless of the citizenship of the parents.

- **BY DESCENT**: Child born abroad, whose father or mother or grandparent was an Irish citizen by birth.

- **MARRIAGE**: Foreigner who marries an Irish citizen can apply for Irish citizenship after three years of marriage.

- **BY NATURALIZATION**: Irish citizenship may be acquired upon fulfillment of the following condition: Person has resided in Ireland for a cumulative period of four years out of eight. The last year of residence before application for citizenship must be continual.

DUAL CITIZENSHIP: RECOGNIZED.

LOSS OF CITIZENSHIP:

- **VOLUNTARY**: Voluntary renunciation of Irish citizenship is permitted by law. Letters of renunciation should be sent to the Department of Justice in Dublin. Contact the Embassy for details and required paperwork.

- **INVOLUNTARY**: The following is grounds for involuntary loss of naturalized citizenship: citizenship was obtained through fraud or false statement.

ANY QUESTIONS concerning citizenship, or requests for renunciation of citizenship, should be directed to the address below:

Embassy of Ireland
Consular Section
2234 Massachusetts Ave., NW
Washington, DC 20008

Embassy/Consular Telephone: 202-462-3939
Fax: 202-232-5993

www.irelandemb.org
www.cso.ie/index.html
www.genuki.org.uk

ISRAEL

CITIZENSHIP: Citizenship is based upon the Citizenship Law of 1952 and amended in 1968.
- Any Jew who immigrated to Israel before July 14, 1952, was granted citizenship after declaring a desire to reside permanently in Israel.
- Any former citizen of Palestine, present in Israel before July 14, 1952, was granted citizenship upon fulfillment of certain (*unspecified*) conditions.
- Any Jew or a member of a family of a Jew who immigrates to Israel after expressing their intention to settle in Israel, if from the date of their arrival as an immigrant, unless, being above the age of eighteen and a foreign citizen, they declare within three months from the date of arrival, that they do not wish to become an Israeli citizen. A "member of a family" of a Jew includes a spouse, a grandchild, and spouses of the child or grandchild of a Jew.

- **BY BIRTH**: Birth within the territory of Israel does not automatically confer citizenship.
  - Being born in Israel to a citizen of Israel.
  - Stateless person, born in Israel after May 14, 1948, is able to apply for citizenship between their 18th and 21st birthdays, provided they have resided in Israel for at least five years before application.

- **BY DESCENT**:
  - Child born on or after July 14, 1952, at least one of whose parents is a citizen of Israel, regardless of the child's country of birth.
  - A person born outside Israel while a parent was an Israeli citizen by Return (a 'renaturalized' Jew), Residence, or Naturalization.

- **BY NATURALIZATION**: Israeli citizenship may be acquired upon fulfillment of the following conditions: Person has resided in Israel a cumulative period of three years, intends to reside permanently in Israel, has some knowledge of Hebrew, and has renounced previous citizenship.

DUAL CITIZENSHIP: RECOGNIZED.
Exception: Naturalized Israeli citizens are not allowed to maintain dual citizenship. Citizens of Israel, who have immigrated to another country but still maintain citizenship with Israel, retain certain military obligations to the state of Israel. These obligations come into force if the person returns to live in Israel for an extended period. The Consulate states that these obligations only affect dual citizens.

LOSS OF CITIZENSHIP:

- **VOLUNTARY**: Voluntary loss of citizenship is permitted by law. Contact the Embassy for details and required paperwork.

- **INVOLUNTARY**: The following are grounds for involuntary loss of naturalized Israeli citizenship: Naturalized citizen either fails to renounce previous citizenship or voluntarily acquires new citizenship after obtaining Israeli citizenship.

ANY QUESTIONS concerning citizenship, should be directed to the address below:

Embassy of Israel
Consular Section
3514 International Dr., NW
Washington, DC 20008

Embassy Telephone: 202-364-5557
Consular Telephone: 202-364-5500
Fax: 202-364-5429

www.israel.org

ITALY

CITIZENSHIP: Citizenship law is based upon the Italian Law on Nationality amended February 5, 1992.

- **BY BIRTH**: Birth within the territory of Italy does not confer citizenship.
  Exceptions: A child born to unknown parents, and a child born in Italy, who resides there legally and uninterruptedly until reaching age 18, and who specifically requests Italian citizenship.

- **BY DESCENT**: Child, at least one of whose parents is an Italian citizen, regardless of the child's country of birth. Italian law makes provisions for citizenship to be granted to persons with specific familial ties to Italy.

- **MARRIAGE**: Person who marries an Italian national is eligible for citizenship unless person has been involved in any criminal proceeding.

- **BY NATURALIZATION**: Certain persons may acquire Italian citizenship upon completion of these periods of legal residency:
  - Three years for those with familial ties to Italy.
  - Four years for nationals of the European Community.
  - Five years for refugees, foreigners of legal age adopted by Italians, and persons who worked abroad in the service of Italy.
  - Ten years for others not falling into above categories.

DUAL CITIZENSHIP: RECOGNIZED. Amendment dated August 16, 1992, states those Italian citizens who acquire U.S. citizenship will retain Italian citizenship unless they voluntarily renounce their Italian citizenship.

LOSS OF CITIZENSHIP:

- **VOLUNTARY**: Voluntary renunciation is permitted by Italian law, though is not required when acquiring a foreign citizenship. Contact Embassy for details and required paperwork.

- **INVOLUNTARY**: The following is grounds for involuntary loss of Italian citizenship: Person voluntarily chooses to serve in the military of a foreign state, especially during a declared state of war.

ANY QUESTIONS concerning citizenship, or requests for renunciation of citizenship, should be directed to the address below:

Embassy of Italy
Consular Section
1601 Fuller St., NW
Washington, DC 20009

Embassy Phone: 202-328-5500
Consular Telephone: 202-328-5553
Fax: 202-328-5593

www.istat.it

JAMAICA

CITIZENSHIP: Citizenship is based upon the Jamaican Nationality Act of 1962, amended March 2, 1993. (UKC-Commonwealth Nation)

- **BY BIRTH**: Child born in the territory of Jamaica, regardless of the nationality of the parents.

- **BY DESCENT**: Child born abroad, at least one of whose parents is a citizen of Jamaica.

- **MARRIAGE**: Person, who marries a citizen of Jamaica, is eligible for Jamaican citizenship.

- **BY NATURALIZATION**: Jamaican citizenship may be applied for upon fulfillment of the following conditions:
  - Person has resided in Jamaica for at least the 12 months prior to the application for citizenship.
  - Person has resided in Jamaica for an aggregate of at least four years during the five year period before the application.
  - Person intends to reside in Jamaica once citizenship is granted.
  - Person is of good character, has a permanent residence and livelihood, and is involved in Jamaican society.

DUAL CITIZENSHIP: RECOGNIZED.
- The Jamaican Constitution does not specifically refer to dual citizenship, but it does not prohibit citizens from acquiring a second nationality.
- Jamaican law states that any Jamaican who acquires a foreign citizenship will be subject to all the responsibilities of the new citizenship and cannot claim any exemptions on the basis of their Jamaican nationality.

LOSS OF CITIZENSHIP:

- **VOLUNTARY**: Jamaican citizens do not lose their Jamaican citizenship upon the acquisition of a foreign citizenship. Any citizen of Jamaica wishing to renounce Jamaican citizenship must be granted permission by the government of Jamaica. Requests for renunciation must be sent to:
    > The Ministry of National Security
    > 12 Ocean Boulevard
    > Kingston Mall, Jamaica

- **INVOLUNTARY**: *No information was provided.*

ANY QUESTIONS concerning citizenship, or requests for renunciation of citizenship, should be directed to the address below:

Embassy of Jamaica
1520 New Hampshire Avenue, NW
Washington, DC 20036

Embassy Telephone: 202-452-0660
Fax: 202-452-0081

www.jamaica.com

JAPAN

CITIZENSHIP: Japanese citizenship is regulated by the Nationality Act of May 4, 1950.

- **BY BIRTH**: Birth within the territory of Japan does not automatically confer Japanese citizenship. Only in the case of a child whose parents are unknown or stateless is the child considered a Japanese citizen.

- **BY DESCENT**:
    - Child, whose father is a citizen of Japan, regardless of the child's country of birth. This law also applies if the father dies before the birth of the child.
    - Child born to Japanese mother and unknown or stateless father.

- **BY NATURALIZATION**: *No information was provided.*

DUAL CITIZENSHIP: NOT RECOGNIZED.
Exception: If a child is born abroad to Japanese parents the child can acquire dual nationality if citizenship is also acquired in the country of birth. Person with dual nationality has to choose one nationality by the age of 22. If dual nationality is acquired between ages 20 and 22, the person must choose one nationality within 2 years. If one does not choose Japanese nationality within these periods, the Minister of Justice can require one to choose a nationality. Failure to comply within one month of this requirement will result in loss of Japanese citizenship.

LOSS OF CITIZENSHIP:

- **VOLUNTARY**: Voluntary renunciation of citizenship can be accomplished at any Japanese consulate abroad. Paperwork will be completed at the Embassy; citizenship will terminate immediately. Renunciations do not have to be further approved by the government.

- **INVOLUNTARY**: The following is grounds for involuntary loss of Japanese citizenship: Person voluntarily acquires foreign nationality.

ANY QUESTIONS concerning citizenship, or requests for renunciation of citizenship, should be directed to the address below:

The Embassy of Japan
Consular Section
2520 Massachusetts Ave., NW
Washington, DC 20008

Embassy/Consular Telephone: 202-238-6700
Fax: 202-328-2187

www.embjap.org
www.mofa.go.jp

JORDAN

CITIZENSHIP: Citizenship laws are based upon the Jordanian Citizenship Act of 1954.

- **BY BIRTH**: Birth within the territory of Jordan does not automatically confer citizenship.

- **BY DESCENT**: Child born of a Jordanian father, regardless of the child's country of birth. **Preference is given** to those of Arab descent. The following are also considered citizens of Jordan:
  - Person of Arab descent who was habitually resident in Transjordan in 1928.
  - Person of Palestinian Arab nationality before May 15, 1948, who was habitually resident in Jordan at the coming into force of the 1954 Act.
  - Person of Arab blood continually resident in Jordan for five years.

- **BY NATURALIZATION**: Jordanian citizenship may be acquired upon fulfillment of the following condition: Person has maintained residence in Jordan for at least 15 years.

DUAL CITIZENSHIP: RECOGNIZED.

LOSS OF CITIZENSHIP: A Jordanian may neither lose Jordanian citizenship nor acquire the nationality of another state (other than an Arab State) without the consent of the Board of Ministers

- **VOLUNTARY**: Jordanian law permits voluntary renunciation, with the permission of the Board of Ministers. Contact the Embassy for details and required paperwork. A fee is assessed and the renunciation must be further approved by the Ministry of the Interior.

- **INVOLUNTARY**: The following are grounds for involuntary loss of Jordanian citizenship, though loss is not recognized until permission is granted by the board of Ministers:
  - Person commits misconduct that undermines the security of the state.
  - Person joins the Armed Forces of another state.

ANY QUESTIONS concerning citizenship, or requests for renunciation of citizenship, should be directed to the address below:

The Embassy of the Hashemite Kingdom of Jordan
3504 International Dr., NW
Washington, DC 20008

Embassy Telephone: 202-966-2664
Consular Telephone: 202-966-2861
Fax: 202-686-4491

www.nic.gov.jo

KAZAKHSTAN

CITIZENSHIP: Citizenship laws are based upon the Law on Citizenship for the Republic of Kazakhstan, dated March 1, 1992.

- **BY BIRTH**: Birth within the territory of Kazakhstan does not automatically confer citizenship. The exception is a child born of unknown or stateless parents.

- **BY DESCENT**:
  - Person born in Kazakhstan before March 1, 1992, who has maintained residence in the country.
  - Child of a Kazak mother or father, regardless of the child's country of birth.

- **OTHER**: Child born abroad, whose mother or father has legal permanent residency in Kazakhstan.

- **BY NATURALIZATION**: Kazak citizenship may be acquired upon fulfillment of the following conditions: Person is familiar with the language, has renounced former citizenship, and has made formal application for citizenship to either the Kazak Embassy or the Foreign Ministry in Kazakhstan.

DUAL CITIZENSHIP: NOT RECOGNIZED.
Exception: There are possible future dual citizenship agreements with some former Soviet Republics. Contact the Embassy for more information.

LOSS OF CITIZENSHIP:

- **VOLUNTARY**: Voluntary renunciation of Kazak citizenship is permitted under the law. Contact Kazakhstan Embassy for details and required paperwork.

- **INVOLUNTARY**: The following is grounds for involuntary renunciation of Kazak citizenship: Person voluntarily acquires foreign citizenship.

ANY QUESTIONS concerning citizenship, or requests for renunciation of citizenship, should be directed to the address below:

Embassy of Kazakhstan
Consular Section
3421 Massachusetts Ave., NW
Washington, DC 20007

Embassy/Consular Telephone: 202-333-4504/07
Fax: 202-333-4509

www.undp.org/missions/kazakhstan

KENYA

CITIZENSHIP: Citizenship laws are contained in the Kenyan Constitution.

- **BY BIRTH**: Every person born in Kenya after December 11, 1963, becomes a citizen of Kenya if, at the date of birth, at least one parent is a citizen of Kenya. This rule does not apply if:
  - The father possesses immunity from lawsuit and legal process as accorded to the envoy of a foreign State accredited to Kenya.
  - The father is a citizen of a country with which Kenya is at war and the birth occurs in a place then under occupation by that other country.

- **BY DESCENT**: Any person born outside Kenya after December 11, 1963, becomes a citizen of Kenya at the date of birth, if at that date, their father is a citizen of Kenya.

- **BY REGISTRATION**: Any woman who has been married to a citizen of Kenya is entitled to be registered as a citizen of Kenya. Certain other (*unspecified*) persons are eligible to be registered as citizens by virtue of other connections with Kenya after December 11, 1963.

- **BY NATURALIZATION**: A person is eligible to be naturalized as a citizen of Kenya if they satisfy the government that they meet these conditions:
  - Has attained the age of 21 years.
  - Has ordinarily and lawfully resided in Kenya for the twelve month period immediately preceding their application.
  - Has ordinarily and lawfully resided in Kenya for a period of, or for periods amounting in the aggregate to, not less than four years in the seven years immediately preceding the most recent 12 months.
  - Is of good character.
  - Has an adequate knowledge of the Swahili language.
  - Intends, if naturalized, to continue to reside in Kenya.

DUAL CITIZENSHIP: Not recognized except for persons under 21 years old.

LOSS OF CITIZENSHIP: Kenyan citizenship may be lost voluntarily or involuntarily.

- **INVOLUNTARY**:
  - The government may, by order after such procedures as may be prescribed by Parliament, deprive of their citizenship of Kenya any person who is a citizen by registration or naturalization on grounds specified (*not identified*) by the Constitution.
  - A person who, upon the attainment of the age of 21 years is a citizen of Kenya and also a citizen of some country other than Kenya, ceases to be a citizen of Kenya upon the specified date unless he has renounced his citizenship of that other country and has taken the oath of allegiance.

- **VOLUNTARY**:
  - Retaining citizenship of another country.
  - Acquiring citizenship of some other country.
  - A citizen of Kenya shall cease to be such a citizen if, having attained the age of 21 years, acquires citizenship of some country other than Kenya by voluntary act (other than Marriage); or, having attained the age of 21 years, otherwise acquires the citizenship of some country other that Kenya and has not, by specified date, renounced citizenship of that other country, taken the oath of allegiance, and made and registered such declaration of intentions concerning residence as may be prescribed by or under an Act of the Kenyan Parliament.

KENYA (cont.)

ANY QUESTIONS concerning citizenship, or requests for renunciation of citizenship, should be directed to the address below:

The Embassy of Kenya
Consular Section
2249 R St., NW
Washington, DC 20008

Embassy/Consular Telephone: 202-387-6101
Fax: 202-462-3829

KIRIBATI (Formerly the Gilbert Islands)

CITIZENSHIP: Citizenship information is based on the Kiribati Independence Order dated July 12, 1979. These persons were eligible for automatic citizenship on Independence Day, July 12, 1979:
- Person of Kiribati descent (i.e., person descended from those born in Kiribati before 1900) who was born in Kiribati and was a citizen of the United Kingdom and Colonies (UKC).
- Person not of Kiribati descent, but who was born in Kiribati.
- Person of Kiribati descent, or a citizen of the UKC, who was naturalized in Kiribati.
- Person of Kiribati descent, a citizen of the UKC, born abroad, whose father was a citizen of Kiribati.
- Foreign woman who was married to person eligible for Kiribati citizenship.

- **BY BIRTH**: Birth within the territory of Kiribati, on or after July 12, 1979, does not automatically confer citizenship. The only exception is a child born to unknown or stateless parents.

- **BY DESCENT**: For persons born on or after July 12, 1979:
  - Child of a native-born Kiribati father, regardless of the child's country of birth.
  - Child born out of wedlock to a Kiribati mother and an unknown father, regardless of the child's country of birth.

- **MARRIAGE**: A foreign wife of a Kiribati citizen is eligible to register for citizenship.

- **BY NATURALIZATION**: *No information was provided.*

DUAL CITIZENSHIP: NOT RECOGNIZED.

LOSS OF CITIZENSHIP:

- **VOLUNTARY**: Voluntary renunciation of Kiribati citizenship is permitted by law.

- **INVOLUNTARY**: There are no grounds for the loss of citizenship for those of Kiribati descent. The following are grounds for involuntary loss of all other forms of Kiribati citizenship:
  - Person voluntarily obtains foreign citizenship, except by marriage.
  - Person exercises rights or privileges, or submits to any requirements, of a foreign state.
  - Naturalized citizenship that was obtained through fraud or falsity.

ANY QUESTIONS concerning Kiribati Citizenship Law should be directed to the addresses below:

Law Library
American-British Law Division Rm. LM 240
Library of Congress/Madison Building
Washington, DC 20540-3020 - Telephone: 202-707-5077 - Fax: 202-707-1820

The Republic of Kiribati does not have an embassy in the United States; the Ambassador for the Marshal Islands is the accredited representative of Kiribati in the United States.

Republic of the Marshall Islands
Attn: Kiribati Interest Section
2433 Massachusetts Ave. NW
Washington, DC 20008 - Embassy Phone: 202-234-5414 - Fax: 202-232-3236

KOREA, NORTH (Democratic People's Republic of Korea)

CITIZENSHIP: Citizenship is based upon the Nationality Law of October 9, 1963. Persons who were citizens of the territory of Korea at the establishment of the People's Republic, May 1, 1948, were granted North Korean citizenship on that date.

- **BY BIRTH**: Birth within the territory of North Korea does not automatically confer citizenship. The exception is a child born of unknown or stateless parents.

- **BY DESCENT**:
  - A child born of a North Korean mother and father, regardless of the child's country of birth.
  - A child born in North Korea, of a North Korean citizen and a foreign national.
  - The citizenship of a child born abroad of parents of mixed nationality, one of whom is a North Korean citizen, is to be determined by the parents.

- **BY NATURALIZATION**: North Korean citizenship is only granted by the Presidium of the Supreme Peoples' Assembly. *Specific requirements were not provided.*

DUAL CITIZENSHIP: NOT RECOGNIZED.
Exception: It is difficult to renounce North Korean citizenship. Most citizens of North Korea who become naturalized citizens of another country will remain unofficial dual citizens, still considered North Korean citizens by the North Korean government.

LOSS OF CITIZENSHIP:

- **VOLUNTARY**: Voluntary renunciation of North Korean Citizenship is technically possible by North Korean Law. Renunciation must be granted by the Peoples' Assembly. Unless renunciation is officially granted, the person will continue to be considered a citizen of North Korea.

- **INVOLUNTARY**: There are no grounds for involuntary loss of North Korean citizenship.

ANY QUESTIONS concerning North Korean citizenship laws should be directed to:

Permanent Representative of the Democratic People's Republic of Korea to the UN
515 East 72nd St, 38-F
New York, N.Y. 10021

Telephone: 212-772-0712/0725/0748
Fax: 212-772-0735 - **prkun@undp.org**

Or

CA/OCS/CCS/EAP RM 4817
U.S. Department of State
2201 C St., NW
Washington, DC 20520-4818

Telephone: 202-647-7717
Fax: 202-647-7388

North Korea does not have diplomatic representation in the United States. Citizenship information was provided by the U.S. State Department's Office of Citizen Consular Services.

KOREA, SOUTH (Republic of Korea)

CITIZENSHIP: Korean citizenship is governed by the Nationality Act of December 13, 1997, later amended.

- **BY BIRTH**: Birth within the territory of the Republic of Korea does not automatically confer citizenship.
  - A person who is born in the Republic of Korea of unknown parents.
  - An abandoned child found in the Republic of Korea is recognized as born in Korea.

- **BY DESCENT**:
  - A person whose father or mother is a national of the Republic of Korea at the time of the child's birth.
  - Child whose father is a Korean national is automatically considered a Korean citizen regardless of the child's place of birth, even if the father died before the child was born.

- **BY NATURALIZATION**: Naturalization falls into two basic categories: Acknowledgment and General Naturalization.

  - **ACKNOWLEDGEMENT**: Laws concerning Acknowledgement are generally invoked when there is some form of blood tie or marital bond involving a citizen of the Republic of Korea. Requirements for citizenship through Acknowledgment vary if the petitioner is a minor or a foreign wife.
    - All petitioners, including minors and foreign wives, must possess no foreign citizenship or must renounce the foreign nationality within 6 months. They also must have resided within the Republic of Korea for at least three years.
    - If the person is a minor (according to the laws of the former home country), their mother or father who is a Korean national must acknowledge them. Acknowledgement by the parent of the child is a prerequisite to naturalization. It is also required that the Korean parent make a simultaneous acknowledgement of their own Korean nationality.
    - A foreigner whose spouse is a national of the Republic of Korea may obtain permission for naturalization if they have been married for 3 years and domiciled in Korea for at least one consecutive year.

  - **GENERAL**: Specific conditions apply when there is no blood or marital tie. Under this circumstance, Korean citizenship will be granted upon the fulfillment of these conditions:
    - Person has resided in the Republic of Korea for five years or more.
    - Person shall be of majority pursuant to the Civil Act of the Republic of Korea.
    - Person shall be of good conduct.
    - Person must have the ability to provide an independent livelihood.
    - Person must have a basic knowledge of the Korean language and understand Korean customs.
    - Person must obtain permission of the Minister of Justice.

DUAL CITIZENSHIP: NOT RECOGNIZED.
A person who has had the nationalities of both the Republic of Korea and a foreign country by birth shall select one nationality before their 22nd birthday.

LOSS OF CITIZENSHIP:

- **VOLUNTARY**: To renounce citizenship, contact the consular office. A processing fee is required. The embassy will process the forms through Korea.

KOREA, SOUTH (cont.)

- **INVOLUNTARY**: The following are grounds for involuntary loss of Korean citizenship:
  - Person acquires the citizenship of a foreign spouse or adoptive parent, or any other voluntary acquisition of foreign citizenship.
  - Person has obtained an annulment or divorce and their Korean citizenship was acquired through marriage.
  - Person, after six months of Korean citizenship, has still not renounced previous citizenship

ANY QUESTIONS concerning citizenship, or requests for renunciation of citizenship, should be directed to the address below:

The Embassy of the Republic of Korea
Consular Office
2320 Massachusetts Ave., NW
Washington, DC 20008

Embassy Telephone: 202-939-5600
Consular Telephone: 202-939-5661/5653 or 202-939-5657
Embassy Fax: 202-797-0595
Consular Fax: 202-342-1597

KUWAIT

CITIZENSHIP: Citizenship laws are based upon the Constitution of Kuwait.

- **BY BIRTH**: Birth within the territory of Kuwait does not automatically confer citizenship. Kuwait has a large number of guest workers living in the country; Kuwaiti law considers them to be citizens of their country of origin. Children born in Kuwait of long term guest residents do not qualify for citizenship. In all cases, unless the child is born to a Kuwaiti citizen, the child is born a citizen of the parents' home country.

- **BY DESCENT**:
  - Child born in wedlock, whose father is a citizen of Kuwait, regardless of the child's country of birth.
  - Child born out of wedlock, to a Kuwaiti mother and an unknown father, regardless of the child's country of birth.

- **MARRIAGE**:
  - A foreign woman who marries a citizen of Kuwait may obtain citizenship after 15 years residency.
  - A foreign man who marries a citizen of Kuwait is not eligible for citizenship.

- **BY NATURALIZATION**: Kuwaiti citizenship may be obtained under the following specific condition: Person is granted citizenship through a special act of government.

DUAL CITIZENSHIP: NOT RECOGNIZED.

LOSS OF CITIZENSHIP:

- **VOLUNTARY**: Voluntary renunciation of Kuwaiti citizenship is permitted by law. Contact the Embassy for details and required paperwork.

- **INVOLUNTARY**: There are no grounds for involuntary loss of Kuwaiti citizenship.

ANY QUESTIONS concerning citizenship, or requests for renunciation of citizenship, should be directed to the address below:

Embassy of the State of Kuwait
Consular Section
2940 Tilden St., NW
Washington, DC 20008

Embassy/Consular Telephone: 202-966-0702
Fax: 202-966-8468

www.kuwait-info.org
www.moc.kw

KYRGYZ REPUBLIC

CITIZENSHIP: Citizenship is based on the draft Constitution, dated May 5, 1993.

- **BY BIRTH**: Birth within the territory of Kyrgyz Republic does not automatically confer citizenship. The exception is a child of unknown or stateless parents who have been permanently residing in the Kyrgyz Republic and who plan to continue residing in the country.

- **BY DESCENT**:
  - Child of both a Kyrgyz mother and father, regardless of the child's country of birth.
  - Child born in the Kyrgyz Republic at least one of whose parents is a citizen of the Kyrgyz Republic.
  - Child born abroad, both of whose parents are Kyrgyz citizens.
  - For a child born abroad, one of whose parents is not a Kyrgyz citizen, the parents choose which nationality the child will possess.

- **BY NATURALIZATION**: Kyrgyz citizenship may be acquired upon fulfillment of the following condition: The person's application for citizenship is approved by the national government.

DUAL CITIZENSHIP: NOT RECOGNIZED.
Exception: *Current information is not available; the Kyrgyz Republic may adopt dual citizenship agreements with former Soviet Republics.*

LOSS OF CITIZENSHIP:

- **VOLUNTARY**: Voluntary renunciation of Kyrgyz citizenship is permitted by law. Contact the Embassy for details and required paperwork.

- **INVOLUNTARY**: The following is grounds for involuntary loss of Kyrgyz citizenship: Person acquires foreign citizenship.

ANY QUESTIONS concerning citizenship, or requests for renunciation of citizenship, should be directed to the Embassy. Citizenship questions concerning Russian or former Soviet nationals living in the Republic should similarly be directed to the Kyrgyz Embassy.

Embassy of the Kyrgyz Republic
Consular Section
1732 Wisconsin Ave., NW
Washington, DC 20007

Embassy/Consular Telephone: 202-338-5141
Fax: 202-338-5139

embassy@kyrgyzstan.org
www.kyrgyzstan.org

LAOS

CITIZENSHIP: Citizenship is based upon the Law of Laotian Citizenship, dated November 29, 1990.

- **BY BIRTH**: Birth within the territory of Laos does not confer citizenship.

- **BY DESCENT**: Child born of a Laotian mother or father, regardless of the child's country of birth.

- **BY NATURALIZATION**: Laotian citizenship may be acquired upon fulfillment of the following conditions: Person must be 18 years or older, be able to speak, read, and write Lao, have established permanent residency, understand the customs of the country, have no criminal record, renounce previous citizenship, and receive final permission from the National Assembly.

DUAL CITIZENSHIP: NOT RECOGNIZED.

LOSS OF CITIZENSHIP:

- **VOLUNTARY**: Voluntary renunciation of Laotian citizenship is permitted by law, however, permission must be granted by the National Assembly. Persons should not assume renunciation of citizenship to be automatically guaranteed. Contact the Embassy for details and required paperwork.

- **INVOLUNTARY**: The following are grounds for involuntary renunciation of Laotian citizenship
  - Person voluntarily acquires a foreign citizenship, though persons in this situation should not assume Laotian citizenship would simply be lost by default.
  - Naturalized citizenship was obtained by fraud or false statement.
  - Naturalized citizen has engaged in behavior detrimental to the state of Laos.

ANY QUESTIONS concerning citizenship, or requests for renunciation of citizenship, should be directed to the address below:

Embassy of the Lao People's Democratic Republic
Consular Section
2222 S St., NW
Washington, DC 20008

Embassy/Consular Telephone: 202-332-6416/17
Fax: 202-332-4923

www.loaembassy.com/discover/index.htm

LATVIA

CITIZENSHIP: The citizenship regulations are set in the Citizenship Law of the Republic of Latvia

- **BY BIRTH**: *Data not provided.*

- **BY DESCENT**:
  - A child whose parents were citizens of Latvia on the day of birth, regardless of the child's place of birth.
  - If, at the time of birth, one of the parents is a citizen of Latvia and the other parent is an alien, if the child was born in Latvia..
  - A child born outside of Latvia, but both parents otherwise permanently reside in Latvia.
  - A child born outside of Latvia, but the parent with whom the child lives otherwise permanently resides in Latvia.
  - If, at the time of birth, one parent is a citizen of Latvia and the other parent is an alien and the permanent place of residence of both parents is outside Latvia, then the child's citizenship shall be decided upon by mutual agreement of the parents.
  - If, at the time of birth, one parent is a Latvian citizen and the other parent is stateless or is unknown, then the child shall be a Latvian citizen regardless of the child's place of birth.

- **BY MARRIAGE**: The marriage of a Latvian citizen to an alien or a stateless person, and the dissolution of such marriage, shall not cause a change in citizenship of Latvian citizens. The acquisition or loss of the citizenship of Latvia by one spouse does not affect the citizenship of the other spouse.

- **BY NATURALIZATION**:
  - A person can be granted the citizenship of Latvia through naturalization, upon their request.
  - The citizenship of Latvia shall be granted through naturalization only to those who are registered in the Residents' Registry and who comply with other (*unspecified*) conditions established by the Citizenship Law.

DUAL CITIZENSHIP: Not recognized. If a citizen of Latvia simultaneously can be considered a citizen or subject of a foreign country in accordance with the laws of that country, the citizen shall be considered solely a citizen of Latvia in relations with the Republic of Latvia.

LOSS OF CITZENSHIP:

- **VOLUNTARY**:
  - Any person, who is a citizen of another state or has been guaranteed the citizenship of another state, shall be entitled to renounce Latvian citizenship.

    An application to renounce citizenship can be denied if the person has not fulfilled obligations to the state or if the person has not fulfilled military service obligations. A decision to deny an application for the renunciation of citizenship can be appealed to the courts.

LATVIA (cont.)

- **INVOLUNTARY**: Latvian citizenship may be revoked by a decision of a Regional Court, if:
  - Person has acquired the citizenship of another state without submitting an application for renunciation of citizenship of Latvia.
  - Person is serving in the armed forces, military forces, security service, police (militia), or is employed in a juridical institution of a foreign state, without permission from the Cabinet of Ministers;
  - Person has intentionally provided false information when verifying their right to hold Latvian citizenship or has illegally obtained the citizenship of Latvia.

  The revocation of Latvian citizenship shall not affect the citizenship of the person's spouse, children, or other family members.

QUESTIONS concerning citizenship, should be directed to the address below:

The Embassy of Latvia
Consular Section
4325 17th St., NW
Washington, DC 20011

Embassy/Consular Telephone: 202-726-8213
Fax: 202-726-6785

www.latvia-usa.org
www.csb.lv

LEBANON

CITIZENSHIP: *The basis for citizenship laws was not provided.*

- **BY BIRTH**: Birth within the Republic of Lebanon does not confer citizenship.

- **BY DESCENT**:
    - A child whose father is a citizen of Lebanon is considered to be a Lebanese citizen.

      A child born in Lebanon to a foreign mother, without acknowledgement by a Lebanese father, obtains the nationality of the mother.

      All children of Lebanese descent born outside of Lebanon must be registered at the Lebanese embassy or the child's Lebanese citizenship will not be automatically granted.

- **BY NATURALIZATION**: Lebanese citizenship can be acquired by fulfilling the following condition: Person has applied for, and been granted, a Decree from the Lebanese Council of Ministers. Naturalized citizenship cannot otherwise be acquired.

DUAL CITIZENSHIP: RECOGNIZED.

LOSS OF CITIZENSHIP:

- **VOLUNTARY**: To voluntarily renounce Lebanese citizenship, person must send a letter of renunciation to the nearest Lebanese embassy or consulate. The embassy will forward the renunciation to Lebanon. The embassy will notify the individual if the renunciation is approved

  Lebanese citizenship, voluntarily renounced, can be reacquired if the reasons for renunciation no longer apply.

- **INVOLUNTARY**: The following are grounds for involuntary loss of Lebanese citizenship:
    - Person engages in the service of a foreign state.
    - Person commits an offense against the security of the Lebanese state.

ANY QUESTIONS concerning citizenship, or requests for renunciation of citizenship, should be directed to the address below:

The Embassy of Lebanon
Consular Section
2560 28th St., NW
Washington, DC 20008

Embassy Telephone: 202-939-6300
Consular Telephone: 202-939-6305
Fax: 202- 939-6324

www.erols.com/lebanon/stat.htm

LESOTHO

CITIZENSHIP: Citizenship is based upon the Lesotho Citizenship Order, dated 1971, and the revised Constitution, dated 1993. Questions concerning persons born on or before October 3, 1966 (independence), should be directed to the Embassy. (UKC-Commonwealth Nation)

- **BY BIRTH**: Child born after October 3, 1966, within the territory of Lesotho, regardless of the nationality of the parents. The exception is a child born of parents who are not citizens and whose father works in a diplomatic capacity.

- **BY DESCENT**:
  - Child born abroad, after October 3, 1966, whose father is a citizen.
  - Child born abroad, after October 3, 1966, whose mother is an unmarried Lesothan citizen.

- **MARRIAGE**:
  - A foreign woman who was already married to a man who became a citizen of Lesotho on October 3, 1966, is granted citizenship upon application.
  - A foreign woman who marries a citizen of Lesotho after October 3, 1966, can apply for citizenship.

- **BY NATURALIZATION**: Lesothan citizenship is acquired upon fulfillment of the following conditions: Person is at least age 21, has resided in Lesotho for five years after October 3, 1966, has renounced previous citizenship, knows the language, is of good character and mental capacity, takes the oath of allegiance, and plans to permanently reside in Lesotho.

DUAL CITIZENSHIP: NOT RECOGNIZED.
Exception: Child born abroad, who obtains the citizenship of the country of birth, may retain dual citizenship until their 21st birthday. Person must renounce other citizenship or Lesothan citizenship will be revoked.

LOSS OF CITIZENSHIP:

- **VOLUNTARY**: Voluntary renunciation of Lesothan citizenship is permitted by law, pending approval by the government. Contact the Embassy for details and required paperwork.

- **INVOLUNTARY**: The following are grounds for involuntary loss of Lesothan citizenship:
  - Any citizen voluntarily acquires a foreign citizenship other than through marriage.
  - Naturalized/Registered (N/R) citizenship…
    - Was obtained through fraud or false statement.
    - Citizen displays acts of disloyalty to Lesotho.
    - Citizen, within five years of citizenship, is convicted of a crime and sentenced to at least five years imprisonment.
    - Citizen has resided abroad more than seven years without registering intention to remain a citizen of Lesotho.
    - Citizen has claimed rights or privileges of citizens of another country.

ANY QUESTIONS concerning citizenship, should be directed to the address below:

Embassy of the Kingdom of Lesotho
Consular Section
2511 Massachusetts Ave., NW
Washington, DC 20008
Embassy/Consular Telephone: 202-797-5533/34/35/36
Fax: 202-234-6815

LIBERIA

CITIZENSHIP: Citizenship laws are based upon the Constitution of the Republic of Liberia. The Liberian Constitution states that, "In order to preserve, foster, and maintain the positive Liberian culture, values, and character, only persons who are Negroes or of Negro descent shall qualify by birth or by naturalization to be citizens of Liberia."

- **BY BIRTH**: Birth within the territory of Liberia does not automatically confer citizenship. The only exception is a child born to unknown parents.

- **BY DESCENT**: Child, at least one of whose parents is a citizen of Liberia, regardless of the child's country of birth.

- **BY NATURALIZATION**: *No information provided beyond the stated constitutional requirements.* .

DUAL CITIZENSHIP: NOT RECOGNIZED.
Exception: Child may keep dual citizenship before reaching the age of majority (18). Upon reaching majority age, the person must renounce any other citizenship.

LOSS OF CITIZENSHIP:

- **VOLUNTARY**: Voluntary renunciation of Liberian citizenship is permitted by law.

- **INVOLUNTARY**: The following is grounds for involuntary loss of Liberian citizenship: Person above the age of majority (18) acquires a foreign citizenship.

ANY QUESTIONS concerning citizenship of Liberia should be directed to the address below:

Embassy of the Republic of Liberia
5201 16th Street, NW
Washington DC 20011

Telephone: 202-723-0437
Fax: 202-723-0436

info@liberiaemb.org

LIBYA

CITIZENSHIP: Information is based upon the Nationality Law #17, dated 1954, and Law #3, dated 1979. Persons born before October 7, 1951 (date of Libyan Constitution), who did not have a previous citizenship and had been residing in Libya, obtained citizenship under the following conditions:

- Person was born in Libya.
- Person was born abroad of a mother or father born in Libya.
- Person had been living in Libya for at least 10 years before October 7, 1951.

- **BY BIRTH**: Birth within the territory of Libya, on or after October 7, 1951, does not automatically confer citizenship.

- **BY DESCENT**: Child born on or after October 7, 1951, of a Libyan mother, father, grandmother, or grandfather, regardless of the child's country of birth.

- **MARRIAGE**: A foreign woman who marries a citizen of Libya may obtain Libyan citizenship if she renounces former citizenship, resides with her husband in marriage for at least two years, and notifies the Minister of Foreign Affairs of her desire to obtain Libyan citizenship. If the marriage ends in divorce, the woman's citizenship will only be removed if she remarries a non-Libyan and leaves the country.

- **BY NATURALIZATION**: Libyan citizenship may be acquired upon fulfillment of the following conditions:
  - Person has renounced previous nationality, is a legal adult, has good morality and mental health, and desires to remain in Libya. Residency requirements vary:
    - Arab man married to a Libyan woman - four years.
    - Person of Arab descent - five years.
    - Children (of father's nationality) of Libyan mother and foreign father - three years.

DUAL CITIZENSHIP: NOT RECOGNIZED.

LOSS OF CITIZENSHIP:

- **VOLUNTARY**: *No information was provided.*

- **INVOLUNTARY**: The following are grounds for involuntary loss of Libyan citizenship:
  - Person obtains new citizenship without government permission.
  - Person enlists in foreign military or attempts to avoid Libyan conscription.
  - Person seeks asylum in another country.
  - Person attempts to smuggle money out of the country.
  - Person converts to a religion other than Islam.
  - Person deserted country after 1969 revolution.
  - Person refuses to return home within 6 months of state request.
  - Person commits treasonous acts against the state.

  - Additional grounds for a naturalized citizen:
    - Person commits crimes against the security of the state.
    - Person remains outside the country more than two years.
    - Person obtained citizenship through fraud or false statement.

LIBYA (cont.)

ANY QUESTIONS concerning Libya should be directed to the address below

NEA/MAG Rm 5250
U.S. Department of State
2201 C St., NW
Washington, DC 20520

Telephone: 202-647-4674
Fax: 202-736-4458

Questions concerning Libyan Citizenship law should be directed to:

Law Library
Near Eastern and African Law Division
Madison Building RM LM 240
101 Independence Ave., NW
Washington, DC 20540-3060

Telephone: 202-707-5073
Fax: 202-707-1820

LITHUANIA

CITIZENSHIP: Citizenship is based upon the Law on Citizenship of the Republic of Lithuania, dated December 5, 1991. Questions concerning persons born before June 15, 1940, should be sent to either the Consulate General of Lithuania in New York or in Chicago.

IMPLEMENTATION OF THE RIGHT TO CITIZENSHIP: Persons who possessed Lithuanian citizenship prior to June 15, 1940, their children and grandchildren, must apply for citizenship to the Consulates in New York or Chicago.

- **BY BIRTH**: Birth within Lithuania does not automatically confer citizenship. The exception is a child of unknown or stateless parents.

- **BY DESCENT**:
    - Child, both of whose parents are citizens of Lithuania, regardless of child's country of birth.
    - Child born abroad, one of whose parents is a citizen of Lithuania.
    - Child born abroad, one of whose parents is a citizen of Lithuania with permanent residence in Lithuania.

- **BY NATURALIZATION**: Lithuanian citizenship may be acquired upon fulfillment of the following conditions: Person has passed examinations in the Lithuanian language and in the basic provisions of the Constitution, has permanently resided in Lithuania for at least 10 years, has a permanent place of employment or a legal source of support, and is a stateless person or has renounced previous citizenship.

- **MARRIAGE**: Foreigner who marries a citizen of Lithuania must fulfill all the basic naturalization requirements except that residency requirement is three years after marriage.

DUAL CITIZENSHIP: Not generally recognized. *Specificity not provided.*

LOSS OF CITIZENSHIP:

- **VOLUNTARY**: Voluntary renunciation of Lithuanian citizenship is permitted by law. Contact Embassy for details and required paperwork.

- **INVOLUNTARY**: The following are grounds for involuntary loss of Lithuanian citizenship:
    - Person voluntarily acquires a foreign citizenship.
    - Person lives abroad over 3 years without government permission.
    - Person enters the civilian or military service of a foreign state.

ANY QUESTIONS concerning citizenship, should be directed to an address below:

Consulate General of Lithuania
420 Fifth Avenue 3rd Floor
New York, NY 10018
    Telephone: 212-354-7840/7849
    Fax: 212-354-7911

Consulate General of Lithuania
211 East Ontario Street, Suite 1500
Chicago, IL 60611
    Telephone: 312-397-0382
    Fax: 312-397-0385

Embassy of the Republic of Lithuania
Consular Section
2622 16th St., NW
Washington, DC 20009
    Telephone: 202-234-5860/2639
    Fax: 202-328-0466

www.std.lt

LUXEMBOURG

CITIZENSHIP: Luxembourg citizenship is governed by the Law of January 1, 1987. This Law is based on the principle of descent (*jus sanguinis*).

- **BY BIRTH**: Birth within the territory of Luxembourg does not automatically confer citizenship.

- **BY DESCENT**:
  - Child whose father or mother is a citizen of Luxembourg, regardless of the child's country of birth.
  - Child born out of wedlock to a foreign mother and Luxembourger father is considered a citizen of Luxembourg if paternity is legally established.

- **BY NATURALIZATION**: Application for Luxembourg citizenship through naturalization falls into two categories:
  - **Naturalization**:
    - Citizenship granted through the Legislature requires a 10-year residency in Luxembourg as well as sufficient (*unspecified*) national assimilation.
  - **Option Policy**:
    - The Option is reserved for various categories of foreigners who have special ties with the country (birth within the territory, adoption, or marriage to a Luxembourg national). Citizenship is granted by declaration, subject to the approval of the Minister of Justice

DUAL CITIZENSHIP: NOT RECOGNIZED.
Exception: Child born abroad to Luxembourg citizens, who acquires another citizenship due to laws in the country of birth. However, at the age of 18 a decision must be made of which nationality the individual wishes to maintain. Upon this decision, the other nationality must be renounced.

LOSS OF CITIZENSHIP:

- **VOLUNTARY**: Voluntary renunciation of Luxembourger citizenship must be done in the country. Persons living in Luxembourg make their declaration before a civil officer in their loca area. In eight days the person will receive a certificate of renunciation. Four days later, the renunciation will be published in the Gazette, making it final. If the person resides out of the country, the declaration must be made in the capital, Luxembourg City, before a civil officer.

- **INVOLUNTARY**: The following are grounds for involuntary loss of Luxembourger citizenship:
  - Voluntary acquisition of a foreign citizenship.
  - Grave crime against the State of Luxembourg (applies only to naturalized citizens).

ANY QUESTIONS concerning citizenship, or requests for renunciation of citizenship, should be directed to the address below:

Embassy of Luxembourg
Consular Section
2200 Massachusetts Ave., NW
Washington, DC 20008

Embassy/Consular Telephone: 202-265-4171/72
Fax: 202-328-8270

MADAGASCAR

CITIZENSHIP: Malagasy citizenship is based upon Ordinance No.60-064, dated July 22, 1960. Malagasy nationality law is based on descent from the father (*jus sanguinis*).

- **BY BIRTH**: Birth within the Republic of Madagascar does not automatically confer citizenship. Citizenship is only granted automatically in cases of abandoned children.

- **BY DESCENT**:
  - Child, born in wedlock, whose father is a citizen of Madagascar.
  - Child, born out of wedlock to Malagasy mother, when the child's father is stateless or unknown

- **MARRIAGE**: Foreign woman, who marries a citizen of Madagascar, can obtain citizenship by declaration. After marriage, wife must make a declaration to an officer of the State of her desire to obtain Malagasy citizenship. Citizenship is granted upon this declaration on a two-year probationary basis.

- **BY NATURALIZATION**: Malagasy citizenship can be obtained upon fulfillment of the following conditions: Person must be at least 18 years of age, be of good character, be in good mental and physical health, and not have been convicted of a crime within the last year.

DUAL CITIZENSHIP: NOT RECOGNIZED.
Exception: Child born abroad, who obtains a foreign citizenship, may keep their dual citizenship until the age of majority (21). At that time the child must choose which citizenship they wish to keep.

A Malagasy citizen, who upon marriage to a foreign spouse obtains a foreign citizenship, is not required to renounce their Malagasy citizenship unless it is a requirement (of their other citizenship).

LOSS OF CITIZENSHIP:

- **VOLUNTARY**: Requests for voluntary renunciation of citizenship may be directed to the nearest Malagasy Embassy.

- **INVOLUNTARY**: The following are grounds for involuntary loss of Malagasy citizenship:
  - Person voluntarily obtains foreign citizenship.
  - Person marries a foreign national and resides permanently abroad.
  - Person convicted of crime against the security of the State.

ANY QUESTIONS concerning citizenship should be directed to the address below:

Embassy of the Republic of Madagascar
Consular Department
2374 Massachusetts Ave., NW
Washington, DC 20008

Embassy/Consular Telephone: 202-265-5525
Fax: 202-483-7603

malagasy@embassy.org
www3.itu.ch/missions/madagascar

MALAWI

CITIZENSHIP: Citizenship is based upon the Malawi Citizenship Act, dated July 6, 1966. Every person who was a citizen of Malawi before July 6, 1966, continues to be a citizen of Malawi. (UKC-Commonwealth Nation)

- **BY BIRTH**: Birth within the territory of Malawi does not automatically confer citizenship. The exception is a child born of unknown parents.

- **BY DESCENT**:
  - Child born in Malawi, on or after July 6, 1966, whose father or mother is a citizen of Malawi and is of African race.
  - Child born abroad, on or after July 6, 1966, one of whose parents is a native-born citizen of Malawi of African race.

- **BY NATURALIZATION**: Malawian citizenship may be acquired upon fulfillment of the following conditions: Person is of an African race or has Commonwealth or Malawian ties, has resided five years in the country, has adequate knowledge of the English language, intends to reside permanently in Malawi, and will renounce previous citizenship. (Aliens without the national ties must have resided for seven years.)

DUAL CITIZENSHIP: NOT RECOGNIZED.
Exception: Child born abroad, who obtains citizenship of country of birth, may maintain dual citizenship until age 21, when the person must renounce the other citizenship within one year or Malawian citizenship will be revoked.
A citizen of Malawi, age 22 or older, who obtains new citizenship through other than voluntary means (for example, marriage) has one year to declare a desire to retain Malawian citizenship or it will be revoked.

LOSS OF CITIZENSHIP:

- **VOLUNTARY**: Voluntary renunciation of Malawian citizenship is permitted by law. Contact the Embassy for details and required paperwork.

- **INVOLUNTARY**: The following are grounds for involuntary loss of naturalized or registered Malawian citizenship:
  - Person exercises rights or privileges of another country.
  - Citizenship was obtained through fraud or false statements.
  - Person has been arrested and imprisoned within seven years of citizenship.
  - Person has shown disloyalty or treason against Malawian government.
  - Person has been resident outside Malawi for seven years or more without proper registration with Consulate.

ANY QUESTIONS concerning citizenship should be directed to the address below:

Embassy of Malawi   Embassy/Consular Telephone: 202-797-1007
Consular Section   Fax: 202-265-0976
2408 Massachusetts Ave., NW
Washington, DC 20008

MALAYSIA

CITIZENSHIP: Citizenship laws are based upon the Constitution of Malaysia.

- **BY BIRTH**: Birth within the territory of Malaysia does not automatically confer right to citizenship.

- **BY DESCENT**:
  - Child born in wedlock, both of whose parents are citizens of Malaysia, regardless of the child's country of birth.
  - Child born in wedlock, in Malaysia, of a Malaysian mother and a foreign father.
  - Child, born in wedlock, abroad, of a Malaysian mother and a foreign father, obtains father's citizenship.
  - Child born out of wedlock, in Malaysia, of a Malaysian mother.
  - A child born out of wedlock, outside of Malaysia, to a Malaysian mother, is not considered a citizen of Malaysia. The child may return to Malaysia with the mother with a permanent residency status and may apply for citizenship later.

- **MARRIAGE**: A foreign woman who marries a citizen of Malaysia may obtain citizenship through registration. However, citizenship is revoked if the marriage is dissolved by divorce or annulment within the first two years.

- **BY NATURALIZATION**: Citizenship by naturalization is not encouraged. *Naturalization conditions were not provided.*

DUAL CITIZENSHIP: NOT RECOGNIZED.

LOSS OF CITIZENSHIP:

- **VOLUNTARY**: Voluntary renunciation of Malaysian citizenship is permitted by law. Contact the Embassy for details and required paperwork.

- **INVOLUNTARY**: The following are grounds for involuntary loss of Malaysian citizenship:
  - Person voluntarily acquires foreign citizenship.
  - Registered or Naturalized citizen…
    - Comes under criminal sentence at home or abroad within five years after gaining citizenship.
    - Shows disloyalty to the country and Government of Malaysia.
    - Works for a foreign government without permission of the Malaysian government.
    - Resides continuously abroad for more than five years without registering with Malaysian Embassies or Consulates.
    - Citizenship was obtained through fraud or false statement.

ANY QUESTIONS concerning citizenship, should be directed to an address below:

Embassy of Malaysia
Consular Section
1900 24th St., NW
Washington, DC 20008

Tel: 202-328-2700
Tel: 202-328-2742
Fax: 202-483-7661
mwwashdc@erols.com

Consulate General of Malaysia
313 East 43rd St
New York, NY 10017

Tel: 212-490-2722
Fax: 212-490-8576
mwnycg@erols.com

Consulate General of Malaysia
550 South Hope St.
Los Angeles, CA 90071

Tel: 213-892-1238
Fax: 213-892-9031
mwla@pacbell.net

MALDIVES

CITIZENSHIP: *Information on the basis of Maldivian citizenship law was not provided.* (UKC-Commonwealth Nation)

- **BY BIRTH**: Birth within the territory of the Maldives does not automatically confer citizenship.

- **BY DESCENT**:
  - Child born of a Maldivian father, regardless of the child's country of birth.
  - Child born of a Maldivian mother and an unknown or stateless father, regardless of the child's country of birth.

- **MARRIAGE**: Foreign spouses of Maldivian citizens are not automatically granted citizenship, and are not required to obtain Maldivian citizenship.

- **BY NATURALIZATION**: Maldivian citizenship may be acquired. The final granting of citizenship is at the discretion of the President of the Republic. The child of a Maldivian mother and a foreign father is eligible to claim Maldivian citizenship upon fulfilling the requirements of the law. *Other specifics not provided.*

DUAL CITIZENSHIP: RECOGNIZED.

LOSS OF CITIZENSHIP:

- **VOLUNTARY**: Voluntary renunciation of Maldivian citizenship is permitted by law. Final permission must be granted by the President of the Republic. Contact the Maldivian Embassy for details and proper paperwork.

- **INVOLUNTARY**: There are no provisions for the involuntary loss of Maldivian citizenship. Persons who acquire a new citizenship should not assume that they have lost their Maldivian citizenship by default.

ANY QUESTIONS concerning citizenship, or requests for renunciation of citizenship, should be directed to the address below:

Permanent Mission to the United Nations
The Republic of the Maldives
820 Second Ave., STE 800C
New York, NY 10017

Mission Telephone: 212-599-6195
Fax: 212-661-6405

www.maldives-info.com
www.undp.org/missions/maldives/

MALI

CITIZENSHIP: Citizenship is based upon the Code of Nationality, regulation No.95-098 of 1995. This regulation replaced No.62-18 of February 3, 1962.

- **BY BIRTH**: Birth within the territory of Mali does not automatically confer citizenship. The exception is a child born to unknown or stateless parents.

- **BY DESCENT**: Child of a Malian mother or father, regardless of the child's country of birth.

- **MARRIAGE**:
  - A foreign woman who marries a citizen of Mali may register for citizenship after the marriage, with no residency requirements.
  - A foreign man who marries a citizen of Mali may register for citizenship three years after the marriage.

- **BY NATURALIZATION**: Malian citizenship may be acquired upon fulfillment of the following conditions: Person has resided for at least five years in the country and has renounced former citizenship.

DUAL CITIZENSHIP: Recognized by Article 38 of the Code of Nationality.

LOSS OF CITIZENSHIP:

- **VOLUNTARY**: Voluntary renunciation of Malian citizenship is permitted by law. Contact the Embassy for details and required paperwork. Any Malian national with permanent residency abroad who has acquired a foreign citizenship can voluntarily renounce Malian citizenship, according to conditions stated in Article 45 of the Code.

- **INVOLUNTARY**: The following are grounds for involuntary loss of Malian citizenship (*pending current review of Dual Citizenship laws*):
  - Malian woman marries a foreign national and adopts her spouse's citizenship.
  - Naturalized Malian citizen commits crimes or other actions not in the interest of the Malian state or people, within the first 10 years of naturalization.

ANY QUESTIONS concerning citizenship, or requests for renunciation of citizenship, should be directed to the address below:

Embassy of the Republic of Mali
Consular Section
2130 R St., NW
Washington, DC 20008

Embassy/Consular Telephone: 202-332-2249 or 202-939-8950
Fax: 202-332-6603

MALTA

CITIZENSHIP: Citizenship for the Republic of Malta is based on the 1964 Constitution, as amended, and the Maltese Citizenship Act. (UKC-Commonwealth Nation)

- **BY BIRTH**:
  - Persons born between September 21, 1964 and January 8, 1989: Child born within the territory of Malta, regardless of the nationality of the parents.
  - Persons Born On or after January 8, 1989: Birth within the territory of Malta does not automatically confer citizenship.
  - Persons born in the territory of Malta, on or before September 21, 1964: Child of a Maltese-born parent.

- **BY DESCENT**:
  - Child born on or before September 21, 1964: Child born abroad, whose father or paternal grandparents were born in Malta and who were also citizens of the United Kingdom and Colonies (UKC).
  - Child born between September 21, 1964 and January 8, 1989: Child born abroad, whose father was a citizen of Malta.
  - Child born on or after January 8, 1989: Child born abroad, at least one of whose parents is a citizen of Malta.
  - Child born between September 21, 1964 and January 8, 1989: Child born abroad, whose mother was a citizen of Malta; conditional citizenship circumstances, contact Embassy)

- **REGISTRATION**: Foreign national who marries a citizen of Malta is eligible to register for Maltese citizenship.

- **BY NATURALIZATION**: Maltese citizenship is acquired upon fulfillment of the following conditions: Person must be 18 years or older, have resided in Malta for at least five years, and have renounced previous citizenship.

DUAL CITIZENSHIP: NOT RECOGNIZED.
Exceptions:
- Child born abroad, who obtains the citizenship of the birth country, is allowed to maintain dual citizenship until age 19. Person then has from age 19 to 20 to renounce foreign citizenship or Maltese citizenship will be revoked.
- Certain native-born Maltese emigrants are permitted to possess dual citizenship. If questions arise, contact the Embassy.

LOSS OF CITIZENSHIP:

- **VOLUNTARY**: Voluntary renunciation of Maltese citizenship is permitted by law. Contact the Embassy for details and required paperwork.

- **INVOLUNTARY**: The following is grounds for involuntary loss of citizenship: Person voluntarily acquires a foreign citizenship.

ANY QUESTIONS concerning citizenship, or requests for renunciation of citizenship, should be directed to the address below:

Embassy of Malta
Consular Section
2017 Connecticut Ave., NW
Washington, DC 20008

Embassy/Consular Telephone: 202-462-3611/12
Fax: 202-387-5470
www.magnet.mt/home/cos

MARSHALL ISLANDS

CITIZENSHIP: Citizenship is based upon the Immigration Law of the Marshall Islands and the Constitution of the Marshall Islands, dated December 21, 1978.

A person, who before December 21, 1978, was a citizen of the Trust Territory of the Pacific Islands became a citizen of the Marshall Islands if either the person or the person's parents had land rights.

- **BY BIRTH**: Birth within the territory of the Marshall Islands does not automatically confer citizenship. The exception is a child born in the Marshall Islands who would otherwise be stateless.

- **BY DESCENT**: A person born on or after December 21, 1978, at least one of whose parents was a citizen of the Marshall Islands.

- **REGISTRATION**: Citizenship by registration is permitted by Marshallese law. *No other information was provided about requirements.*

- **BY NATURALIZATION**: Marshallese citizenship can be applied for upon fulfillment of the following conditions:
    - Person has resided in the country for at least five years.
    - Person is of good character, is able to speak and understand Marshallese, and understands the customs and traditions of the country.
    - Person has a viable means of support.
    - Person has renounced previous citizenship.

DUAL CITIZENSHIP: NOT RECOGNIZED.
Exception: Child born abroad of Marshallese parents who obtains the citizenship of the country of birth is allowed to retain dual citizenship until the age of 17. Upon reaching 17, the person has one year to renounce the other citizenship or Marshallese citizenship will be lost.

LOSS OF CITIZENSHIP:

- **VOLUNTARY**: Voluntary renunciation of Marshallese citizenship is permitted by law. Proof of new citizenship is required. Contact the Embassy for details and required paperwork.

- **INVOLUNTARY**: The following are grounds for involuntary loss of Marshallese citizenship:
    - Person has voluntarily acquired foreign citizenship, other than through marriage to a foreign national.
    - Registered or Naturalized citizen…
        - Citizenship was gained through fraud or false statement.
        - Advocated the overthrow of the Marshallese government.
        - Commits treason or espionage against the government.

ANY QUESTIONS concerning citizenship should be directed to the address below:

Embassy of the Republic of the Marshall Islands
Consular Section
2433 Massachusetts Ave., NW
Washington, DC 20008

Embassy/Consular Telephone: 202-234-5414
Fax: 202-232-3236

MAURITANIA

CITIZENSHIP: Citizenship laws are governed by the Nationality Code of June 12, 1961.

- **BY BIRTH**: Birth within the territory of Mauritania does not automatically confer citizenship. **Exceptions**:
  - Child born in Mauritania of a parent who, though not a citizen, was also born in Mauritania.
  - Child born in Mauritania to non-citizen parents (citizenship after a five year waiting period).

- **BY DESCENT**: Child, at least one of whose parents is a citizen of Mauritania, regardless of the child's country of birth.

- **MARRIAGE**: A foreign woman who marries a citizen of Mauritania is immediately granted citizenship, upon request.

- **BY NATURALIZATION**: Mauritanian citizenship may be acquired upon fulfillment of the following conditions: The person has resided in the country for at least five years, has had no law violations, and has become acquainted with the language and customs of Mauritania.

DUAL CITIZENSHIP: NOT RECOGNIZED, in most circumstances (*specificity not provided*).
Exception: Mauritanian woman who marries a foreign national and must take the nationality of her husband does not lose her Mauritanian citizenship unless she formally requests removal.

LOSS OF CITIZENSHIP:

- **VOLUNTARY**: Voluntary loss of Mauritanian citizenship is permitted by law. Contact the Embassy for details and proper paperwork.

- **INVOLUNTARY**: The following are grounds for involuntary loss of Mauritanian citizenship: Person voluntarily acquires a foreign citizenship and does not fall into any exempted categories.

ANY QUESTIONS concerning citizenship, or requests for renunciation of citizenship, should be directed to the address below:

Embassy of the Islamic Republic of Mauritania
Consular Section
2129 Leroy Pl., NW
Washington, DC 20008

Embassy/Consular Telephone: 202-232-5700
Fax: 202-319-2623

MAURITIUS

CITIZENSHIP: Citizenship laws are based upon the Mauritius Independence Order of March 4, 1968. (UKC-Commonwealth Nation)

- **BY BIRTH**: Child born in the territory of Mauritius, regardless of the nationality of the parents.

- **BY DESCENT:**
  - Child born abroad in wedlock, whose father is a citizen of Mauritius.
  - Child born abroad and out of wedlock, whose mother is a citizen of Mauritius.
  - All citizen-children born abroad must be registered in Mauritius.

- **MARRIAGE**:
  - A foreign woman who marries a citizen of Mauritius is automatically granted citizenship by registration.
  - A foreign man who marries a citizen of Mauritius can be granted citizenship on an individual case basis.

- **BY NATURALIZATION**: Acquisition of Mauritian citizenship is severely limited and actively discouraged. No policy for naturalization is now in effect.

DUAL CITIZENSHIP: RECOGNIZED.
Exception: Dual citizenship is recognized for any native-born Mauritian age 21 or older.

LOSS OF CITIZENSHIP:

- **VOLUNTARY**: Voluntary renunciation of Mauritian citizenship is permitted by law. Contact the Embassy for details and proper paperwork.

- **INVOLUNTARY**: There is no current Mauritian policy concerning the involuntary loss of citizenship.

ANY QUESTIONS concerning citizenship, or requests for renunciation of citizenship, should be directed to the address below:

Embassy of Mauritius
Consular Section
4301 Connecticut Ave., NW STE 441
Washington, DC 20008

Embassy/Consular Telephone: 202-244-1491/92
FAX: 202-966-0983

www.embassy.org/mauritius

MEXICO

CITIZENSHIP: Mexican citizenship is based on the Federal Constitution as amended March 20, 1998.

- **BY BIRTH**: Child born within the territory of Mexico, regardless of the nationality of the parents.

- **BY DESCENT**:
  - Child born abroad to Mexican parents.
  - Child born aboard military/civilian Mexican ship or plane.

- **BY NATURALIZATION**: Mexican citizenship may be applied for upon fulfillment of the following:
  - Submit an application requesting Mexican nationality at the Mexican Ministry of Foreign Affairs.
  - Prove knowledge of the history of the Mexico, speak Spanish, and be integrated into the national culture.
  - Prove residence in Mexico for the last five years before submitting the application, unless…
    - Married to a Mexican citizen
    - Have a Mexican parent or child
    - Have been adopted by a Mexican citizen
    - Have contributed distinctively to Mexico
    - Renounce the citizenship of origin once the application has been approved.

DUAL CITIZENSHIP: (*Not specified.*) Mexican law establishes a distinction between nationality and citizenship. The 1998 Amendment recognized Mexican nationality transmitted by birth, restricting nationality to the first generation born abroad. It also preserved Mexican nationality by birth, when adopting a foreign nationality. Mexicans abroad holding Mexican nationality will be treated with legal equality in Mexico; specifically, they will keep patrimonial rights, access to reserved areas of investment, and the ability to inherit without restriction.

LOSS OF CITIZENSHIP:

- **VOLUNTARY**: Person sends letter of renunciation to Mexican Foreign Affairs representative.

- **INVOLUNTARY**: The following are grounds for involuntary loss of Mexican citizenship:
  - Person receives a foreign title or honor.
  - Person who has been naturalized lives for 5 years in original country of birth.
  - Person who has been naturalized attempts to pass as a foreigner on public documents or uses a foreign passport.

ANY QUESTIONS concerning citizenship, should be directed to the address below:

Consulate of Mexico
Consular Section
2827 16th St., NW
Washington, DC 20009

Embassy Telephone: 202-728-1600
Consular Telephone: 202-736-1000/01/02
Fax: 202-797-1793
www.embassyofmexico.org
www.inegi.gob.mx/homeing/homeoneg/homeing.html
consulwas@aol.com

MICRONESIA

CITIZENSHIP: Citizenship is based upon the Citizenship and Naturalization Act of May 10, 1979 (date of independence). All persons who were citizens of the Trust Territory of the Pacific Islands prior to the date of independence are considered citizens of Micronesia.

- **BY BIRTH**: Birth within the territory of Micronesia does not automatically confer citizenship.

- **BY DESCENT**: Child, at least one of whose parents was a citizen of the Trust Territory before independence or was a citizen of Micronesia after independence.

- **BY NATURALIZATION**: Micronesian citizenship is acquired upon fulfillment of the following conditions:
    - Person has resided in the country for at least five years.
    - Person is the child or spouse of a citizen of Micronesia
    - Person is a permanent resident of Micronesia.
    - Person is competent in one of the languages of the country.
    - Person has renounced previous citizenship.

DUAL CITIZENSHIP: NOT RECOGNIZED.
Exception: Dual citizenship was recognized before the constitution was adopted. According to the constitution, anyone who possessed dual citizenship prior to May 10, 1979, has up to three years after their 18th birthday, or three years after the acceptance of the constitution, whichever is later, to retain Micronesian citizenship and renounce other citizenship. Those who do not renounce other citizenship will become a "national" (*permanent resident*) of Micronesia.

LOSS OF CITIZENSHIP:

- **VOLUNTARY**: Voluntary renunciation of Micronesian citizenship is permitted by law. Contact the Embassy for details and required paperwork.

- **INVOLUNTARY**: The following are grounds for involuntary loss of Micronesian citizenship:
    - Person voluntarily acquires foreign citizenship.
    - Person declares formal allegiance to a foreign state.
    - Person enters the service of foreign armed forces. (Service in the armed forces of the United States is permitted in certain cases.)
    - Person votes in a political election of a foreign state.

ANY QUESTIONS concerning citizenship, or requests for renunciation of citizenship, should be directed to the address below:

Embassy of the Federated States of Micronesia
Consular Section
1725 N St., NW
Washington, DC 20036

Embassy/Consular Telephone: 202-223-4383
Fax: 202-223-4391

MOLDOVA

CITIZENSHIP: Citizenship is based upon the Law of Citizenship, dated June 23, 1990. All who resided in the territory of Moldova before June 23, 1990, and have a viable means of support, may obtain citizenship automatically upon request.

- **BY BIRTH**: Birth within the territory of Moldova does not automatically confer citizenship.

- **BY DESCENT**: Child, at least one of whose parents is a citizen of Moldova, regardless of the child's country of birth.

- **REGISTRATION**: Citizenship may be granted by registration for the following persons:
    - Foreign national who has been married to a citizen of Moldova for at least three years.
    - Child, 18 and under, who has been adopted by citizens of Moldova.

- **BY NATURALIZATION**: Moldovan citizenship may be acquired upon fulfillment of the following conditions: Person must be at least 19 years old, have renounced previous citizenship, and have resided in the country for at least 10 years.

DUAL CITIZENSHIP: NOT RECOGNIZED.
Exception: A foreign citizen can be granted Moldovan citizenship by Special Presidential Decree without renouncing former citizenship.

LOSS OF CITIZENSHIP:

- **VOLUNTARY**: Voluntary renunciation of Moldovan citizenship is permitted by law. Contact the Embassy for details and required paperwork.

- **INVOLUNTARY**: *No information was provided.* The Law on Citizenship states that Moldovan citizenship may be revoked for certain (*unspecified*) reasons.

ANY QUESTIONS concerning citizenship, or requests for renunciation of citizenship, should be directed to the address below:

Embassy of the Republic of Moldova
2101 S Street, NW
Washington, DC 20008

Telephone: 202-667-1130
FAX: 202-667-1204
www.moldova.org

MONACO

CITIZENSHIP: Based upon the Acquisition of Monegasque Nationality, dated January 1, 1987.

- **BY BIRTH**: Birth within the territory of Monaco does not automatically confer citizenship. The only exception is a child born in Monaco to unknown parents.

- **BY DESCENT**:
  - Child born in wedlock, whose father is a citizen of Monaco, regardless of the child's country of birth.
  - Child born out of wedlock, whose mother is a citizen of Monaco and whose father is unknown.
  - Child born out of wedlock to Monegasque citizens -- citizenship granted upon marriage of parents.
  - Children of naturalized citizens are automatically granted citizenship.

- **MARRIAGE**:
  - A foreign woman who marries a Monegasque man is automatically eligible for Monegasque citizenship.
  - A Monegasque woman who marries a foreigner retains her Monegasque citizenship unless prevented by the laws of her husband's country.

- **BY NATURALIZATION**: Monegasque citizenship may be acquired upon fulfillment of the following conditions: Person has resided in the country for 10 years after reaching the age of 21, has proof of loss of previous citizenship, and has been freed from any obligation to perform military service abroad.

  - Children of naturalized citizens are automatically granted citizenship.

DUAL CITIZENSHIP: NOT RECOGNIZED.

LOSS OF CITIZENSHIP:

- **VOLUNTARY**: Permitted under Monegasque law. *Additional information was not provided.*

- **INVOLUNTARY**: The following are grounds for involuntary loss of Monegasque citizenship:
  - Person voluntarily acquires foreign citizenship.
  - Person voluntarily performs military service abroad.

ANY QUESTIONS concerning citizenship, or requests for renunciation of citizenship, should be directed to the address below:

Consulate General of Monaco
565 Fifth Avenue
New York, NY 10017

Telephone: 212-286-0500
Fax: 212-286-1574
consulate@monaco1.org
www.monaco.mc/usa

MONGOLIA

CITIZENSHIP: Citizenship is based upon the Constitution of Mongolia, dated January 13, 1992, to be updated. *Information herein was characterized by the Mongolian Consul as the best information available.*

- **BY BIRTH**: Birth within the territory of Mongolia does not automatically confer citizenship. Children of unknown or stateless parents may apply to the President for citizenship, but citizenship will not be granted automatically.

- **BY DESCENT**:
  - Child, both of whose parents are citizens of Mongolia, regardless of the child's country of birth.
  - Child, one of whose parents is a citizen of Mongolia, is not automatically granted citizenship; the parents have the option of requesting Mongolian citizenship for the child from the President's Office.

- **BY NATURALIZATION**: Mongolian citizenship may only be acquired by submitting a request directly to the President's Office. Final authority for granting citizenship rests with this office.

DUAL CITIZENSHIP: NOT RECOGNIZED.

LOSS OF CITIZENSHIP:

- **VOLUNTARY**: Voluntary renunciation of Mongolian citizenship is permitted by law. Request must be sent for approval to the President's Office. Contact the Embassy for details and required paperwork.

- **INVOLUNTARY**: There are no grounds for involuntary loss of Mongolian citizenship.

ANY QUESTIONS concerning citizenship, or requests for renunciation of citizenship, should be directed to the address below:

Embassy of Mongolia
Consular Section
2833 M St., NW
Washington, DC 20007

Embassy/Consular Telephone: 202-333-7117
Fax: 202-298-9227

www.mongoliaonline.mn/english

MOROCCO

CITIZENSHIP: Citizenship is governed by the code of Moroccan Nationality, dated September 6, 1958.

- **BY BIRTH**: Birth within the territory of Morocco does not automatically confer citizenship.

- **BY DESCENT**:
  - Child of a Moroccan father, regardless of the child's country of birth.
  - Child of a Moroccan mother and an unknown or stateless father, regardless of the child's country of birth.

- **MARRIAGE**: A foreign woman who marries a Moroccan citizen can become a Moroccan citizen by declaration after two years residency and marriage.

- **BY NATURALIZATION**: Moroccan citizenship may be acquired upon fulfillment of the following conditions: Person has continually resided in the country for five years and is of full age. Citizenship must be approved by Cabinet decree.

DUAL CITIZENSHIP: RECOGNIZED.
Exception: Moroccan law recognizes dual citizenship, but permission must be granted by the government before a second citizenship is acquired. Dual citizenship by default is not recognized

LOSS OF CITIZENSHIP:

- **VOLUNTARY**: Voluntary renunciation of Moroccan citizenship is permitted by law. Renunciation is not automatic and must be approved by the Ministry of Justice. Contact the Embassy for details and required paperwork.

- **INVOLUNTARY**: The following are grounds for involuntary loss of Moroccan citizenship (unless the government has previously permitted the activity):
  - Person voluntarily acquires a foreign citizenship.
  - Moroccan woman marries a foreign national and acquires the husband's citizenship.
  - Person serves in the military or public employment of a foreign state and refuses the Moroccan government's demand that they resign.

ANY QUESTIONS concerning citizenship, or requests for renunciation of citizenship, should be directed to the address below:

Embassy of the Kingdom of Morocco
Consular Section
1601 21st St., NW
Washington, DC 20009

Embassy/Consular Telephone: 202-462-7979 through 82
Fax: 202-462-7643

MOZAMBIQUE

CITIZENSHIP: Citizenship is based upon the Law of Nationality, of 1975, amended November 1990.

- **BY BIRTH**: Birth within the territory of Mozambique does not automatically confer citizenship.
  Exceptions:
  - A child of foreign citizens, born in the territory of Mozambique, is eligible to register for citizenship upon turning age 18.
  - A child born in Mozambique of non-citizens, both of whom were also born in Mozambique, is granted citizenship.

- **BY DESCENT**:
  - Child born in Mozambique, at least one of whose parents is a citizen of Mozambique.
  - Child born abroad, whose father is a citizen of Mozambique. (Child of a foreign father and Mozambican mother obtains father's citizenship if child is born abroad.)
  - Child born abroad of a Mozambican mother and an unknown father.

- **MARRIAGE**:
  - A foreign woman who marries a Mozambican man may register for citizenship immediately
  - A foreign man who marries a Mozambican woman must reside in Mozambique for five years before registering for citizenship.

- **BY NATURALIZATION**: Mozambican citizenship may be acquired upon fulfillment of the following conditions: Person is at least 18 years old, has resided in the country for five years, and has renounced former citizenship.

DUAL CITIZENSHIP: NOT RECOGNIZED
Exception: Child born abroad, who acquires the citizenship of the country of birth, may retain dual citizenship until the age of 18. Then, foreign citizenship must be renounced or Mozambican citizenship will be revoked.

LOSS OF CITIZENSHIP:

- **VOLUNTARY**: Voluntary renunciation of Mozambican citizenship is permitted by law. Contact the Embassy for details and required paperwork.

- **INVOLUNTARY**: The following are grounds for involuntary loss of Mozambican citizenship:
  - Person voluntarily acquires a new citizenship.
  - Person becomes an agent of a foreign country without the permission of the government.

ANY QUESTIONS concerning citizenship, or requests for renunciation of citizenship, should be directed to the address below:

Embassy of the Republic of Mozambique
Consular Section
1990 M St., NW STE 570
Washington, DC 20036

Embassy/Consular Telephone: 202-293-7146
Fax: 202-835-0245

www.mbendi.cd.za/cymzcy.htm

MYANMAR (Formerly Burma)

CITIZENSHIP: *Information on the basis for Myanmar citizenship law was not provided.*

- **BY BIRTH**: Birth within the territory of Myanmar does not automatically confer citizenship.

- **BY DESCENT**:
  - Child, both of whose parents are citizens of Myanmar, regardless of the child's country of birth.
  - Child born in Myanmar of a Myanmar mother and an unknown father

- **BY NATURALIZATION**: Acquisition of Myanmar citizenship by foreign nationals is limited. Foreign nationals who marry citizens of Myanmar are not allowed to obtain citizenship, but may be granted a permit to live in the country.

DUAL CITIZENSHIP: NOT RECOGNIZED.

LOSS OF CITIZENSHIP:

- **VOLUNTARY**: Voluntary renunciation of Myanmar citizenship is permitted. Contact the Myanmar Embassy for details and required paperwork.

  The Myanmar Embassy states that most citizens of Myanmar wishing to relinquish citizenship, rather than formally renouncing citizenship, simply fail to renew their internally required passports. Once a passport has expired, citizenship is automatically lost.

- **INVOLUNTARY**: The following is grounds for involuntary loss of Myanmar citizenship: Person acquires a foreign citizenship.

ANY QUESTIONS concerning citizenship, or requests for renunciation of citizenship, should be directed to the address below:

Embassy of the Union of Myanmar
Consular Section
2300 S St., NW
Washington, DC 20008

Embassy/Consular Telephone: 202-332-9044/45
Fax: 202-332-9046

www.myanmar.come/e-index.html

NAMIBIA

CITIZENSHIP: Citizenship laws are based upon the Constitution of the Republic of Namibia, dated March 21, 1990, the date of independence. (UKC-Commonwealth Nation)

- **BY BIRTH**: Birth within the territory of Namibia does not automatically confer citizenship. The exception is a child of unknown parents.

- **BY DESCENT**:
  - Persons born before March 21, 1990, born in Namibia, of parents who were legal residents in Namibia.
  - Persons born after March 21, 1990, born in wedlock, at least one of whose parents is a citizen of Namibia, regardless of the child's country of birth.
  - Child born out of wedlock to a Namibian mother and an unknown or stateless father.

- **MARRIAGE**: Foreigner who marries a citizen of Namibia may apply for citizenship two years after marriage.

- **REGISTRATION**: Persons were eligible to register for citizenship up to one year after independence if they were ordinarily resident in Namibia at the time of independence, had lived in the country for at least five years, and had renounced their previous citizenship.

- **BY NATURALIZATION**: Namibian citizenship may be acquired upon fulfillment of the following conditions: Person has resided continually in the country for at least five years, and has renounced previous citizenship.

DUAL CITIZENSHIP: NOT RECOGNIZED.
Exception: Namibian child born abroad who gains citizenship of the country of birth may retain dual citizenship until age 18.

LOSS OF CITIZENSHIP:

- **VOLUNTARY**: Voluntary renunciation of Namibian citizenship is permitted by law. Contact the Embassy for details and required paperwork.

- **INVOLUNTARY**: The following are grounds for involuntary loss of Namibian citizenship:
  - Person has voluntarily acquired foreign citizenship
  - Person has volunteered to serve in the armed forces of another country without government permission.
  - Person has lived abroad more than two years without written permission of the Namibian government.

ANY QUESTIONS concerning citizenship should be directed to the address below:

Embassy of the Republic of Namibia
Consular Section
1605 New Hampshire Ave., NW
Washington, DC 20009

Embassy/Consular Telephone: 202-986-0540
Fax: 202-986-0443

NAURU

CITIZENSHIP: Citizenship is based upon the Nauruan Community Ordinance of 1956 - 1966, as well as the Constitution of Nauru, dated January 30, 1968. (UKC-Commonwealth Nation)

According to the 1968 Constitution, a person who, on January 30, 1968, was included in one of the classes of persons who constituted the Nauruan Community in the Nauruan Community Ordinance, is a citizen of Nauru.

- **BY BIRTH**: Birth within the territory of Nauru does not automatically confer citizenship. Only in the case of persons born in the territory who would otherwise be stateless is citizenship automatically granted.

- **BY DESCENT**:
- Child born on or after January 31, 1968, one of whose parents was a Nauruan citizen at the time of the child's birth, even if the parent dies before the child is born.
- Child born on or after January 31, 1968 of a marriage between a Nauruan citizen and a Pacific Islander and neither parent has within seven days after birth declared that the child is not a Nauruan citizen.

- **MARRIAGE**: A woman, who is not a Nauruan citizen, who marries a Nauruan citizen, is entitled to apply to become a Nauruan citizen.

- **BY NATURALIZATION**: Parliament may make provisions for acquisition of Nauru citizenship by an individual who is not otherwise eligible to be a Nauru citizen.

DUAL CITIZENSHIP: NOT RECOGNIZED.
Exception: Nauruan woman who receives a second citizenship upon her marriage to a foreign national, does not lose her Nauruan citizenship.

LOSS OF CITIZENSHIP:

- **VOLUNTARY**: Parliament may make a provision for renunciation of an individual's Nauruan citizenship. *Other information about renunciation of Nauruan citizenship was not provided.*

- **INVOLUNTARY**: The following is grounds for involuntary loss of Nauruan citizenship: Voluntary acquisition of foreign citizenship.

ANY QUESTIONS concerning citizenship should be directed to the address below:

Library of Congress
Law Library, Directorate of Legal Research
Western Law Division
James Madison Memorial Building, Rm. LM-240
Washington, DC 20540-3230

Telephone: 202-707-7850
Fax: 202-707-1820

Nauru has no diplomatic representation in the United States. It has a consulate in Agana, Guam.

NEPAL

CITIZENSHIP: Nepalese citizenship is based on the Constitution of the Kingdom of Nepal, updated and amended in 1990, and the Nepal Citizenship Act of 1964.

- **BY BIRTH**: Child born in Nepal, regardless of the citizenship of the parents.

- **BY DESCENT**:
  - A child whose father is a citizen of Nepal at the time of the child's birth.
  - Child found within the Kingdom of Nepal whose parents are not known, until the father of the child can be traced.

- **BY NATURALIZATION**: Nepalese citizenship can be acquired upon fulfillment of the following conditions:
  - Person can read and write the national language of Nepal.
  - Person is engaged in any occupation in Nepal.
  - Person has resided in Nepal for no less than 15 years.
  - Person has taken steps to renounce the citizenship of their former country.

  - **OTHER**:
    - Woman married to a citizen of Nepal, who has initiated steps to renounce her previous citizenship.
    - Person is an internationally distinguished professional who has applied for Nepalese citizenship, and is granted an honorary Nepalese citizenship.
    - Whenever any territory is incorporated into the Kingdom of Nepal, every person having domicile within such territory shall become a citizen of Nepal.

DUAL CITIZENSHIP: NOT RECOGNIZED.

LOSS OF CITIZENSHIP:

- **VOLUNTARY**:
  - Voluntary renunciation of citizenship, when living in Nepal, may be directed to the Office of the Chief District Officer in any major city.
  - If abroad, renunciations may be sent to the nearest consular section of a Nepalese embassy.

- **INVOLUNTARY**: The following is grounds for involuntary loss of Nepalese citizenship: Voluntary acquisition of foreign citizenship.

ANY QUESTIONS concerning citizenship, should be directed to the address below:

Royal Nepalese Embassy
Consular Section
2131 Leroy Place., NW
Washington, DC 20008

Embassy/Consular Telephone: 202-667-4550
Fax: 202-667-5534

www.info-nepal.com

NETHERLANDS

CITIZENSHIP: Dutch citizenship is based upon the Nationality Act of 1984.

- **BY BIRTH**: Birth within the territory of the Netherlands does not automatically confer citizenship.

- **BY DESCENT**:
  - Child born in wedlock, one of whose parents is a Dutch citizen.
  - Child adopted, one of whose parents is a Dutch citizen and the adoption is in accordance with Dutch law.
  - Child born out of wedlock whose mother is a Dutch citizen.
  - Child born out of wedlock, of a foreign mother and Dutch father -- citizenship will not be granted until the child is legitimized and recognized by the Dutch father.

- **BY NATURALIZATION**: Dutch citizenship may be acquired upon fulfillment of the following conditions:
  - Having resided continually in the country for at least five years and able to speak the Dutch language.
  - Foreign spouses of Dutch nationals may apply for citizenship after three years of marriage, provided they are able to speak the Dutch language.

DUAL CITIZENSHIP: NOT RECOGNIZED.
Exceptions:
- Dutch child born abroad who acquires the citizenship of country of birth. Upon reaching the age of majority, person must chose which nationality to keep.
- Person, who involuntarily obtains another citizenship may not be asked to renounce Dutch citizenship.

Questions concerning dual citizenship and what constitutes involuntary acquisition of a foreign citizenship are not entirely clear in Dutch courts. In cases where the status of Dutch dual citizenship is unclear, contact the Dutch consulate for clarification.

LOSS OF CITIZENSHIP:

- **VOLUNTARY**: Voluntary renunciation of Dutch citizenship may be accomplished in the Netherlands or abroad. Dutch citizens living abroad may send letters of renunciation to the nearest Dutch embassy or consulate.

- **INVOLUNTARY**: The following is grounds for involuntary loss of Dutch citizenship: Voluntary acquisition of foreign citizenship.

ANY QUESTIONS concerning citizenship, or requests for renunciation of citizenship, should be directed to the address below:

Royal Netherlands Embassy
Consular Section
4200 Linnean Ave., NW
Washing ton, DC 20008

Chicago	713-622-8000
Houston	312-256-0110
Los Angeles	310-268-8169
New York	212-246-1429

Embassy Telephone: 202-244-5300
Fax: 202-364-2410
www.cbs.nl/enindex.htm
Email messages are not permitted. Contact nearest Consulate-General by telephone.

NEW ZEALAND

CITIZENSHIP: Citizenship is based upon the Constitution of New Zealand, dated January 1, 1949 New Zealand is a member of the British Commonwealth (See United Kingdom); thus, New Zealanders born before January 1, 1949, have had a variety of citizenship status under British and New Zealand law. Questions concerning persons born before January 1, 1949, should be directed to the Embassy. (UKC-Commonwealth)

- **BY BIRTH**: Child born in the territory of New Zealand after January 1, 1949, regardless of the nationality of the parents.
  Exception: Child born to foreign diplomats while they are posted to New Zealand, unless one parent is a New Zealand citizen.

- **BY DESCENT**: Birth outside of New Zealand on or after January 1, 1978, and at the time of birth, one parent was a New Zealand citizen other than by descent (such as by birth in New Zealand or through a Grant of Citizenship). Application for official recognition of this status must be made before the person attains the age of 22.

- **REGISTRATION**: New Zealand citizenship may be granted to persons in the following categories:
  - Foreign national who marries a citizen of New Zealand and intends to establish residency in the country.
  - Child born abroad, at least one of whose parents is a citizen by descent.

- **BY NATURALIZATION**: New Zealand citizenship may be acquired upon fulfillment of the following conditions: Person is at least 18 years old, has been resident in country for at least three years, is of good character, knows the language and customs, and intends to permanently settle in the country.

  - **GRANT OF CITIZENSHIP**: A person may apply for a Grant of New Zealand Citizenship after having resided as a permanent resident in New Zealand for a least three consecutive years. This applies to spouses of New Zealand citizens.

  - **SECTION 10 GRANT OF CITIZENSHIP**: The Minister shall authorize the grant of New Zealand Citizenship to any person who was born outside of New Zealand from January 1, 1949, to January 1, 1978, and whose mother was a New Zealand citizen other than by descent.

DUAL CITIZENSHIP: RECOGNIZED.

LOSS OF CITIZENSHIP:

- **VOLUNTARY**: Voluntary loss of citizenship is permitted by law. Renunciation of citizenship requires that a person be 18 years of age or older, of full mental capacity at the time of application, and recognized by another country as a citizen. The Embassy should be contacted for required paperwork.

- **INVOLUNTARY**: There are no laws concerning involuntary loss of New Zealand citizenship. Given that New Zealand recognizes dual citizenship, those concerned with the possibility of dual citizenship should not assume naturalization by another country caused their previous citizenship to be lost by default.

NEW ZEALAND (cont.)

ANY QUESTIONS concerning citizenship, or requests for renunciation of citizenship, should be directed to the address below:

Embassy of New Zealand
Consular Section
37 Observatory Circle, NW
Washington, DC 20008

Embassy/Consular Telephone: 202-328-4800
Fax: 202-667-5227

www.stats.govt.nz/statsweb.nsf

NICARAGUA

CITIZENSHIP: Citizenship laws are based upon the Constitution of Nicaragua.

- **BY BIRTH**:
    - Child born within the territory of Nicaragua, regardless of the nationality of the parents. **Exception**: Children of foreign officials serving international organizations or their own countries, unless the parents choose to solicit Nicaraguan citizenship for the child.
    - Child born to unknown parents, found within the territory, until parentage becomes known.

- **BY DESCENT**:
    - Child born abroad, one of whose parents is a citizen of Nicaragua.
    - Child born abroad, whose mother or father was formerly Nicaraguan, if the child applies for citizenship after reaching the age of majority.

- **BY NATURALIZATION**:
    - Child of foreign parents, born on a Nicaraguan boat or airplane, if the parents apply for naturalization of the child.
    - Child born abroad, whose mother or father was formerly Nicaraguan.

DUAL CITIZENSHIP: NOT RECOGNIZED.
Exception: Countries of Central America and other countries with which Nicaragua has agreements of dual citizenship. No agreement exists with the United States.

LOSS OF CITIZENSHIP:

- **VOLUNTARY**: Letters of renunciation may be sent to the nearest Nicaraguan embassy. Passport should be included with the letter.

- **INVOLUNTARY**: The following is grounds for involuntary loss of Nicaraguan citizenship: Person voluntarily acquires a foreign citizenship, other than with the countries with which Nicaragua has dual nationality agreements.

ANY QUESTIONS concerning citizenship, or requests for renunciation of citizenship, should be directed to the address below:

Embassy of Nicaragua
Consular Section
1627 New Hampshire Ave., NW
Washington, DC 20009

Embassy Telephone: 202-939-6570
Fax: 202-939-6542

NIGER

CITIZENSHIP: *Information on the basis for Nigerienne citizenship laws was not provided.*

- **BY BIRTH**: Child born within the territory of Niger, regardless of the nationality of the parents.

- **BY DESCENT**: Child, at least one of whose parents is a Nigerienne citizen, regardless of the child's country of birth.

- **BY NATURALIZATION**: Acquisition of Nigerienne citizenship is possible upon grant by Presidential Decree.

DUAL CITIZENSHIP: NOT RECOGNIZED.

LOSS OF CITIZENSHIP:

- **VOLUNTARY**: Voluntary renunciation of Nigerienne citizenship is permitted by law. Contact Embassy for details and required paperwork.

- **INVOLUNTARY**: The following is grounds for involuntary loss of Nigerian citizenship: Person voluntarily acquires foreign citizenship.

ANY QUESTIONS concerning citizenship, or requests for renunciation of citizenship, should be directed to the address below:

Embassy of the Republic of Niger
Consular Section
2204 R St., NW
Washington, DC 20008

Embassy/Consular Telephone: 202-483-4224/25/26/27
Fax: 202-483-3169

NIGERIA

CITIZENSHIP: Citizenship is based upon the Constitution of the Federal Republic of Nigeria, dated 1989. (UKC-Commonwealth Nation)

Those born before or on the date of independence, October 1, 1960, whose parents or grandparents were born in Nigeria and who were legally residing in Nigeria at the time, are considered citizens of Nigeria.

- **BY BIRTH**: Birth within the territory of Nigeria does not automatically confer citizenship.

- **BY DESCENT**: Child, at least one of whose parents is a citizen of Nigeria, regardless of the child's country of birth.

- **REGISTRATION**: The following persons are eligible to become citizens through registration:
    - A foreign woman who marries a citizen of Nigeria.
    - Person who is of adult age (17), born outside Nigeria, any of whose grandparents is or was a citizen of Nigeria.
    - A foreign child adopted by Nigerian parents.

- **BY NATURALIZATION**: Nigerian citizenship may be acquired upon fulfillment of the following conditions: Person is of full age (17), has resided in Nigeria for at least 15 years, is of good character, plans to remain in Nigeria, is familiar with Nigerian language and customs, has a viable means of support, and has renounced previous citizenship.

DUAL CITIZENSHIP: RECOGNIZED.
Exception: Dual citizenship is only recognized for Nigerian citizens by descent.

LOSS OF CITIZENSHIP:

- **VOLUNTARY**: Voluntary renunciation of Nigerian citizenship is permitted by law. Contact the Embassy for details and required paperwork.

- **INVOLUNTARY**: The following are grounds for involuntary loss of Nigerian citizenship:
    - Registered or Naturalized citizen voluntarily acquires the citizenship of a foreign country.
    - Naturalized citizen, before seven years of residence, sentenced to prison for three years or more.
    - Registered or Naturalized citizen is convicted of acts of disloyalty to the Republic of Nigeria.

ANY QUESTIONS concerning citizenship should be directed to the address below:

Embassy of the Federal Republic of Nigeria
Consular Section
2201 M St., NW
Washington, DC 20037

Embassy Telephone: 202-822-1500
Consular Telephone: 202-822-1539/40/41
Fax: 202-775-1385

NORWAY

CITIZENSHIP: Defined by the Norwegian Nationality Act of December 8, 1950.

- **BY BIRTH**: Birth within the territory of Norway does not automatically confer citizenship. Only in rare cases will citizenship be granted. Abandoned children of unknown parents are considered Norwegian citizens.

- **BY DESCENT**:
  - Child born in wedlock acquires Norwegian nationality if the father or mother is a Norwegian national.
  - Child born out of wedlock acquires Norwegian nationality if the mother is a Norwegian national.

- **BY NATURALIZATION**: Norwegian citizenship may be granted upon fulfillment of the following conditions:
  - Person is at least 18 years of age.
  - Person has resided in Norway for the past seven years and has a record of good conduct.
  - Does not owe more than NOK 20,000 in connection with child maintenance payments.
  - Residence time limit for individuals married to a Norwegian national is computed thus: Take the period of time the individual has been married and add the period of time of residence in Norway. To be eligible for naturalization, the total must amount to at least eight years.
  - Nordic nationals (from Denmark, Finland, Iceland, Sweden) are granted Norwegian nationality after living in Norway for two years.
  - Children are included in a parent's application; adopted children are included, provided the adoption can be approved in Norway.

DUAL CITIZENSHIP: NOT RECOGNIZED.
Exceptions: The Norwegian Nationality Act permits an individual to be a national of more than one country in the following cases:
- If the individual acquired dual nationality at birth from their parents.
- If the individual was born of Norwegian parents in a country where a second nationality is based on birth in the country.
- If an individual is granted Norwegian nationality in accordance with the provision relating to "Notification through the County Governor's Office" and "Persons born before 1979" whereby the former nationality is not automatically lost.

LOSS OF CITIZENSHIP:

- **VOLUNTARY**: Voluntary renunciation of citizenship is granted under the condition that a new citizenship has been granted or soon will be granted. Letters of renunciation may be sent to nearest Norwegian Embassy.

- **INVOLUNTARY**: The following is grounds for involuntary loss of Norwegian citizenship: Person voluntarily obtains foreign citizenship.

ANY QUESTIONS concerning citizenship should be directed to the address below:

Royal Norwegian Embassy
Consular Office
2720 34th St., NW
Washington, DC 20008-2714

Embassy Telephone: 202-333-6000
Consul Telephone: 202-944-8920-24/8937
Fax: 202-337-0870
www.norway.org
www.ssb.no/www-open/english

OMAN

CITIZENSHIP: *Basis for Omani citizenship law was not provided.*

- **BY BIRTH**: Birth within the territory of Oman does not automatically confer citizenship.

- **BY DESCENT**:
  - Child of an Omani father, regardless of the child's country of birth.

  Child of an Omani mother and an unknown or stateless father is not granted citizenship; the child is given an internal passport and is considered a resident alien.

- **MARRIAGE**:
  - Foreign woman who marries a citizen of Oman is granted citizenship by registration after a few (*unspecified*) years of marriage and residency in the country.

  - Foreign man who marries a citizen of Oman is not eligible for Omani citizenship.

- **BY NATURALIZATION**: Naturalization as an Omani citizen is only available to women through marriage to an Omani, and by special decree for men.

DUAL CITIZENSHIP: NOT RECOGNIZED.
Exception: Though Dual Citizenship is not recognized, Omani law does not specifically forbid the acquiring of a second citizenship. If the person begins to exercise the rights and privileges of the second citizenship, steps to remove the person's Omani citizenship may be initiated.

LOSS OF CITIZENSHIP:

- **VOLUNTARY**: Voluntary renunciation of Omani citizenship is permitted by law. Contact the Embassy for details and required paperwork.

- **INVOLUNTARY**: There are no grounds for the automatic involuntary loss of Omani citizenship.

ANY QUESTIONS concerning citizenship, or requests for renunciation of citizenship, should be directed to the address below:

Embassy of the Sultanate of Oman
Consular Section
2535 Belmont Ave., NW
Washington, DC 20008

Embassy/Consular Telephone: 202-387-1980/81/82
Fax: 202-745-4933

PAKISTAN

CITIZENSHIP: Citizenship laws are based upon the Pakistan Citizenship Act of April 13, 1951. (UKC-Commonwealth Nation)

- **BY BIRTH**: Child born after April 13, 1951, in the territory of Pakistan, regardless of the country of birth. The exceptions are the children of certain diplomatic personnel.
  - Persons born in Pakistani territory on or before April 13, 1951 are granted citizenship
  - Person who was born in Pakistan or whose parents or grandparents were born in Pakistan and who had permanently resided in the country since August 14, 1947.
  - A person naturalized as a British subject in Pakistan, and who had renounced any foreign citizenship acquired after birth.
  - Person who before April 13, 1951 had migrated to Pakistan from the Indo-Pakistan subcontinent with the intention of residing permanently in Pakistan.

- **BY DESCENT**:
  - Child born after April 13, 1951 of a native-born Pakistani father, regardless of the child's country of birth.
  - Child born abroad after April 13, 1951, of a Pakistani father not born in Pakistan, is a citizen only if the child is registered at the nearest Pakistani Consulate or Mission.

- **MARRIAGE**: A foreign woman who marries a citizen of Pakistan is eligible for Pakistani citizenship.

- **BY NATURALIZATION**: *No information was provided.*

DUAL CITIZENSHIP: NOT RECOGNIZED.
Exception: Child born abroad who obtains the citizenship of the country of birth may retain dual citizenship until age 21. The person must then renounce the other citizenship or Pakistani citizenship will be revoked.

LOSS OF CITIZENSHIP:

- **VOLUNTARY**: Voluntary renunciation of Pakistani citizenship is permitted by law. Contact the Embassy for details and required paperwork.

- **INVOLUNTARY**: The following are grounds for involuntary loss of Pakistani citizenship:
  - Person obtains foreign citizenship.
  - Naturalized citizenship was obtained through fraud or falsity.
  - Naturalized citizen shows disloyalty to government.
  - Naturalized citizen is convicted of a crime in first five years of citizenship.
  - Citizen has resided outside the country for over seven years without registering with the Pakistani Consulate.

ANY QUESTIONS concerning citizenship should be directed to the address below:

Embassy of Pakistan
Consular Section
2315 Massachusetts Ave., NW
Washington, DC 20008

Embassy Telephone: 202-939-6200
Consular Telephone: 202-939-6261
Fax: 202-387-0484

www.pakistan-embassy.com
www.pak.gov.pk

PALAU

CITIZENSHIP: Palau became an independent nation in 1994; citizenship laws are taken from the 1994 Constitution.

- **BY DESCENT**: Child born abroad, at least one of whose parents is a citizen of Palau.

- **BY NATURALIZATION**: No opportunity for naturalized citizenship.

DUAL CITIZENSHIP: NOT RECOGNIZED.

LOSS OF CITIZENSHIP:

- **VOLUNTARY**: Palauan citizens may renounce their citizenship at 21 years of age.

- **INVOLUNTARY**: The following are grounds for involuntary loss of Palauan citizenship:
    - Person voluntarily acquires a foreign citizenship.
    - Person has willfully lied or concealed information in applying for citizenship.
    - Person advocates or participates in actions against the security of the nation of Palau.
    - Person fraudulently or illegally entered the Island of Palau prior to or after naturalization.

ANY QUESTIONS concerning citizenship should be directed to the address below:

Embassy of the Republic of Palau
1150 18th Street NW, #790
Washington, DC 20415

Telephone: 202-452-6814
Fax: 202-452-6281

PALESTINE, PALESTINE NATIONAL AUTHORITY FOR THE WEST BANK AND GAZA

CITIZENSHIP: *Citizenship laws are being developed for the region governed by the Palestine National Authority. The Oslo Agreement of 1993 empowered the Palestine National Authority for the West Bank and Gaza to issue Palestinians passports for this region.*

The Agreement of 1993 authorized the following people to be issued passports from the Palestine National Authority:
- Current residents of the West Bank
- Current residents of Gaza
- Palestinian refugees returning to the Palestine Authority

DUAL CITIZENSHIP: Laws are under development.

ANY QUESTIONS concerning citizenship should be directed to the address below:

The Palestine National Authority Office
Consular Section
1730 K Street NW #1004
Washington, DC 20006

Telephone: 202-785-8394
Fax: 202-887-5337

PANAMA

CITIZENSHIP: Citizenship regulations are outlined in the Panamanian Constitution.

- **BY BIRTH**: Child born within the territory of the Republic of Panama, regardless of the nationality of the parents.

- **BY DESCENT**: (Citizenship by descent is contingent upon person having established residency in Panama, either through parents or self.)
  - Child born abroad, one of whose parents is a Panamanian by birth.
  - Child born abroad, one of whose parents is a Panamanian by naturalization. Child must declare their intention to elect Panamanian nationality no later than one year after reaching age 18.

- **BY NATURALIZATION**: Panamanian citizenship may be acquired upon fulfillment of the following conditions:
  - Person has lived in Panama for at least five years, has a command of the Spanish language, is knowledgeable of Panamanian history, and has renounced their previous citizenship.
  - Child under age seven, born abroad and adopted by Panamanian nationals, does not need naturalization certification. Child, however, must declare their intention to elect Panamanian nationality not more than one year after reaching age 18

  - Nationals by birth of Spain, or of any Latin American state, become citizens of Panama under different conditions. Rather than follow the general requirements, the petitioner is instead obligated to fulfill the same conditions that would apply to a Panamanian national wishing to seek citizenship in the petitioner's country of origin.

DUAL CITIZENSHIP: NOT RECOGNIZED.
Exception: A child born abroad to Panamanian parents, who obtains citizenship of country of birth, may retain it until reaching the age of majority (18). Person must then decide which citizenship they wish to retain.

LOSS OF CITIZENSHIP:

- **VOLUNTARY**: Letters of renunciation should be presented personally or by representative to the Ministry of Government and Justice.

- **INVOLUNTARY**: The following are grounds for involuntary loss of Panamanian citizenship:
  - Person voluntarily acquires foreign citizenship.
  - Person enters the service of an enemy state.

ANY QUESTIONS concerning citizenship, or requests for renunciation of citizenship, should be directed to the address below:

Embassy of the Republic of Panama
Consular Section
2862 McGill Terr., NW
Washington, DC 20008

Embassy/Consular Telephone: 202-483-1407
Fax: 202-483-8413

PAPUA NEW GUINEA

CITIZENSHIP: Citizenship is based upon the Citizenship Act, dated February 13, 1976, and the Constitution, dated September 16, 1975. (UKC-Commonwealth Nation)

- **BY BIRTH**:
    - Persons born before September 16, 1975: Person born in the country, whose maternal and paternal grandparents were also born in the country.
    - Children of unknown or stateless parents.

- **BY DESCENT**:
    - Person born before September 16, 1975: Person born abroad, whose maternal and paternal grandparents were born in the country. Person must also have been registered and, if over 19, have renounced any other citizenships.
    - Person born on or after September 16, 1975: Child, at least one of whose parents is a citizen, regardless of the child's country of birth; however, child born abroad must be registered no later than one year after birth.

- **BY NATURALIZATION**: Papua New Guinean citizenship may be acquired upon fulfillment of the following conditions: Person has resided for eight years in the country, has renounced previous citizenship, intends to remain in the country, is of good character, respects the local customs and culture, can speak the local language, and has a reliable source of income or support.

DUAL CITIZENSHIP: NOT RECOGNIZED.
Exception: Child-citizen born abroad, who obtains the citizenship of the country of birth, may retain dual citizenship until the age of 18. Then the person has one year to renounce the foreign citizenship or Papua New Guinean citizenship will be revoked.

LOSS OF CITIZENSHIP:

- **VOLUNTARY**: Voluntary renunciation of Papua New Guinean citizenship is permitted by law. Contact the Embassy for details and paperwork. Person must be at least 19 years old and plan to obtain a new citizenship.

- **INVOLUNTARY**: The following are grounds for involuntary loss of Papua New Guinean citizenship: (These rules do not apply when the action is under the compulsion of another country's laws.)
    - Person voluntarily obtains foreign citizenship, other than through marriage.
    - Person exercises the rights of a citizen of a foreign country.
    - Person takes an oath of allegiance to another country.
    - Person joins a foreign armed force without government permission.
    - Person travels under the passport of another country.
    - Naturalized citizenship was obtained through fraud.

ANY QUESTIONS concerning citizenship should be directed to the address below:

Embassy of Papua New Guinea
Consular Section
1779 Massachusetts Ave., NW #805
Washington, DC 20036

Phone: 202-745-3680
Fax: 202-745-3679

www.pngembassy.org

PARAGUAY

CITIZENSHIP: Citizenship is based upon the Paraguayan Constitution.

- **BY BIRTH**: Child born within the territory of the Republic of Paraguay, regardless of the nationality of the parents.

- **BY DESCENT**:
  - Child born abroad, one of whose parents is a natural-born Paraguayan and who is in the service of the Republic.
  - Child born abroad, one of whose parents is a natural-born Paraguayan, if the child takes up permanent residency in Paraguay and has not exercised rights or complied with obligations inherent in the citizenship of the country of birth.

- **BY NATURALIZATION**: Persons seeking Paraguayan citizenship through naturalization fall into two categories (*further naturalization requirements were not provided*):
  - Has ties to Paraguay (must declare intention to become citizen):
    - Child born abroad, one of whose parents is a native-born Paraguayan, who has exercised rights or complied with obligations required of their country of birth.
    - Child born abroad to non-Paraguayan parents who are in the service of the Republic and have established residency in Paraguay.
  - Has no ties to Paraguay:
    - Must be at least 18 years of age, have resided in Paraguay for at least three years, exhibited good conduct, and have continued gainful employment.

DUAL CITIZENSHIP: RECOGNIZED (only native-born Paraguayans may hold dual citizenship).

LOSS OF CITIZENSHIP: No native-born Paraguayan may be involuntarily deprived of their citizenship, but may voluntarily relinquish it. Neither marriage nor the dissolution of a marriage shall alter the nationality of a spouse or that of their children.

- **VOLUNTARY**: Letters of renunciation may be sent to the nearest Paraguayan Embassy abroad.

- **INVOLUNTARY**: The following are conditions for the involuntary loss of naturalized Paraguayan citizenship:
  - Voluntary acquisition of a foreign citizenship.
  - Unjustified absence from the country for more than three years.

ANY QUESTIONS concerning citizenship, or requests for renunciation of citizenship, should be directed to the address below:

Embassy of the Republic of Paraguay
Consular Section
2400 Massachusetts Ave., NW
Washington, DC 20008

Embassy/Consular Telephone: 202-483-6960/61/62
Fax: 202-234-4508

PERU

CITIZENSHIP: Citizenship laws are based upon the Constitution of Peru dated October 31, 1993, and Nationality Law No.26574 dated January, 1996.

- **BY BIRTH**:
  - Persons born in the territory of the Republic of Peru are citizens; eligible for registration at age 18.
  - Person younger than 16 years old, in a state of abandonment, who reside in the territory of Peru.

- **BY DESCENT**: Child born abroad, whose father or mother is a citizen of Peru. The granted right of citizenship by descent is recognized to the descendants until the third generation.

- **REGISTRATION**:
  - Foreign woman or man who marries a citizen of Peru; the spouse naturalized by marriage does not lose Peruvian nationality in the event of divorce or the spouse's death.
  - Person (18 years or older), born in Peru, but whose parents were not citizens of Peru.
  - Person (18 years or older), born in wedlock outside of Peru to Peruvian mother or father.

- **BY NATURALIZATION**: Peruvian citizenship may be acquired upon fulfillment of the following conditions:
  - Person has resided in Peru for two consecutive years.
  - Works regularly in a professional, artistic, occupational, or managerial activity.
  - Possesses good behavior and moral solvency with no penal antecedents.
  - Foreign persons who live in the territory of the Republic, with distinguished services to the Peruvian Nation, may be granted citizenship by legislative resolution.

DUAL CITIZENSHIP: RECOGNIZED. Peruvians by birth who adopt the nationality of another country do not lose their Peruvian nationality unless they express renunciation before competent government authority.

LOSS OF CITIZENSHIP: Acquired Peruvian nationality granted under Nationality Law No.26574 is lost for expressed renunciation before the General Address of Migrations or consular offices overseas, and for the following reasons:
- For crimes against the State and the national defense.
- For crimes against the Public Security by illicit traffic of drugs.
- For crimes of terrorism and betrayal of the nation.

- Peruvians by birth who adopt the nationality of another country do not lose their Peruvian nationality unless they express renunciation before competent government authority.

Other information, relating to Voluntary or Involuntary loss of citizenship, was not provided.

ANY QUESTIONS concerning citizenship, or requests for renunciation of citizenship, should be directed to the address below:

The Embassy of Peru
Consular Section
1625 Massachusetts Ave., NW
Washington, DC 20036

Consular Telephone: 202-462-1084 or 1085
Consular Fax: 202-462-1088

PHILIPPINES

CITIZENSHIP: Citizenship laws are based upon the Constitution of the Philippines dated February 2, 1987. Citizens of the Philippines prior to the adoption of the Constitution are still citizens.

- **BY BIRTH**: Birth within the territory of the Philippines does not automatically confer citizenship.

- **BY DESCENT**:
    - Child, at least one of whose parents is a citizen of the Philippines, regardless of the child's country of birth.
    - Child born before January 17, 1973, of a Filipino mother, who elects Philippine citizenship upon reaching the age of majority (21).

- **BY NATURALIZATION**: Filipino citizenship may be acquired upon fulfillment of the following conditions:
    - Person has resided in the Philippines for at least 10 years.
    - Person has proof of livelihood and permanent residence.
    - Person has shown familiarity with the customs and language of the Philippines.

DUAL CITIZENSHIP: NOT RECOGNIZED.
Exceptions:
- Child born abroad to Filipino parents, who acquires the citizenship of the country of birth. This child is not obliged to choose a preferred citizenship until the age of majority (21).
- Filipino citizens who marry a foreign national and acquire the citizenship of their spouse become unofficial dual citizens. In all cases, the Filipino citizenship would take legal precedence.

LOSS OF CITIZENSHIP:

- **VOLUNTARY**: Voluntary renunciation of Filipino citizenship may be made at the nearest Philippines Embassy or consulate. Person must provide Philippines passport and proof of acquisition of new citizenship.

- **INVOLUNTARY**: The following are grounds for involuntary loss of Filipino citizenship: Person voluntarily acquires foreign citizenship.

ANY QUESTIONS concerning citizenship, or requests for renunciation of citizenship, should be directed to the address below:

The Philippines Embassy
Consular Section
1617 Massachusetts Ave., NW
Washington, DC 20036

Consular Telephone: 202-467-9324 or 200-467-9387
Fax: 202-467-9417

www.census.gov.ph

POLAND

CITIZENSHIP: Citizenship is governed by the Constitution of the Republic of Poland and the Citizenship Act of February 15, 1962.

- **BY BIRTH**: Birth within the territory of the Republic of Poland does not automatically confer citizenship. A child who was born in or is found within the territory of Poland acquires citizenship if both parents are unknown, whose citizenship cannot be established, or who is stateless.

- **BY DESCENT**:
  - Child acquires citizenship regardless of the child's country of birth if both parents are citizens of Poland, or if one of the parents is a citizen of Poland and the other is not known, of unknown citizenship, or is stateless.
  - Child, one of whose parents is a citizen of a foreign country, and the child acquires Polish citizenship by birth: The child's parents must submit an affidavit explaining these circumstances to Polish authorities within three months of the child's birth. The parents may choose foreign citizenship for the child if the laws of the foreign country grant the child citizenship based on descent from the foreign parent. Formal recognition of Polish citizenship by descent can be granted to this child at age 16 if an affidavit expressing the child's will to become a Polish citizen is executed before, and submitted to, the Polish authorities.

- **BY NATURALIZATION**: Citizenship can be granted by the President of the Republic of Poland. An alien is eligible to apply for citizenship if:
  - They have resided in Poland as a lawful resident for at least 5 years.
  - They submit of evidence of the loss (or renunciation) of foreign citizenship.

DUAL CITIZENSHIP: NOT RECOGNIZED. Poland does not recognize dual citizenship of its citizens. Polish law does not forbid a Polish citizen from becoming the citizen of a foreign state but Polish authorities will only recognize the Polish citizenship.

LOSS OF CITIZENSHIP:

- **VOLUNTARY**: Voluntary renunciation of citizenship may be in Poland or through the nearest Polish embassy. A Polish citizen may gain foreign citizenship after receiving permission from the President of the Republic of Poland to renounce Polish citizenship. The loss of citizenship is effective on a date it is granted; Polish citizens with promissory citizenship in a foreign state would be then be stateless if they had not yet acquired that citizenship.

- **INVOLUNTARY**: The Constitution prohibits an involuntary loss of Polish citizenship.

ANY QUESTIONS concerning citizenship should be directed to the address below:

Embassy of the Republic of Poland
Consular Division
2224 Wyoming Ave., NW
Washington, DC 20008

Embassy Telephone: 202-234-3800/01/02
Consular Telephone: 202-232-4528 or 202-234-2501
Fax: 202-328-2152
www.polishworld.com

PORTUGAL

CITIZENSHIP: Citizenship is based upon Citizenship Law #37/81, dated 1981, and regulated by Decree Law #322/82.

- **BY BIRTH**: Birth within the territory of Portugal does not automatically confer citizenship.

- **BY DESCENT**: Child, at least one of whose parents is a citizen of Portugal, regardless of the child's country of birth. Parents of a child born abroad must make a declaration of desire for Portuguese citizenship for the child and register the child either at a Portuguese consulate abroad or at government offices in Portugal.

- **REGISTRATION**: The following are eligible for citizenship by registration:
  - Foreign spouses who have been married to a Portuguese citizen for over 3 years.
  - Foreign child adopted by Portuguese citizens.

- **BY NATURALIZATION**: Portuguese citizenship may be acquired upon fulfillment of the following conditions:
  - Person is at least 21 years old.
  - Person has resided in Portugal for at least six years if originally from a Portuguese speaking country or for 10 years for other nationals.
  - Person has a working knowledge of Portuguese.
  - Person possesses a good moral character and civil record.
  - Person has a viable means of support.

DUAL CITIZENSHIP: RECOGNIZED.
Exception: Portuguese citizens who obtained a second citizenship prior to October of 1981 lost their Portuguese citizenship under the previous Citizenship Law #2098, dated July, 1959. Upon adoption of the new law, # 37/81, these persons were able to petition for the return of their Portuguese citizenship.

LOSS OF CITIZENSHIP:

- **VOLUNTARY**: Voluntary renunciation of Portuguese citizenship is permitted by law. Contact the Embassy for details and required paperwork.

- **INVOLUNTARY**: The following is grounds for involuntary loss of Portuguese citizenship: Upon reaching age 21, dual citizen does not formally express their desire to maintain their Portuguese citizenship.

ANY QUESTIONS concerning citizenship, or requests for renunciation of citizenship, should be directed to the address below:

Embassy of Portugal
Consular Section
2310 Tracy Place NW
Washington, DC 20008

Embassy/Consular Telephone: 202-332-3007
Fax: 202-387-2768

www.infoline.ine.pt/si/english/port.html

QATAR

CITIZENSHIP: Qatari nationality is regulated by Law #2 of 1961, amended by Law #19 of 1963 and Law #17 of 1966. Citizenship is automatic for a person who resided in Qatar prior to 1930.

- **BY BIRTH**: Birth within the State of Qatar does not confer citizenship.

- **BY DESCENT**:
  - Child born to a Qatari father, regardless of the child's country of birth.

- **BY NATURALIZATION**: Qatari citizenship can be granted upon fulfillment of the following conditions:
  - Person must have lawfully continued residence in Qatar for a period of not less than 20 years before the date of their application.
    - For Arab nationals of another Arab country, the residence period is 15 years.
  - Person must have a lawful means of living and must be of good character.
  - Person must have a fair command of the Arabic language.

DUAL CITIZENSHIP: NOT RECOGNIZED.

LOSS OF CITIZENSHIP:

- **VOLUNTARY**: Permitted under Qatari Law. Letters of renunciation should be sent to any Qatari embassy abroad.

- **INVOLUNTARY**: The following are grounds for involuntary loss of Qatari citizenship:
  - Person joins the military service of a foreign country against the wishes of the Qatari government.
  - Person acquires a foreign nationality.
  - Person works for the interests of a foreign government that is in a state of war with Qatar

ANY QUESTIONS concerning citizenship, or requests for renunciation of citizenship, should be directed to the address below:

Embassy of the State of Qatar
Consular Section
4200 Wisconsin Ave., NW
Washington, DC 20037

Embassy/Consular Telephone: 202-274-1600
Fax: 202-237-9880
www.mofa.gov.qa

ROMANIA

CITIZENSHIP: Romanian citizenship law is based on Law 21 dated 1991.

- **BY BIRTH**: Birth within the territory of Romania does not automatically confer citizenship.

- **BY DESCENT**: Child, at least one of whose parents is a citizen of Romania, regardless of the child's country of birth.

- **BY NATURALIZATION**: Romanian citizenship may be acquired upon fulfillment of the following conditions:
  - Person must have resided in Romania at least five years.
  - Person must be proficient in the Romanian language.
  - Person must pass a test on Romanian culture and history.

- **MARRIAGE**: Foreign national who marries a Romanian citizen must reside in Romania for three years, but fulfill the other naturalization conditions.

DUAL CITIZENSHIP: RECOGNIZED. Due to Romanian recognition of dual citizenship, a child born to parents of differing nationalities is permitted by Romanian law to be a dual citizen. Restrictions might exist in the laws of the non-Romanian parent's country.

LOSS OF CITIZENSHIP: Under current Romanian law there are no grounds for involuntary loss of Romanian citizenship. Three months after voluntarily renouncing citizenship, a former citizen may reapply for Romanian citizenship.

- **VOLUNTARY**: Voluntary renunciation is permitted by law, but is not required unless the laws of a second country demand. Contact the Romanian Embassy for details and proper paperwork.

- **INVOLUNTARY**: There are no grounds for involuntary loss of Romanian citizenship.

ANY QUESTIONS concerning citizenship should be directed to the addresses below:

Embassy of Romania
Consular Section
1607 23rd St., NW
Washington, DC 20008

Embassy Telephone: 202-332-4846/48/51
Consular Telephone: 202-202-332-9678 ext. 117,118, or 119
Fax: 202-232-4748
office@reoembus.org
www.roembus.org and **www.embassy.org/romania**

Consul General of Romania in New York
200 East 38th Street
New York, NY 10016

Telephone: 212-682-9120
Fax: 212-972-8463
economic@romconsny.org
www.romconsny.org

Consul General of Romania in Los Angeles
11766 Wilshire Blvd. #1230
Los Angles, CA 90025

Telephone: 310-444-0043
Fax: 310-445-0043

RUSSIAN FEDERATION

CITIZENSHIP: Citizenship laws are based upon the Law on Citizenship dated February 6, 1992.

- **BY BIRTH**: If either parent is a citizen of the Russian Federation, and the other is a stateless person, their child shall be a citizen of the Russian Federation, irrespective of the child's place of birth.

- **BY DESCENT**:
  - If both parents are citizens of the Russian Federation, irrespective of the child's place of birth.
  - If one parent is a citizen of the Russian Federation and the other is of another citizenship, the child's citizenship shall be decided, irrespective of the child's place of birth, by a written agreement between the parents. (In the absence of such agreement, the child shall acquire citizenship of the Russian Federation if it were born on the territory of the Russian Federation or if it would otherwise become a stateless person.)

- **BY REGISTRATION**:
  - Persons whose spouse or direct ancestor is a citizen of the Russian Federation.
  - Person who acquired other citizenship by birth, either of whose parents was a citizen of the Russian Federation, may register for citizenship within five years after their 18th birthday.
  - Children of former Russian Federation citizens, born after the termination of parents' Russian Federation citizenship, may register for citizenship within five years after their 18th birthday.
  - Former citizens of the USSR who resided on the territory of the former USSR and who came to reside on the territory of the Russian Federation after February 6, 1992, if they declared their intention to acquire citizenship of the Russian Federation by December 31, 2000.
  - Stateless persons permanently residing on the territory of the Russian Federation on the day of enactment of the present Law, or on the territory of other republics of the former USSR as of September 1, 1991, both of whom within one year of enactment of the present Law declare their intention to acquire citizenship of the Russian Federation.
  - Foreign citizens and stateless persons, irrespective of their domicile, who themselves are, or one of whose direct ancestors were, a subject of Russia by birth, and who, within one year of enactment of the present Law, declare their intention to acquire the Russian Federation citizenship.

- **BY NATURALIZATION**: Russian Federation citizenship may be acquired upon fulfillment of the following conditions:
  - Be at least 18 years old.
  - Have permanent residence for a total of five years, or three years of continuous residence immediately prior to filing an application:
    - For refugees recognized as such by the Russian Federation, the time periods shall be halved.

(The period of residence is considered continuous when a person has traveled outside the borders of the Russian Federation for study or medical treatment for longer than three months.)

DUAL CITIZENSHIP: RECOGNIZED. A Russian Federation citizen may be permitted, on petition, to be in simultaneous citizenship of another state with which the Russian Federation has a pertinent treaty.

LOSS OF CITIZENSHIP: *No information concerning Involuntary loss was provided.*

RUSSIAN FEDERATION (cont.)

- **VOLUNTARY**: Renunciation of citizenship of the Russian Federation will be granted upon application for another citizenship when the individual is not in receipt of papers for military ca or indictment in a criminal case.

ANY QUESTIONS concerning citizenship, or requests for renunciation of citizenship, should be directed to the address below:

Embassy of the Russian Federation
Consular Division
2641 Tunlaw Road, NW
Washington, DC 20007

Consular Telephone: 202-939-8907/13/18
Fax: 202-483-7579
Office Hours: 9:00 am to 12:30 pm

www.undp.org/missions/russianfed

RWANDA

CITIZENSHIP: Citizenship laws are based upon the Code of Rwandese Nationality dated September 28, 1963.

- **BY BIRTH**: Birth within the territory of Rwanda does not automatically confer citizenship. The exception is a child born within the territory of Rwanda to unknown parents.

- **BY DESCENT**:
  - Child whose father is a citizen of Rwanda, regardless of the child's country of birth.
  - Child whose mother is a citizen of Rwanda and whose father is unknown or stateless.

- **BY NATURALIZATION**: Rwandese citizenship may be acquired upon fulfillment of the following conditions: Person has resided in Rwanda for at least 10 years and is not hostile to the democratic and republican ideals of Rwanda

- **MARRIAGE**: Person who marries a Rwandese citizen is eligible for citizenship by naturalization.

DUAL CITIZENSHIP: NOT RECOGNIZED.
Exception: Rwandese child born abroad, who obtains the citizenship of the country of birth, is allowed to retain dual citizenship until reaching the age of majority (18), at which time one citizenship must be chosen.

LOSS OF CITIZENSHIP:

- **VOLUNTARY**: Voluntary renunciation of citizenship is permitted under Rwandese law. Rwandese passports may be turned in at the nearest Rwandese Embassy.

- **INVOLUNTARY**: The following is grounds for involuntary loss of Rwandese citizenship: Voluntary acquisition of foreign citizenship.

ANY QUESTIONS concerning citizenship, or requests for renunciation of citizenship, should be directed to the address below:

Embassy of the Republic of Rwanda
Consular Section
1714 New Hampshire Ave., NW
Washington, DC 20009

Embassy/Consular Telephone: 202-232-2882
Fax: 202-232-4544
www.rwandemb.org/rwanda

ST. KITTS AND NEVIS

CITIZENSHIP: Citizenship laws are based upon the Constitution of St. Kitts and Nevis. Categories of citizenship are divided by the date of independence, September 19, 1983. (UKC-Commonwealth Nation)

- **BY BIRTH**: Child of unknown parents is granted citizenship.
  - Persons born before September 19, 1983: Birth within the territory of St. Kitts and Nevis does not automatically confer citizenship.
  - Person born on or after September 19, 1983: Child born in the territory of St. Kitts and Nevis, regardless of the citizenship of the parents.

- **BY DESCENT**:
  - Person born before September 19, 1983: Any person living in St. Kitts, who was at that time a British Dependent Territory Citizen (BDTC) or a British Citizen was eligible for St. Kittsian citizenship.
    - Their child born abroad or adopted.
    - Their foreign national spouse.
  - Persons born on or after September 19, 1983: Child born abroad, at least one of whose parents was a citizen of St. Kitts and Nevis.

- **BY NATURALIZATION**: Person seeking St. Kittsian citizenship is not required to renounce previous citizenship. *Other information was not provided*.

DUAL CITIZENSHIP: RECOGNIZED.

LOSS OF CITIZENSHIP:

- **VOLUNTARY**: Voluntary renunciation of St. Kittsian citizenship is permitted by law. Letter of renunciation must be sent to the Attorney General of St. Kitts. Contact the Embassy for proper procedures concerning letter of renunciation.

- **INVOLUNTARY**: The following are grounds for involuntary loss of naturalized St. Kittsian citizenship:
  - Person's naturalized citizenship was obtained by fraud, false representation, or willful concealment of information.
  - Person commits act of treason against the government.

ANY QUESTIONS concerning citizenship, or requests for renunciation of citizenship, should be directed to the address below:

The Embassy of St. Kitts and Nevis
Consular Section
3216 New Mexico Avenue, NW 3rd Floor
Washington, DC 20016

Embassy/Consular Telephone: 202-686-2636
ax: 202-686-7623

ST. LUCIA

CITIZENSHIP: Citizenship is based upon the Citizenship Act of St. Lucia, dated June 5, 1979. (UKC-Commonwealth Nation) The following categories of persons were granted St. Lucian citizenship upon the date of independence (February 22, 1979):

- A citizen of the United Kingdom and Colonies (UKC) naturalized or registered in St. Lucia.
- A Commonwealth citizen who resided in St. Lucia for seven years.
- A foreign woman married to a man who was eligible for citizenship.

- **BY BIRTH**:
  - Person born in the territory of St. Lucia before February 22, 1979, who was a citizen of the UKC.
  - Person born in the territory of St. Lucia after February 22, 1979, regardless of the nationality of the parents.
  - **Exception**: Child born to foreign representatives or diplomats.

- **BY DESCENT**: Child born abroad, before or after independence, at least one of whose parents is a citizen, or was eligible for citizenship at the time of independence.

- **REGISTRATION**: A foreigner married to a citizen of St. Lucia, either living or deceased, is eligible to request citizenship by registration, subject to the approval of the government.

- **BY NATURALIZATION**: St. Lucian citizenship may be acquired upon fulfillment of the following conditions: Person is of good character, is familiar with the language and customs, has resided in the country for eight years before submitting application, intends to reside in St. Lucia, and has renounced previous citizenship.

DUAL CITIZENSHIP: RECOGNIZED.

LOSS OF CITIZENSHIP:

- **VOLUNTARY**: Voluntary renunciation of St. Lucian citizenship is permitted by law. Contact the Embassy for details and required paperwork.

- **INVOLUNTARY**: The following are grounds for involuntary loss of St. Lucian citizenship:
  - Naturalized citizenship is gained through fraud or falsehoods.
  - Citizen is convicted of treason against the government.

ANY QUESTIONS concerning citizenship, or requests for renunciation of citizenship, should be directed to the address below:

Embassy of St. Lucia
Consular Section
3216 New Mexico Avenue NW
Washington, DC 20016

Embassy/Consular Telephone: 202-364-6792 through 6795
Fax: 202-364-6723

ST. VINCENT AND THE GRENADINES

CITIZENSHIP: Citizenship Laws are based upon the Saint Vincent Constitution, dated October 27, 1979 and the Citizenship Act of 1984. As a member of the British Commonwealth, Saint Vincent has specific laws and rules for British and Commonwealth citizens. (UKC-Commonwealth)

- **BY BIRTH**: Child born within the territory of Saint Vincent, regardless of the nationality of the parents. The exception is a child, one of whose parents is employed in a foreign diplomatic post.

- **BY DESCENT**: Child born abroad or adopted child under age 18, at least one of whose parents is a citizen of Saint Vincent.

- **REGISTRATION**: The following may apply for citizenship by registration:
    - Foreigner who has married a citizen of Saint Vincent.
    - Citizen of the British Commonwealth who has resided in Saint Vincent for at least seven years.
    - Person who had previously renounced Saint Vincentian citizenship.
    - Stepchild or adopted child of Saint Vincentians, under age 21.

    The following are requirements for registering for citizenship: Person has resided in the country for at least 12 months preceding registration, has lived in the country continuously for at least nine years, is of good character, has knowledge of the English language and citizenship responsibilities, and plans to make Saint Vincent a permanent home.

- **BY NATURALIZATION**: Same as Registration. Some foreign nationals may be required to renounce previous citizenship.

DUAL CITIZENSHIP: RECOGNIZED in these special categories:
- Person born abroad of St. Vincentian parents, who obtained citizenship of the country of birth.
- Child born in St. Vincent of foreign parents.
- Citizen of St. Vincent married to a foreign national.
- Naturalized citizens.

LOSS OF CITIZENSHIP:

- **VOLUNTARY**: Permitted by law for all citizens 18 years and older. Contact Embassy for details and required paperwork.

- **INVOLUNTARY**: The following are grounds for involuntary loss of Saint Vincentian citizenship
    - Person obtains naturalization or registration by fraud.
    - Person has shown disloyalty to the country.
    - Person has lived continuously abroad for at least five years.

ANY QUESTIONS concerning citizenship should be directed to the address below:

Embassy of St. Vincent and The Grenadines
3216 New Mexico Ave., NW
Washington, DC 20016

Embassy Telephone: 202-364-6730
Fax: 202-364-6736
www.heraldsvg.com

SAMOA (Formerly Western Samoa)

CITIZENSHIP: Citizenship is based upon the Citizenship Act of 1972, dated August 9, 1972. All persons who were citizens of Samoa under the 1959 Citizenship of Western Samoa Ordinance continued to be citizens of Samoa. (UKC-Commonwealth Nation)

- **BY BIRTH**: Child born on or after August 9, 1972, in the territory of Western Samoa, regardless of the nationality of the parents.

- **BY DESCENT**:
  - Child born abroad, on or after August 9, 1972, of a Samoan father.
  - Child born abroad, out of wedlock, on or after August 9, 1972, of a Samoan mother.

- **REGISTRATION**: British Commonwealth citizens may register for Samoan citizenship upon fulfillment of the following conditions: Person has resided in the country for at least three years, is of good character, understands the language and customs of the country, and intends to continue to reside in the country.

- **MARRIAGE**: A foreign woman married to a citizen of Samoa may register for citizenship.

- **BY NATURALIZATION**: Samoan citizenship may be acquired upon fulfillment of the following conditions: Person has resided in the country for at least five years, is of good character, understands the language and customs of the country and intends to continue to reside in the country.

DUAL CITIZENSHIP: NOT RECOGNIZED.
Exception: A person who involuntarily acquires dual citizenship by marriage to a foreign national.

LOSS OF CITIZENSHIP:

- **VOLUNTARY**: Voluntary renunciation of Western Samoan citizenship is permitted by law. Contact the Mission for details and required paperwork.

- **INVOLUNTARY**: The following are grounds for involuntary loss of Western Samoan citizenship:
  - Person voluntarily obtains new citizenship, except by marriage.
  - Shows disloyalty to the country by:
    - Joining a foreign armed force
    - Carrying a foreign passport
    - Exercising rights of another citizenship
    - Taking oath of loyalty to a foreign country
  - Person has continuously resided abroad for more than six years and shows no interest in returning to reside in Samoa.
  - Naturalized or Registered citizenship obtained through fraud.

ANY QUESTIONS concerning citizenship, or requests for renunciation of citizenship, should be directed to the address below:

Samoan Permanent Mission to the United Nations
820 Second Ave., STE 800D
New York, NY 10017

Mission Telephone: 212-599-6196
Fax: 212-599-0797

SAO TOME AND PRINCIPE

CITIZENSHIP: Citizenship is based upon the Law of Nationality, dated September 13, 1990.

- **BY BIRTH**: Birth within the territory of Sao Tome does not automatically confer citizenship. The exceptions are as follows:
  - Child born in the territory of Sao Tome of (non-diplomatic) foreign parents who have settled in the country. (*The "settled" qualification is ambiguous; more specificity was not provided.*)
  - Child born to unknown or stateless parents.

- **BY DESCENT**:
  - Child born in Sao Tome, at least one of whose parents is a citizen.
  - Child born abroad, at least one of whose parents is a citizen, if parents register the child as a citizen.

- **MARRIAGE**: The foreign spouse of a citizen of Sao Tome may obtain citizenship upon renouncing previous citizenship, establishing residency in the country, and declaring their desire to obtain Sao Tomean citizenship.

- **BY NATURALIZATION**: Sao Tomean citizenship may be acquired upon fulfillment of the following conditions: Person has resided in the country for at least five years, is a legal adult, knows the language, is of good morality and integrity, has renounced previous citizenship, has a viable means of support, and obtains the approval of the Ministry of Justice.

DUAL CITIZENSHIP: NOT RECOGNIZED.

LOSS OF CITIZENSHIP:

- **VOLUNTARY**: Voluntary renunciation of citizenship is permitted by law. Contact the UN Mission for details and required paperwork.

- **INVOLUNTARY**: The following are grounds for involuntary loss of Sao Tomean citizenship:
  - Person voluntarily acquires foreign citizenship.
  - Person enlists in a foreign armed force.
  - Naturalized citizen fails to adapt to the country's customs.
  - Person commits a crime or dangerous act against the state.

ANY QUESTIONS concerning citizenship, or requests for renunciation of citizenship, should be directed to the address below:

Permanent Mission to the United Nations
Democratic Republic of Sao Tome and Principe
400 Park Avenue
New York, NY 10022

Mission Telephone: 212-317-0533
Fax: 212-317-0580

SAUDI ARABIA

CITIZENSHIP: Citizenship is based upon the Saudi Nationality Law.

- **BY BIRTH**: Birth within the territory of Saudi Arabia does not automatically confer citizenship.

- **BY DESCENT**:
  - Child of a Saudi father, born in wedlock, regardless of the child's country of birth.
  - Child of a Saudi father and foreign mother, born out of wedlock, will obtain the citizenship of the mother.
  - Child born in Saudi Arabia, out of wedlock, to a Saudi mother and unknown father.

  - Child born out of wedlock to a Saudi mother, born outside the country, will not be granted citizenship by descent.

- **MARRIAGE**:

  - Foreign woman who marries a citizen of Saudi Arabia may apply for citizenship by registration. Residency requirements vary from case to case, up to five years. Citizenship is not automatically granted.

  - Foreign man who marries a citizen of Saudi Arabia is able to apply for citizenship, granted on a case by case basis.

- **BY NATURALIZATION**: Saudi Arabia does not automatically grant rights to apply for naturalization. For persons who otherwise qualify (*unspecified*) for permanent residency, naturalization conditions include: Residence in the country for five years, no criminal record, and renunciation of previous citizenship.

DUAL CITIZENSHIP: NOT RECOGNIZED.
Exception: A Saudi woman who marries a foreign citizen may retain her Saudi citizenship unless prohibited by the laws of the spouse's home country.

LOSS OF CITIZENSHIP:

- **VOLUNTARY**: Voluntary renunciation of Saudi citizenship is permitted by law. Contact the Embassy for details and required paperwork.

- **INVOLUNTARY**: The following are grounds for involuntary loss of Saudi citizenship:
  - Person voluntarily acquires a foreign citizenship.
  - Naturalized citizenship was obtained through fraud or falsehood.

ANY QUESTIONS concerning citizenship, or requests for renunciation of citizenship, should be directed to the address below:

Embassy of Saudi Arabia
Consular Section
601 New Hampshire Ave., NW
Washington, DC 20037

Embassy Telephone: 202-342-3800
Consular Telephone:
Fax: 202-944-5983

SENEGAL

CITIZENSHIP: Citizenship is based upon the Code of Nationality, dated 1960, amended in 1989.

- **BY BIRTH**: Birth within the territory of Senegal does not automatically confer citizenship.

- **BY DESCENT**:
  - Child born of a Senegalese father, regardless of the child's country of birth.
  - Child born of a Senegalese mother and an unknown father, regardless of the child's country of birth.

- **MARRIAGE**: Foreigner who marries a Senegalese is granted permanent residency and can apply for citizenship by naturalization.

- **BY NATURALIZATION**: Senegalese citizenship may be acquired upon fulfillment of the following conditions: Person has sought and received the permission of the Department of Justice for permanent residency, has resided in the country for at least five years, is of good moral character, and does not have a criminal record.

DUAL CITIZENSHIP: NOT RECOGNIZED.
Exception: Senegal does not remove a person's citizenship upon acquiring a new citizenship. If a Senegalese citizen acquires a second citizenship, in the eyes of Senegalese law the person remains a citizen of Senegal. Second citizenships will not be formally recognized until the person is legally released from their Senegalese citizenship.

LOSS OF CITIZENSHIP:

- **VOLUNTARY**: Voluntary renunciation of Senegalese citizenship is permitted by law. Though the Senegalese Embassy may assist, the renunciation process must be handled by the individual in person, in Senegal, through the court system. Applications for renouncing Senegalese citizenship must be processed through the Ministry of Justice.

  - Due to Senegal's non-recognition policy concerning second citizenships, persons should not assume Senegalese citizenship has been lost by default. The person should similarly not assume that voluntary renunciation of citizenship will automatically be granted.

- **INVOLUNTARY**: The following is grounds for involuntary loss of Senegalese citizenship: Person is convicted of acts contrary to the interests of the government of Senegal.

ANY QUESTIONS concerning citizenship, or requests for renunciation of citizenship, should be directed to the address below:

Embassy of the Republic of Senegal
Consular Section
2112 Wyoming Ave., NW
Washington, DC 20008

Embassy/Consular Telephone: 202-234-0540/41
Fax: 202-332-6315

SEYCHELLES

CITIZENSHIP: Citizenship laws are based upon the Citizenship of Seychelles Act, dated June 29, 1976, and the Constitution of Seychelles, dated 1970. Questions concerning persons born before June 29, 1976, should be directed to the Seychellois Mission. (UKC-Commonwealth Nation)

- **BY BIRTH**: Birth within the territory of Seychelles does not automatically confer citizenship. The exception is a child born of unknown or stateless parents.

- **BY DESCENT**:
  - Child born in wedlock and in Seychelles, at least one of whose parents is a citizen of Seychelles.
  - Child born out of wedlock in Seychelles, whose mother is a citizen of Seychelles and whose father is unknown or stateless.

- **REGISTRATION**: Child born abroad, at least one of whose parents is a citizen of Seychelles, may acquire citizenship through registration.

- **MARRIAGE**: Person who marries a citizen of Seychelles is eligible for citizenship through naturalization without meeting other requirements.

- **BY NATURALIZATION**: Seychellois citizenship may be acquired upon fulfillment of the following conditions: Person has continuously resided in country for five years, is of good character, is knowledgeable of English or French, is intent on remaining in the country, and has renounced former citizenship.

DUAL CITIZENSHIP: NOT RECOGNIZED
Exception: The government of Seychelles only recognizes dual citizenship in specific cases concerning native born citizens of Seychelles who later obtain another citizenship for domestic or economic convenience (such as to work abroad) or involuntarily through marriage to a foreign citizen.

LOSS OF CITIZENSHIP:

- **VOLUNTARY**: Voluntary renunciation of Seychellois citizenship is permitted by law. Contact the mission for details and required paperwork.

- **INVOLUNTARY**: The following are grounds for involuntary loss of Seychellois citizenship by registration or by naturalization:
  - Person fails to renounce previous citizenship or obtains new citizenship.
  - Person was absent from the country seven years without registering.
  - Person obtained citizenship through false means.

ANY QUESTIONS concerning citizenship should be directed to the address below:

Permanent Mission to the UN
The Republic of the Seychelles
820 Second Ave., STE 900F
New York, NY 10017

Mission Telephone: 212-687-9766/67
Fax: 212-922-9177

SIERRA LEONE

CITIZENSHIP: Citizenship is based upon the Law of Citizenship, dated 1961. (UKC-Commonwealth Nation)

- **BY BIRTH**: Persons of African Negro (*sic; Constitution*) descent, born in Sierra Leone on or before April 26, 1961, who fell into the following categories, were granted Sierra Leonean citizenship:
    - Citizen of the United Kingdom and Colonies (UKC)
    - British Protected Person

    Child born in Sierra Leone on or before April 26, 1961, none of whose parents or grandparents were born in Sierra Leone, is not eligible for citizenship.

- **BY DESCENT**: Child whose father and a grandfather were Sierra Leoneans of African Negro descent, regardless of the child's country of birth.

- **REGISTRATION**: Person, either of whose parents is a Negro of African descent, may apply to register as a citizen of Sierra Leone.

- **BY NATURALIZATION**: Sierra Leonean citizenship may be acquired upon fulfillment of the following conditions: Person has resided in the country for at least five years, has observed the laws, and has contributed to the development of the country.

DUAL CITIZENSHIP: NOT RECOGNIZED.

LOSS OF CITIZENSHIP:

- **VOLUNTARY**: Voluntary renunciation of Sierra Leonean citizenship is permitted by law. The renunciation must be in Sierra Leone. Contact the Office of the Attorney General or Minister of Justice, Guma Building, Lamina Sankoh Street, Freetown, Sierra Leone.

- **INVOLUNTARY**: *No information was provided.*

ANY QUESTIONS concerning citizenship, or requests for renunciation of citizenship, should be directed to the address below:

Embassy of Sierra Leone
Consular Section
1701 19th St., NW
Washington, DC 20009

Embassy/Consular Telephone: 202-939-9261
Fax: 483-1793

www.sierra-leone.org

SINGAPORE

CITIZENSHIP: Citizenship laws are based upon the Constitution of Singapore, dated August 9, 1965. All questions dealing with persons born before August 9, 1965, should be directed to the Embassy of Singapore. (UKC-Commonwealth Nation)

- **BY BIRTH**: Birth within the territory of Singapore does not automatically confer citizenship.

- **BY DESCENT**:
  - Child born after August 9, 1965, in the territory of Singapore, at least one of whose parents was a citizen of Singapore.
  - Child born abroad after August 9, 1965, whose father was a citizen of Singapore by birth or registration. Child must be registered in Singapore or abroad within one year of birth.

- **MARRIAGE**: A foreign woman who marries a citizen of Singapore may be registered as a citizen under the following conditions: She has continuously resided in Singapore for two years, is of good character, and intends to reside permanently in Singapore.

- **BY NATURALIZATION**: Singaporean citizenship may be acquired upon fulfillment of the following conditions: Person must be at least 21 years old, have resided in Singapore for the sum of 10 years – continuously at least the twelve months immediately before the application, be of good character, have a knowledge of the language, and intend to permanently reside in the country.

DUAL CITIZENSHIP: NOT RECOGNIZED.
Exception: Child born abroad of Singaporean parents, who acquires the citizenship of the country of birth, may maintain dual citizenship until the age of 21 years. Then the person has 12 months to take the Oath of Allegiance and Loyalty and renounce the foreign citizenship, or their Singaporean citizenship will be revoked.

LOSS OF CITIZENSHIP:

- **VOLUNTARY**: Voluntary renunciation of citizenship is permitted by law for all citizens over the age of 21. Contact the Singaporean Embassy for details and appropriate paperwork. Required submissions include proof of new citizenship, birth certificate, identity card, and passport.

- **INVOLUNTARY**: The following are grounds for involuntary loss of Singaporean citizenship:
  - Person over age 22 has voluntarily acquired new citizenship.
  - Naturalized citizenship was obtained through fraud.
  - Naturalized citizen has lived over 5 years in a foreign country.,

ANY QUESTIONS concerning citizenship, or requests for renunciation of citizenship, should be directed to the address below:

The Embassy of the Republic of Singapore
Consular Section
3501 International Place, NW
Washington, DC 20008

Embassy/Consular Telephone: 202-537-3100
Fax: 202-537-7086
singemb@bellatlantic.net
www.singstat.gov.sg

SLOVAK REPUBLIC

CITIZENSHIP: Citizenship Law is based upon the National Council of the Slovak Republic Law No.40, dated January 19, 1993. Persons who were citizens of the Slovak Republic up to December 31, 1992, are considered citizens of Slovakia.

- **BY BIRTH**: Birth within the territory of Slovakia does not automatically confer citizenship.
  Exceptions:
  - Child born in Slovakia to parents who are unknown or stateless.
  - Child born in Slovakia who did not automatically receive the citizenship of foreign parents.

- **BY DESCENT**:
  - Child, one of whose parents is a citizen of Slovakia, regardless of the child's country of birth.
  - Child adopted by a citizen of Slovakia.

- **BY NATURALIZATION**: Slovak citizenship is acquired upon fulfillment of the following conditions: Person has been permanently residing in the territory for at least five years, has a command of the Slovak language, and has not been pronounced guilty of a deliberate crime within the last five years. Foreigners married to Slovak nationals need not fulfill these requirements.

DUAL CITIZENSHIP: RECOGNIZED. If a citizen of Slovakia holds another citizenship, their Slovak citizenship is considered to be dominant.

LOSS OF CITIZENSHIP:

- **VOLUNTARY**:
  - Voluntary renunciation of citizenship is possible only on the condition that the applicant is able to prove citizenship of another state or that the granting of citizenship can be reasonably assumed. Release of Slovak citizenship is possible only upon an individual's own petition. Decisions regarding release from citizenship are made by the District Offices Citizenship is cancelled upon receipt of the document of renunciation.

  - Persons involved in criminal proceedings, serving a prison term, or who are delinquent in their taxes or debts are not allowed to renounce citizenship.

- **INVOLUNTARY**: Slovak citizenship cannot be revoked by a decision of any state authority.

ANY QUESTIONS concerning citizenship, or requests for renunciation of citizenship, should be directed to the address below:

Embassy of the Slovak Republic
Consular Section
3900 Linnean Ave., NW
Washington, DC 20008

Embassy/Consular Telephone: 202-965-5160
Fax: 202-965-5166
www.slovakemb.com/index.html

SLOVENIA

CITIZENSHIP: Slovenian citizenship is based on the Citizenship Act of June 25, 1991.

- **BY BIRTH**:
  - Child born in the Republic of Slovenia with at least one parent a citizen.
  - Child born in the Republic of Slovenia with unknown parents, or parents with no citizenship.

- **BY DESCENT**: Children born abroad to Slovenian citizens must meet the following requirements to be granted citizenship:
  - Both parents must be citizens of Slovenia.
  - One parent is unknown or has no citizenship, but the other parent is a citizen of Slovenia.
  - Child must either be registered with appropriate authorities or return home to Slovenia as a permanent resident before the age of 18.
  - After age 18, a person who was not registered and is now considered a legal adult, can still obtain Slovenian citizenship by personally declaring for Slovenian citizenship before the age of 23.

- **BY NATURALIZATION**: Slovenian citizenship can be acquired by fulfillment of the following conditions.
  - Person must be at least 18 years old.
  - Person must have lived in the Republic for at least 10 years, the most recent five years prior to the petition for citizenship without interruption.
    - Descendants of Slovenian expatriates, up to the third generation, and foreign spouses of Slovenian citizens, need only reside for one year.
  - Person must have an assured residence and means of support.
  - Person must prove by examination a working knowledge of the Slovenian language.
  - Person must have been released from previous citizenship or can prove that such a release will be granted if the person acquires citizenship of the Republic of Slovenia.
  - The person has not been sentenced for a criminal offence anywhere for a prison term longer than one year.
  - There must be no ban on the person's residence in the Republic of Slovenia.
  - Acceptance into citizenship must present no threat to public order or the security and defense of the State.
  - The person must have all tax duties paid.
  - A Citizen of another republic who had permanent residence in the Republic of Slovenia on December 23, 1990 may apply for citizenship.

DUAL CITIZENSHIP: NOT RECOGNIZED.
Exception: Slovenian expatriates who may had involuntarily fled the country, as well as their descendants, are the only categories of people in the dual citizenship category. *This policy is now in flux; any questions regarding the possibility of dual citizenship should be directed to the Slovenian Consul.*

LOSS OF CITIZENSHIP:

- **VOLUNTARY**: Renunciation of citizenship is permitted if the conditions listed below are met:
  - Person is over 18 and lives in a foreign country.
  - Person has no military service obligations.
  - All debts and legal obligations have been satisfied.
  - The person faces no pending criminal proceedings.
  - Person has proof that foreign citizenship will be granted.
  - If new citizenship is not adopted within one year, decree of dismissal may be cancelled.

SLOVENIA (cont.)

- Children (under 18) lose their citizenship upon the request of their parents. If the child is older than 14 years, the child must give their consent to the loss of citizenship.
- The petition for loss of citizenship can be rejected if the interests of the State take precedence.

- **INVOLUNTARY**: A citizen of Slovenia, residing in a foreign country and in possession of foreign citizenship, may involuntarily be deprived of Slovenian citizenship if any of the following apply:
  - The person is a member of any organization engaged in activities to overthrow the government of the Republic of Slovenia.
  - The person is a member of a foreign intelligence service jeopardizing the interests of the Republic, or harms such interests by serving under a government authority or organization of a foreign state.
  - If a person is frequently sentenced for criminal offences or prosecuted for public order offences.
  - If a person declines to fulfil duties that are mandatory for a citizen of the Republic of Slovenia.

ANY QUESTIONS concerning citizenship, or requests for renunciation of citizenship, should be directed to the address below:

Embassy of the Republic of Slovenia
1525 New Hampshire Ave. NW
Washington, DC 20036

Embassy Telephone: 202-667-5363
Fax: 202-667-4563

SOLOMON ISLANDS

CITIZENSHIP: Citizenship is based upon the Solomon Islands Independence Order No.783, dated July 7, 1978. The Solomon Islands, a former British Colony and a Commonwealth Nation, have a variety of categories of person eligible for citizenship. (UKC-Commonwealth)

The following categories of people were automatically eligible for citizenship at the time of Independence, July 7, 1978:
* Person who belonged to a people indigenous to the Solomon Islands.
* Any woman who was married to an indigenous Solomon Islander.

The following categories of people were eligible to register as citizens of the Solomon Islands up to two years after Independence Day:
* Citizen of the United Kingdom and Colonies (UKC) or a British Protected Person (BPP), as well as their spouse and children, who was born in the Solomon Islands.
* Citizen of the UKC or a BPP, as well as their spouse and children, who had resided in the Solomon Islands for at least seven years.

* **BY BIRTH**: Birth within the territory of the Solomon Islands does not automatically confer citizenship.

* **BY DESCENT**: Child born on or after July 7, 1978, at least one of whose parents is a citizen of the Solomon Islands, regardless of the child's nation of birth.

* **BY NATURALIZATION**: *No information was provided.*

DUAL CITIZENSHIP: NOT RECOGNIZED.
Exceptions:
* Non-indigenous citizens of the Solomon Islands who possess a second citizenship have two years --or until the person reaches age 18, whichever comes later-- to renounce this second citizenship or Solomon Island citizenship will be revoked.
* Persons who obtain Solomon Island citizenship have six months to renounce their former citizenship or Solomon Island citizenship will be revoked.

LOSS OF CITIZENSHIP:

* **VOLUNTARY**: Voluntary renunciation of Solomon Island citizenship is permitted by law. Contact the UN Mission for details and required paperwork.

* **INVOLUNTARY**: Only under Dual Citizenship restrictions.

ANY QUESTIONS concerning citizenship, or requests for renunciation of citizenship, should be directed to the address below:

Permanent Mission to the UN
Solomon Islands
800 Second Ave. 4th Floor
New York, NY 10017-4709

Mission Telephone: 212-599-6192/3
Fax: 212-661-8925
www.solomons.com

SOMALIA, SOMALI REPUBLIC

No information was provided.

Since 1995 Somalia has had no functioning central government; armed factions control different regions. Since 1999 a joint United Nations police force has been operating in the capital, Mogadishu, but much of the nation is in disarray facing continued violence and famine.

www.//gaia.info.usaid.gov/horn/somalia/somalia

SOUTH AFRICA

CITIZENSHIP: Citizenship is based upon the South African Citizenship Act, 1995 (Act No.88 of 1995), as amended, with an effective date of October 6, 1995. The South African Citizenship Act of 1949 has been repealed.

- **BY BIRTH**: Birth within the territory of South Africa does not automatically confer citizenship. A person may claim South African citizenship by birth if:
  - One parent was a South African citizen.
  - One parent had been lawfully admitted to the Republic for permanent residence when the child was born.
  - For a child born out of wedlock before October 6, 1995, the mother must have been a South African citizen at the time of the birth of the child.
  - Any person born in the Republic of South Africa who is not regarded a South African by birth, shall become a South African citizen by birth if adopted in accordance with the Child Care Act, 1083, by parents of which one is a South African citizen and the birth is registered in South Africa.

- **BY DESCENT**: Any person born outside South Africa, at least one of whose parents is a South African citizen at the time of the child's birth, and whose birth is registered in the terms of the Births and Deaths Registration Act, 1922, shall be a South African citizen by descent.

- **BY NATURALIZATION**: A person can become a South African citizen by naturalization if:
  - They are a minor;
  - Have been lawfully admitted to the Republic for permanent residence;
  - Have been resident for a continuous period of not less than one year immediately preceding the date of application;
    - They, in addition, have been resident in the Republic for a further period of not less than four years during the eight years immediately preceding the date of the application.

- **RESUMPTION OF SOUTH AFRICAN CITZENSHIP**: In some cases, persons who have lost or forfeited their South African citizenship, and who are residing permanently in South Africa, may apply for resumption of their South African citizenship. Contact the South African Embassy for more details.

DUAL CITIZENSHIP: RECOGNIZED.
A South African citizen who is an adult shall cease to be a South African citizen if they acquire the citizenship of another country by one or another voluntary and formal act. However, South African law recognizes dual citizenship if the person requests permission of the Department of Home Affairs to retain or acquire another citizenship. When a person acquires the citizenship of another country automatically by virtue of marriage, they shall not cease to be a South African citizen

LOSS OF CITIZENSHIP:

- **VOLUNTARY**: Voluntary renunciation of South African citizenship is permitted by law. Contact the South African Embassy for details and required paperwork.

- **INVOLUNTARY**: The following are grounds for involuntary loss of South African citizenship:
  - Person acquires a foreign citizenship without permission.
  - Naturalized or Registered citizen continually resides outside the country for seven years or more.
  - A person who also has citizenship of any other country and serves in the armed forces of such a country while the country is at war with the Republic.

SOUTH AFRICA (cont.)

QUESTIONS concerning citizenship, or requests for renunciation of citizenship, should be directed to:

Embassy of South Africa
Consular Section
3051 Massachusetts Ave., NW
Washington, DC 20008

Embassy/Consular Telephone: 202-232-4400
Fax: 202-244-9417

consular@southafrica.net
www.southafrica.net
www.statssa.gov/za

SPAIN

CITIZENSHIP: The basis for Spanish citizenship law is Articles 17 through 26 of the "Codigo Civil" that was modified by Laws 18/1990 and 29/1995.

- **BY BIRTH**: Birth within the territory of Spain does not automatically confer citizenship. The exception is a child born to unknown or stateless parents.

- **BY DESCENT**:
    - Child, at least one of whose parents is a citizen of Spain, regardless of the child's country of birth.
    - Child born of non-Spanish citizen parents, provided at least one of the parents was born in Spain.

- **BY NATURALIZATION**: Spanish citizenship may be acquired upon fulfillment of conditions which vary according to the person involved.
    - Persons with no ties to Spain must reside in the country for at least 10 years.
    - Persons who are former nationals of Portugal, the Philippines, or certain South American countries need only reside for two years.
    - Persons who were born in Spain, who have married a citizen of Spain, or who were born outside of Spain of a mother or father who was originally Spanish, need only reside one year.

DUAL CITIZENSHIP: NOT RECOGNIZED.
Exception: Spain has dual citizenship treaties with the following countries: Bolivia, Chile, Ecuador, Costa Rica, Guatemala, Nicaragua, Paraguay, Peru, the Dominican Republic, Argentina, and Honduras. Spaniards residing in the above countries do not lose their rights as Spaniards if they adopt the nationality of the country of residence. For all other countries, Spanish citizenship is revoked upon the acquisition of foreign citizenship.

LOSS OF CITIZENSHIP:

- **VOLUNTARY**: Voluntary renunciation of Spanish citizenship is permitted by law. Submission of a Letter of renunciation and passport is required. Contact the Spanish Embassy for more details and required paperwork.

- **INVOLUNTARY**: The following is grounds for involuntary loss of Spanish citizenship: Person voluntarily acquires citizenship of a country with which Spain does not have a dual citizenship agreement.

ANY QUESTIONS concerning citizenship, or requests for renunciation of citizenship, should be directed to the address below:

Consulate General of Spain
2375 Pennsylvania Ave., NW
Washington, DC 20037-1736

Embassy/Consular Telephone: 202-728-2330
Fax: 202-728-2302

www.docuweb.ca/sispain

SRI LANKA (Formerly Ceylon)

CITIZENSHIP: Citizenship laws are based upon the Citizenship Act of Sri Lanka, dated May 22, 1972, and amended in 1987. All who were citizens of Ceylon are considered citizens of Sri Lanka.

- **BY BIRTH:** Birth within the territory of Sri Lanka does not automatically confer citizenship. The exception is a child born of unknown parents.

- **BY DESCENT:**
  - Child born before May 22, 1972:
    - Child born in wedlock whose father, paternal grandfather, or paternal great-grandfather was born in Sri Lanka, regardless of the child's country of birth.
    - Child born out of wedlock is granted citizenship if the mother, maternal grandfather, or maternal great-grandfather is a citizen.
  - Child born on or after May 22, 1972:
    - Child born in wedlock whose father is a citizen of Sri Lanka regardless of the child's country of birth.
    - Child born out of wedlock is granted citizenship if the mother is a citizen of Sri Lanka.
    - A child born abroad must be registered with the proper authorities within one year.

- **REGISTRATION:** Certain persons with paternal or maternal blood ties to Sri Lanka may apply for citizenship by registration provided they are at least 22 years old and intend to permanently reside in Sri Lanka.

- **BY NATURALIZATION:** *No information was provided.*

DUAL CITIZENSHIP: NOT RECOGNIZED.
Exception: Exception to the dual citizenship laws is made if it is felt to be of benefit to Sri Lanka.

LOSS OF CITIZENSHIP: Loss applies to spouse and minor children as well.

- **VOLUNTARY:** Voluntary renunciation of Sri Lankan citizenship is permitted by law. Contact the Embassy for details and required paperwork.

- **INVOLUNTARY:** The following are grounds for involuntary loss of Sri Lankan citizenship:
  - Person voluntarily acquires a foreign citizenship.
  - Citizen by descent, whose father is a citizen by registration, will lose citizenship at age 22 unless they express a desire to retain it.
  - Citizen by registration who…
    - gave false information
    - resided abroad more than five years without government permission
    - was convicted of certain crimes
    - declared loyalty to a foreign government.

ANY QUESTIONS concerning citizenship, or requests for renunciation of citizenship, should be directed to the addresses below:

Embassy of Sri Lanka, Consular Section
2148 Wyoming Ave., NW
Washington, DC 20008

Telephone: 202-483-4025 through 4029
Fax: 202-232-7181

UN Permanent Mission of Sri Lanka
630 3rd Avenue (20th Floor)
New York, NY 10017

Telephone: 212-986-7040, -1,- 2,- 3
Fax: 212-986-1838

SUDAN

CITIZENSHIP: Citizenship is based upon the Law of Sudanese Nationality #22, dated 1957, Law #55, dated 1970, and Law #47, dated 1972.

- **BY BIRTH**:
    - Person born on or before January 1, 1957:
        - Child born in the territory of Sudan, whose parents had established residency in Sudan.
    - Person born after January 1, 1957:
        - Birth in the territory of Sudan does not automatically confer citizenship. The exception is a child born to unknown parents.

- **BY DESCENT**:
    - Person born on or before January 1, 1957:
        - Person whose father and paternal grandfather had been permanently residing in the Sudan since 1924.
    - Person Born after January 1, 1957:
        - Child of a native-born Sudanese father, regardless of the child's country of birth.
        - Child of a naturalized Sudanese father, regardless of the child's country of birth, if the father was naturalized before child's birth.

- **MARRIAGE**: Foreign woman who marries a citizen of the Sudan may obtain citizenship provided she is married according to Sudanese Law, lives in marriage with her husband for at least two years, and renounces her former citizenship.

- **BY NATURALIZATION**: Sudanese citizenship may be acquired upon fulfillment of the following conditions: Person is a legal adult, has resided in Sudan for 10 years, knows the Arabic language, is of good morality, has committed no crimes, desires to remain in the country, renounces previous citizenship, is in good health, and declares loyalty to the country.

DUAL CITIZENSHIP: NOT RECOGNIZED.

LOSS OF CITIZENSHIP:

- **VOLUNTARY**: Voluntary renunciation of Sudanese citizenship is permitted by law. Contact the Embassy for details and required paperwork.

- **INVOLUNTARY**: The following are grounds for involuntary loss of Sudanese citizenship:
    - Person obtains new citizenship.
    - Naturalized citizenship obtained through fraud or falsity.
    - Naturalized citizen lives abroad more than 5 years, without registering.

ANY QUESTIONS concerning citizenship, or requests for renunciation of citizenship, should be directed to the address below:

Embassy of Sudan
2210 Massachusetts Avenue
Washington DC 20008

Telephone: 202-338-8565
www.sudanembassyus.org

SURINAME

CITIZENSHIP: *Information concerning the basis for Surinamer citizenship was not provided.*

ANY QUESTIONS concerning citizenship, or requests for renunciation of citizenship, should be directed to the addresses below:

Embassy of the Republic of Suriname
Consular Section
4301 Connecticut Ave., NW STE 108
Washington, DC 20008

Embassy/Consular Telephone: 202-244-7488/90/91/92
Fax: 202-244-5878

[Department of State Desk Officer for Suriname:
202-647-2620]

SWAZILAND

CITIZENSHIP: *Information on the basis for Swaziland citizenship laws was not provided.* (UKC-Commonwealth Nation)

- **BY BIRTH**: Birth within the territory of Swaziland does not automatically confer citizenship.

- **BY DESCENT**: Child, both of whose parents are citizens of Swaziland, regardless of the child's country of birth.

- **BY NATURALIZATION**: Swazi citizenship by naturalization may be acquired by at least two categories of persons:
  - Person has lived in the country for at least five years and has contributed to the development of the country.
  - Person is a foreign investor who wants to open a business in Swaziland that would employ Swazi citizens.

- **REGISTRATION**: Foreign woman who marries a citizen of Swaziland, or a foreign child adopted by Swazi parents, may obtain citizenship through registration.

DUAL CITIZENSHIP: NOT RECOGNIZED.

LOSS OF CITIZENSHIP:

- **VOLUNTARY**: Voluntary renunciation of citizenship is permitted by law. Contact the Swazi Embassy for details and proper paperwork.

- **INVOLUNTARY**: The following are grounds for involuntary loss of naturalized or registered citizenship; citizenship by birth can only be voluntarily renounced.
  - Person has failed to renounce previous citizenship.
  - Female national has ended marriage to Swazi citizen.
  - Person has become unacceptable to Swazi society by involvement in a serious criminal act.

ANY QUESTIONS concerning citizenship, or requests for renunciation of citizenship, should be directed to the address below:

Embassy of the Kingdom of Swaziland
Consular Section
3400 International Drive. NW STE 3M
Washington, DC 20008-3006

Embassy/Consular Telephone: 202-362-6683
Fax: 202-244-8059

www.realnet.co.sz

SWEDEN

CITIZENSHIP: Citizenship is based upon the Swedish Nationality Law.

- **BY BIRTH**: Birth within the territory of Sweden does not automatically confer citizenship.

- **BY DESCENT**:
    - Child born in wedlock, whose father is a citizen of Sweden, regardless of the child's country of birth.
    - Child born out of wedlock, whose mother is a citizen of Sweden and whose father is unknown or stateless, regardless of the child's country of birth.

- **BY NATURALIZATION**: Swedish citizenship may be acquired upon fulfillment of the following conditions: Person is at least 18 years of age, has resided in Sweden for at least five years, has led a respectable life, and has renounced former citizenship.

DUAL CITIZENSHIP: NOT RECOGNIZED.
Exceptions: Child who obtains a foreign citizenship through birth abroad or by having parents of different nationalities may retain dual citizenship. However, if the child was born abroad and has never resided in Sweden, Swedish citizenship will be lost at age 22 unless an application to retain it is made.

Any Swedish citizen can retain dual citizenship, as long as dual citizenship was not obtained through a conscious desire to voluntarily obtain a foreign citizenship.

LOSS OF CITIZENSHIP: Loss of a person's citizenship also applies to any of the person's minor children.

- **VOLUNTARY**: Voluntary renunciation of citizenship is permitted under Swedish law. Person must present proof of new citizenship. Contact the Swedish Embassy for details and required paperwork.

- **INVOLUNTARY**: The following is grounds for involuntary loss of Swedish citizenship: Person voluntarily acquires a foreign citizenship and does not fall into a category of dual citizenship exception.

ANY QUESTIONS concerning citizenship, or requests for renunciation of citizenship, should be directed to the address below:

The Embassy of Sweden
Consular Section
600 New Hampshire Ave., NW
STE 715 and 1200
Washington, DC 20037

Embassy/Consular Telephone: 202-467-2600
Fax: 202-342-1319

www.scb.se/scbeng/keyeng.htm

SWITZERLAND

CITIZENSHIP: Citizenship laws are based upon the Swiss Citizenship Law dated September 29, 1952, amended in 1984 and 1990.

- **BY BIRTH**: Birth within the territory of Switzerland does not automatically confer citizenship. The exception is a child born to unknown parents.

- **BY DESCENT**:
  - Child born in wedlock, at least one of whose parents is a citizen of Switzerland, regardless of the child's country of birth.
  - Child born out of wedlock, whose mother is a Swiss citizen, regardless of the child's country of birth.
  - Child born abroad to Swiss parents must be registered before the age of 22 or the child wi not be a citizen of Switzerland.

- **BY NATURALIZATION**: Swiss citizenship may be acquired upon fulfillment of the following conditions:
  - Person has resided a total of 12 years in Switzerland, three of which within the last five years prior to application.
    - The twelve-year requirement is adjusted if the time during which the applicant lived in Switzerland was between the ages of 10 and 20; in this case, time counts double as does the time during which the person lived in Switzerland while married to a person who is Swiss by birth.
  - Person is integrated into Swiss life, and is knowledgeable of its customs and laws.
  - Person is not a threat to the security of Switzerland.
  - A foreigner, after marrying a Swiss citizen, can apply for a simplified naturalization if they have lived in Switzerland for a total of five years, have lived in Switzerland for the most recent one year, and lived with the Swiss spouse for at least three years.

Swiss law provides for exceptions to these requirements in situations of blood ties to Swiss citizens, Swiss military service, and adoption by Swiss citizens.

DUAL CITIZENSHIP: RECOGNIZED.

LOSS OF CITIZENSHIP: If one parent decides to renounce Swiss citizenship, their spouse and al children under 20 years of age must also renounce their citizenship. However, a foreign woman who gained Swiss citizenship through marriage does not lose her Swiss citizenship in the event of the termination of the marriage, if she entered the marriage in good faith.

- **VOLUNTARY**: Voluntary renunciation of Swiss citizenship is permitted by law. Upon request, a Swiss citizen will be released from Swiss citizenship if they do not have residence in Switzerland, are at least 18 years old, and have another nationality or have been assured of one. Contact the Swiss Embassy for details and proper paperwork.

- **INVOLUNTARY**: According to the Swiss Consulate, there are no "realistic" conditions for the involuntary loss of Swiss Citizenship. Therefore, Swiss citizens should not assume that the acquisition of a new citizenship would cause their Swiss citizenship to be removed by default.

SWITZERLAND (cont.)

ANY QUESTIONS concerning citizenship, or requests for renunciation of citizenship, should be directed to the address below:

The Embassy of Switzerland
Consular Section
2900 Cathedral Ave., NW
Washington, DC 20008-3449

Embassy/Consular Telephone: 202-745-7900
Fax: 202-387-2564

embassy@was.rep.admin.ch
www.swissemb.org/legal
www.swissembassy.org.uk
www.admin.ch/bfs/eindex.htm

SYRIA

CITIZENSHIP: *Information on the basis for Syrian citizenship laws was not provided.*

- **BY BIRTH**: Birth within the territory of Syria does not automatically confer citizenship.

- **BY DESCENT**:
  - Child born of a Syrian father, regardless of the child's country of birth.
  - Child born of a Syrian mother and an unknown or stateless father.

- **BY NATURALIZATION**: Naturalized citizenship may only be acquired upon marriage to a Syrian citizen and by living in the country for over 10 years.

DUAL CITIZENSHIP: RECOGNIZED.
Exception: Though Syrian law recognizes dual citizenship, it also states that a Syrian citizen with dual citizenship is considered a Syrian first.

LOSS OF CITIZENSHIP:

- **VOLUNTARY**: Though voluntary renunciation of Syrian citizenship is permitted by law, the Syrian Information Office stated that it is so complicated that it is best not to attempt the process. In effect, according to that Office, the process is complicated in order to discourage renunciation of Syrian citizenship. Former citizens of Syria probably maintain an unofficial dua citizenship status and would be subject to Syrian law as citizens should they return to Syria.
- **Exception**: Persons of military service age are not permitted to renounce citizenship.

- **INVOLUNTARY**: *No information was provided.*

ANY QUESTIONS concerning citizenship, or requests for renunciation of citizenship, should be directed to the address below:

Embassy of the Syrian Arab Republic
Consular Section
2215 Wyoming Ave., NW
Washington, DC 20008

Embassy/Consular Telephone: 202-232-6313
Fax: 202-234-9548

TAIWAN (Republic of China)

CITIZENSHIP: Based on the Nationality Law of the Republic of China, dated February 5, 1929. Citizenship is based primarily on descent from the father (*jus sanguinis*).

- **BY BIRTH**: Birth within the territory of Taiwan does not automatically confer citizenship. Only when a child of unknown parentage is found is citizenship granted. This citizenship is removed, upon legitimization by a foreign parent.

- **BY DESCENT**:
  - Child whose father is, at the time of that child's birth, a Taiwanese national, even if the father died before birth.
  - Child whose father is unknown or stateless but whose mother is a Taiwanese national.
  - Child born out of wedlock to foreign woman and Taiwanese national father who has been legitimatized (recognized) by the father.

- **MARRIAGE**: Person who is the foreign wife of a Taiwanese national, except when the law of her own country requires that she retain her original citizenship.

- **BY NATURALIZATION**: Citizenship of Taiwan, Republic of China, can be acquired upon fulfillment of the following conditions: Person has resided in the territory for at least five years, has reached the age of 20 years, is of good character, and has sufficient property or skill to make an independent living.

- The spouse and non-majority age children of a naturalized citizen acquire the Taiwanese citizenship unless it is contrary to the law of the spouse's, or children's, original country.

DUAL CITIZENSHIP: NOT RECOGNIZED.

LOSS OF CITIZENSHIP:

- **VOLUNTARY**: Voluntary renunciation of Taiwanese citizenship is permitted for any persons over the age of 20, except for...
  - Persons of military age who have not yet performed their service
  - Persons who are in active military service
  - Persons who hold military or civilian office.

- **INVOLUNTARY**: The following is grounds for involuntary loss of Taiwanese citizenship: Voluntary acquisition of foreign citizenship. A Taiwanese woman who acquires foreign citizenship through marriage may return to Taiwan as a citizen if the marriage dissolves or she is widowed.

ANY QUESTIONS concerning citizenship, or requests for renunciation of citizenship, should be directed to the address below:

Coordination Council for North American Affairs
Taiwan, Republic of China
4201 Wisconsin Ave., NW
Washington, DC 20016-2137

Service Division Telephone: 202-895-1800   **www.gio.gov.tw**
Fax: 202-966-8639

TAJIKISTAN

CITIZENSHIP: *Information on Tajikistani citizenship laws was not provided.*

ANY QUESTIONS concerning citizenship law should be directed to the address below

Permanent Mission to the United Nations
Republic of Tajikistan
136 E 67th St., 9th floor
New York, NY 10021

Mission Telephone:
Fax: 212-472-7645

[Department of State Desk Officer for Tajikistan
202-647-6757]

www.soros.org/tajkstan.html

TANZANIA (Formerly Tanganyika and Zanzibar)

CITIZENSHIP: All laws are based upon the Tanzanian Citizenship Act No.6 of October 1995. (UKC-Commonwealth Nation)

- **BY BIRTH**: Birth within the territory of Tanzania, either before or after independence, does not automatically confer citizenship.

- **BY DESCENT**:
  - Person Born before December 9, 1961:
    - Person living in Tanzania, who was either a citizen of the United Kingdom and Colonies (UKC) or a British Protected Person (BPP) and at least one of whose parents was born in Tanzania.
    - Person born abroad, who was either a citizen of the UKC or a BPP and whose father was eligible for Tanzanian citizenship.
  - Person Born after December 9, 1961:
    - Child born in Tanzania, at least one of whose parents is a citizen of Tanzania.
    - Child born abroad, whose father is a citizen of Tanzania.

- **MARRIAGE**: A foreign woman who marries a citizen of Tanzania may register for citizenship.

- **BY NATURALIZATION**: Tanzanian citizenship may be acquired upon fulfillment of the following conditions: Person is 21 years old, has renounced former citizenship, and has resided in the country for at least five years.

DUAL CITIZENSHIP: NOT RECOGNIZED.
Exceptions:
- Tanzanian child born abroad who obtained the citizenship of the country of birth is allowed to retain the dual citizenship until age 21. Then, one citizenship must be chosen or Tanzanian citizenship will be revoked.
- Tanzanian who marries a foreign national and involuntarily acquires spouse's citizenship is allowed to retain Tanzanian citizenship.

LOSS OF CITIZENSHIP:

- **VOLUNTARY**: Voluntary renunciation of Tanzanian citizenship is permitted by law. Contact the Embassy for details and required paperwork.

- **INVOLUNTARY**: The following is grounds for involuntary loss of Tanzanian citizenship: Person over age 21 voluntarily acquires foreign citizenship.

ANY QUESTIONS concerning citizenship, or requests for renunciation of citizenship, should be directed to the address below:

Embassy of the United Republic of Tanzania
Consular Section
2139 R St., NW
Washington, DC 20008

balozi@tanzaniaembassy.org
www.tanzania_us.org

Embassy/Consular Telephone: 202-939-6125 or 202-884-1080
Fax: 202-797-7408

THAILAND

CITIZENSHIP: Citizenship laws are based on the Nationality Act of 1965 with Amendment No.2 AD 1992 and Amendment No.3 AD 1993.

- **BY BIRTH**: Birth within the territory of Thailand does not automatically confer citizenship.
    - A person born of a father or mother of Thai nationality, whether within or outside the Thai Kingdom.
    - A person born within the Thai Kingdom except a person of alien parents if, at the time of birth, the father was not married to the mother, unless the mother was given leniency for temporary residence or had been permitted to stay temporarily in the Thai Kingdom, unless she had entered the Kingdom without permission.

- **BY DESCENT**:
    - Child born in wedlock, either of whose parents is a citizen of Thailand, regardless of the child's country of birth.
    - Child born out of wedlock, whose mother is a citizen of Thailand and whose father is unknown or stateless, regardless of the child's country of birth.

- **BY NATURALIZATION**: Before being able to apply for Thai citizenship, the person must have the following qualifications:
    - Have displayed good behavior.
    - Have a regular occupation.
    - Have a domicile in the Thai Kingdom for a consecutive period of not less than five years.
    - Have knowledge of Thai language.

DUAL CITIZENSHIP: NOT RECOGNIZED.
Exceptions:
- Child born abroad to Thai parents, who obtains the citizenship of the foreign country of birth, may retain dual citizenship until reaching the age of majority (18). At this point, person must choose which citizenship to retain.
- A Thai woman who marries a foreign national and acquires her husband's citizenship has technically lost her Thai citizenship. Should the marriage end in death or divorce, the Thai national woman could regain her Thai citizenship. This is an unofficial dual citizenship designed to protect female Thai nationals.

LOSS OF CITIZENSHIP:

- **VOLUNTARY**: Voluntary renunciation of citizenship is permitted by Thai law. Contact the Embassy for details and proper paperwork. If a person of Thai nationality who was born of an alien father and has acquired the nationality of their father desires to retain the other nationality, they must renounce Thai nationality within one year after attaining the age of twenty years.

- **INVOLUNTARY**: The following are grounds for involuntary loss of Thai citizenship:
  Person voluntarily acquires foreign citizenship. When there exist circumstances suitable for maintaining the security or interests of the State, the government is empowered to revoke Thai nationality of a person who had acquired Thai nationality through naturalization.

THAILAND (cont.)

ANY QUESTIONS concerning citizenship, or requests for renunciation of citizenship, should be directed to the address below:

Embassy of Thailand
Consular Section
1024 Wisconsin Ave., NW
Washington, DC 20007

Embassy/Consular Telephone: 202-944-3600
Fax: 202-944-3611

http://emailhost.ait.ac.th/asia/info.html

TOGO

CITIZENSHIP: Citizenship is administered through the Ministry of Territorial Administration and Security, and the Ministry of Justice.

- **BY BIRTH**: Birth with the territory of Togo does not automatically confer citizenship.

- **BY DESCENT**:
  - Child of a Togolese father, regardless of the child's country of birth.
  - Child of a Togolese mother and an unknown father, regardless of the child's country of birth.

- **MARRIAGE**: A foreign citizen who marries a citizen of Togo may register for citizenship.

- **BY NATURALIZATION**: Togolese citizenship may be acquired upon fulfillment of the following conditions: Person has legally resided in Togo for at least five years and has no criminal record.

DUAL CITIZENSHIP: RECOGNIZED.

LOSS OF CITIZENSHIP:

- **VOLUNTARY**: Voluntary renunciation of Togolese citizenship is permitted by law. The person must either write a letter to the proper Ministry in Togo or return to Togo and personally enter the petition for loss of citizenship. The Togolese Embassy may render assistance, but cannot act as a representative for the person.

  Person should not assume that loss of citizenship is automatic or guaranteed.

- **INVOLUNTARY**: There are no grounds for involuntary loss of Togolese citizenship.

ANY QUESTIONS concerning citizenship, or requests for renunciation of citizenship, should be directed to the address below:

Embassy of the Republic of Togo
Consular Section
2208 Massachusetts Ave., NW
Washington, DC 20008

Embassy/Consular Telephone: 202-234-4212/13
Fax: 202-232-3190

TONGA

CITIZENSHIP: Citizenship laws are based upon the Nationality Act dated and amended 1915 through 1988; 2 Laws of Tonga, Chapter 59 (1988 rev. Ed.).

- **BY BIRTH**: Birth within the territory of Tonga does not automatically confer citizenship.

- **BY DESCENT**:
  - Child born in Tonga whose father is a citizen of Tonga.
  - Child born abroad, whose father was born in Tonga.
  - Child born out of wedlock in Tonga whose mother is a citizen of Tonga.

- **MARRIAGE**: A foreign woman who marries a citizen of Tonga is eligible for citizenship 12 months after marriage.

- **BY NATURALIZATION**: Tongan citizenship may be acquired upon fulfillment of the following conditions: Person has resided in the country for at least five years, is of good character, adequately knows the Tongan language, intends to reside in Tonga, and has been granted a letter of naturalization from the King of Tonga. The grant of naturalization is at the absolute discretion of the King.

DUAL CITIZENSHIP: NOT RECOGNIZED.

LOSS OF CITIZENSHIP:

- **VOLUNTARY**: Voluntary renunciation of Tongan citizenship is permitted by law. Tonga does not have diplomatic representation in the United States; renunciation must occur in Tonga or be initiated in a Tongan consulate elsewhere.

- **INVOLUNTARY**: The following are grounds for involuntary loss of Tongan citizenship:
  - Person acquires foreign citizenship.
  - Naturalized citizenship was obtained through fraud.

ANY QUESTIONS concerning Tongan citizenship law should be directed to the address below:

Library of Congress
Law Library, Directorate of Legal Research
Western Law Division
James Madison Memorial Building, Rm. LM-240
Washington, DC 20540-3230

Telephone: 202-707-7850
Fax: 202-707-1820

TRINIDAD AND TOBAGO

CITIZENSHIP: Citizenship is based upon the Citizenship Act of August 30, 1962 (Independence Day), and the revised Constitution, dated 1976. All persons who were granted citizenship at the time of Independence remained citizens under the 1976 Constitution. (UKC-Commonwealth Nation)

- **BY BIRTH**: Child born in Trinidad and Tobago, on or after August 30, 1962, regardless of the nationality of the parents. The exception is a child born to foreign diplomatic personnel, neither of whom is a citizen of Trinidad and Tobago.

- **BY DESCENT**: Child born abroad on or after August 30, 1962, either of whose parents are citizens of Trinidad and Tobago.

- **REGISTRATION**: The following are eligible for citizenship by registration:
  - Commonwealth citizens, citizens of Ireland, British Protected Persons (BPP), and foreign husbands of Trinidad and Tobagoan wives who are of good character, know English, have resided in the country for five years, and have renounced previous citizenship.
  - Foreign woman married prior to August 30, 1962, to a citizen of Trinidad and Tobago, the marriage continuing to the present.

- **BY NATURALIZATION**: Trinidad and Tobagoan citizenship may be acquired upon fulfillment of the following conditions: Person is of good character, knows English, has resided for eight years in the country, plans to continue to reside in Trinidad and Tobago and has renounced former citizenship. This applies to foreign husbands of Trinidad and Tobagoan wives not eligible for citizenship by registration.

DUAL CITIZENSHIP: RECOGNIZED. Beginning July 29, 1988, citizens by birth or descent are permitted to hold dual citizenship. Persons who lost or renounced citizenship before that date may reapply for their citizenship.
Exception: Dual citizenship is not recognized in the case of naturalized or registered citizens.

LOSS OF CITIZENSHIP:

- **VOLUNTARY**: Voluntary renunciation of Trinidad and Tobagoan citizenship is permitted by law. Contact the Embassy for details and required paperwork.

- **INVOLUNTARY**: The following are grounds for involuntary loss of Trinidad and Tobagoan citizenship by naturalization or registration:
  - Citizenship was obtained through fraud or false statements.
  - Person voluntarily acquires a foreign citizenship.
  - Person continues to exercise the rights and privileges of a citizen of their former country.

ANY QUESTIONS concerning citizenship, or requests for renunciation of citizenship, should be directed to the address below:

Embassy of the Republic of Trinidad and Tobago
Consular Section
1708 Massachusetts Ave., NW
Washington, DC 20036

Embassy/Consular Telephone: 202-467-6490
Fax: 202-785-3130

TUNISIA

CITIZENSHIP: Citizenship laws are based upon the Code of Nationality dated January 26, 1956.

- **BY BIRTH**: Birth within the territory of Tunisia does not necessarily confer citizenship.
  Exceptions:
  - A child born to stateless or unknown parents
  - A child born in Tunisia, of a Tunisian mother and foreign father.

- **BY DESCENT**:
  - Child whose father is a citizen of Tunisia, regardless of the child's country of birth.
  - Child of a Tunisian mother and a foreign father may obtain Tunisian citizenship upon the request of the father.
  - Child whose mother is a citizen of Tunisia and whose father is unknown or stateless, regardless of the child's country of birth.

- **MARRIAGE**:
  - Foreign woman, whose country demands that their citizenship be renounced in order to marry, is granted citizenship at the time of her marriage to the Tunisian spouse.
  - Foreign woman, whose country does not demand renouncement of citizenship, may apply for Tunisian citizenship in two years.

- **NATURALIZATION**: Tunisian citizenship may be acquired upon fulfillment of the following conditions: Person has resided in a fixed residence in the country for at least five years, has no criminal record, is knowledgeable of the Arabic language, is in good health, and is of good character. The residence requirement is less than five years for those with blood or marital ties to Tunisian citizens.

DUAL CITIZENSHIP: RECOGNIZED.

LOSS OF CITIZENSHIP:

- **VOLUNTARY**: Voluntary renunciation of citizenship is permitted by law upon receiving permission by Presidential Decree, routine in most situations. Contact the Embassy for details and required paperwork.

- **INVOLUNTARY**: The following are grounds for involuntary loss of Tunisian citizenship:
  - Person has committed a crime.
  - Treason.
  - Person has avoided military service.
  - Person gave false information to naturalization office.

  - Citizenship acquired through marriage is revoked upon annulment of the marriage.

ANY QUESTIONS concerning citizenship, or requests for renunciation of citizenship, should be directed to the address below:

Embassy of Tunisia
Consular Section
1515 Massachusetts Ave., NW
Washington, DC 20036

Embassy/Consular Telephone: 202-862-1850   **www.tunsisiaonline.com**
Fax: 202-862-1858

TURKEY

CITIZENSHIP: Citizenship laws are based upon Article 66 of the Turkish Constitution and regulated in Law 403 of the Turkish Citizenship Law of 1964.

- **BY BIRTH**: Birth within the territory of Turkey does not automatically confer citizenship. **Exception**: A child born to unknown or stateless parents.

- **BY DESCENT**: Child, at least one of whose parents is a citizen of Turkey, regardless of the child's country of birth.

- **MARRIAGE**: A foreign woman who marries a citizen of Turkey may acquire Turkish citizenship upon making a declaration of intent.

- **BY NATURALIZATION**: Turkish citizenship may be acquired upon fulfillment of the following conditions:
    - Person has resided in Turkey for at least five years.
    - Person has shown intent to remain in Turkey.
    - Person is familiar with the Turkish language.
    - Person has sufficient means for self-support.
    - Person has no illness considered threatening to public health.

  The following persons may be eligible for citizenship without fulfilling the residency requirement:
    - Persons of Turkish descent, their spouses, and minor children.
    - The child of a person who, regardless of circumstances, has lost citizenship.
    - Spouse of a Turkish citizen and the spouse's minor children.

DUAL CITIZENSHIP: RECOGNIZED.

LOSS OF CITIZENSHIP:

- **VOLUNTARY**: Voluntary renunciation of citizenship is permitted by law. Contact the Turkish Embassy for details and proper paperwork.

- **INVOLUNTARY**: The following is grounds for involuntary loss of naturalized Turkish citizenship: Person is involved in activities threatening to the security of Turkey.

ANY QUESTIONS concerning citizenship, or requests for renunciation of citizenship, should be directed to the address below:

Embassy of the Republic of Turkey
Consular Section
2525 Massachusetts Ave., NW
Washington, DC 20036

Embassy Telephone: 202-612-6700
Consular Telephone: 202-612-6740 (only 2:30-4:00 p.m.; not in service 10:00 a.m. – 2:30 p.m.)
Fax: 202-612-6744
www.Turkey.org

TURKMENISTAN

CITIZENSHIP: *Information concerning Turkmenistani citizenship was not provided.*

ANY QUESTIONS concerning citizenship, or requests for renunciation of citizenship, should be directed to the addresses below:

Embassy of Turkmenistan
2207 Massachusetts Ave NW
Washington DC 20008

Embassy Telephone: 202-588-1500

Permanent Mission to the United Nations
Republic of Turkmenistan
136 E 67th St., 9th floor
New York, NY 10021

Mission Telephone: 212-472-5921
Fax: 212-628-0252

[Department of State Desk Officer for Turkmenistan
202-647-6831]

www.turkmenistan.org
www.turkmen@earthlink.net

TUVALU

CITIZENSHIP: Citizenship is based upon the Constitution of Tuvalu Ordinance, dated September 15, 1986, and the Citizenship Ordinance 1979.

- **BY BIRTH**: Child born on or after September 15, 1986 in Tuvalu, regardless of the nationality of the parents. The exception is a child whose parents are not citizens, and whose father is a diplomatic representative.

- **BY DESCENT**: Child born abroad on or after September 15, 1986, at least one of whose parents is a citizen of Tuvalu.

- **MARRIAGE**: Foreign national, who marries a citizen of Tuvalu, may register for citizenship.

- **BY NATURALIZATION**: *No information was provided.*

DUAL CITIZENSHIP: RECOGNIZED.

LOSS OF CITIZENSHIP:

- **VOLUNTARY**: Voluntary renunciation of Tuvaluan citizenship is permitted by law. Tuvalu does not have diplomatic representation in the United States; renunciation will have to be initiated elsewhere.

- **INVOLUNTARY**: *No information was provided.*

ANY QUESTIONS concerning Tuvalu Citizenship Law should be directed to the address below:

Library of Congress
Law Library, Directorate of Legal Research
Western Law Division
James Madison Memorial Building, Rm. LM-240
Washington, DC 20540-3230

Telephone: 202-707-7850
Fax: 202-707-1820

www.emulateme.com/tuvalu.htm

UGANDA

CITIZENSHIP: Citizenship is based upon the Constitution of Uganda. Every person who was a citizen of Uganda on or before October 9, 1962, the date of independence, is considered a citizen of Uganda. (UKC-Commonwealth Nation)

- **BY BIRTH**: Birth within the territory of Uganda does not automatically confer citizenship. Questions concerning those born before October 9, 1962, should be directed to the Embassy.

- **BY DESCENT**:
  - Person born in Uganda after October 9, 1962, at least one of whose parents or grandparents is a citizen of Uganda.
  - Person born abroad after October 9, 1962, whose father was a citizen of Uganda.

- **REGISTRATION**: A foreign woman who marries a citizen of Uganda is eligible to register for Ugandan citizenship. This includes women who were married to Ugandans before the date of independence, even if their husband died before that date.

- **BY NATURALIZATION**: *No information was provided.*

DUAL CITIZENSHIP: NOT RECOGNIZED.
Exception: Child born abroad of Ugandan parents, who obtains the citizenship of the country of birth, is allowed to maintain dual citizenship until age 18.

Ugandan law maintains that one citizenship should be chosen at age 18, but this is a rarely enforced law. Unless an individual brings their dual citizenship to the attention of the government, both nationalities may be maintained by default.

LOSS OF CITIZENSHIP:

- **VOLUNTARY**: Voluntary renunciation of Ugandan citizenship is permitted by law. Contact the Embassy for details and required paperwork.

- **INVOLUNTARY**: The following is grounds for involuntary loss of Ugandan citizenship: Person voluntarily acquires foreign citizenship. Unless the government is informed, the citizenship will not be revoked.

ANY QUESTIONS concerning citizenship, or requests for renunciation of citizenship, should be directed to the address below:

Embassy of the Republic of Uganda
Consular Department
5909 16th St., NW
Washington, DC 20011

Embassy Telephone: 202-726-7100/02
Consular Telephone: 202-726-0416
Fax: 202-726-1727

www. nic.ug

UKRAINE

CITIZENSHIP: Citizenship for Ukraine is based upon the 1991 Statute on Citizenship. All those who resided in Ukraine until the approval of this statute retain their citizenship.

- **BY BIRTH**: Birth within the territory of Ukraine does not automatically confer citizenship.

- **BY DESCENT**:
  - Child born within the territory of Ukraine with at least one parent a citizen of Ukraine.
  - Child born abroad, having permanent residence in Ukraine, with at least one parent a citizen of Ukraine.

- **REGISTRATION**: Citizenship may be granted by registration for the following persons:
  - Children adopted by citizens of Ukraine.
  - Persons who have no other citizenship and at least one parent or grandparent Ukrainian by birth.
  - Foreign persons and persons without citizenship, under certain conditions (*unspecified*) listed in the Statute on Citizenship.

- **BY NATURALIZATION**: Ukrainian citizenship may be acquired upon fulfillment of the following conditions: Person does not possess any foreign citizenship, has resided in Ukraine for at least five years, is able to function in the Ukrainian language, and is knowledgeable of the Ukrainian Constitution.

DUAL CITIZENSHIP: NOT RECOGNIZED.

LOSS OF CITIZENSHIP:

- **VOLUNTARY**: Voluntary renunciation of Ukrainian citizenship is permitted by law. Contact the Ukrainian Embassy for details and proper paperwork.

- **INVOLUNTARY**: The following are grounds for involuntary loss of Ukrainian citizenship: Person voluntarily acquires a foreign citizenship. Person enrolls for military service, security service, law enforcement activities, judicial bodies, or other bodies of state power of a foreign state.

ANY QUESTIONS concerning citizenship, or requests for renunciation of citizenship, should be directed to the address below:

Embassy of Ukraine
Consular Office
3350 M St., NW
Washington, DC 20007

Consular Telephone: 202-333-7507
Fax: 202-333-7510
www.rada.kiev.ua

UNITED ARAB EMIRATES

CITIZENSHIP: Citizenship laws are based upon Nationality Law #17, dated January 1, 1972, and amended by Law #10, dated 1975. On December 2, 1971, all persons who were legal citizens of the separate Emirates obtained United Arab Emirate's citizenship upon the unionization of the country.

- **BY BIRTH**: Birth within the territory of the United Arab Emirates does not automatically confer citizenship. The exception is a child born of unknown parents.

- **BY DESCENT**: Applies to persons born on or after January 1, 1972.
    - Child of a United Arab Emirates father, regardless of the child's country of birth. Child born out of wedlock will obtain citizenship upon being legally recognized by the father.
    - Child of a United Arab Emirates mother and an unknown father, regardless of the child's country of birth.

- **MARRIAGE**:
    - A foreign woman who marries a United Arab Emirates citizen may obtain citizenship, provided the woman resides three years in the country after application for citizenship, has given up previous citizenship, and has obtained approval of the Ministry of the Interior.
    - A foreign husband is not eligible for citizenship.

- **BY NATURALIZATION**: Citizenship may be acquired by various groups of persons under the following conditions:
    - Citizens of Qatar, Oman, and Bahrain must reside for three years.
    - Citizens of Arab descent must reside for seven years.
    - All other persons must reside in the country for at least 30 years, 20 of those years occurring after January 1, 1972.

DUAL CITIZENSHIP: NOT RECOGNIZED.

LOSS OF CITIZENSHIP:

- **VOLUNTARY**: Voluntary renunciation of United Arab Emirates citizenship is permitted by law. Contact the Embassy for details and required paperwork.

- **INVOLUNTARY**: The following are grounds for involuntary loss of United Arab Emirates citizenship:
    - Person obtains new citizenship
    - Person joins foreign armed forces without government permission.
    - Naturalized citizen…
        - Citizenship was obtained through fraud.
        - Commits crime in the country.
        - Lives over four years outside the country.
        - Acts against the security of the country.

ANY QUESTIONS concerning citizenship should be directed to the address below:

Embassy of the United Arab Emirates
Consular Section
1255 22 Street NW, Room 700
Washington, DC 20037

www.uae.org.ae
www.emirates.org

Telephone: 202-955-7999
Embassy Fax: 202-337-7029 -- Consular Fax: 202-333-3246

UNITED KINGDOM

UNITED KINGDOM OF GREAT BRITAIN AND NORTHERN IRELAND; (ENGLAND, WALES, SCOTLAND, AND NORTHERN IRELAND)

["*British*" refers to "*of the United Kingdom*"]

CITIZENSHIP: Nationality is regulated by the British Nationality Act of 1984.

Due to Great Britain's historic relationship with its former colonies and the British Commonwealth, certain groups of peoples fall into special categories. Citizenship requirements and special considerations for these groups are frequently different than for those considered to be foreign nationals and, to a degree, are different from category to category. Persons included in these special categories are:

- British Dependent Territories Citizens
- British Overseas Citizens
- British Subjects
- British Protected Persons
- Commonwealth Citizens
- Citizens of the Republic of Ireland.

After January 1, 1983, the following qualify for British citizenship:

- **BY BIRTH**:
  - Child born in the United Kingdom, at least one of whose parents is a British citizen or has settled in the United Kingdom.
  - Child born in the United Kingdom whose parents are unknown.

- **BY DESCENT**:
  - Child born overseas to a British citizen if at least one of his parents is a British citizen other than by descent.
  - Child born overseas to a British citizen in service to the Crown.
  - Child born outside of the United Kingdom with certain family connections (*unspecified*) to the United Kingdom.

- **OTHER**:
  - Child adopted by Order of the Court of the United Kingdom.
  - Person registered by the Secretary of State as a British citizen. (Often used for children born abroad to British citizens.)

- **SPECIAL CATEGORIES**: Persons falling into these categories may be registered as British citizens if they have lived in the United Kingdom lawfully for five years; the twelve months preceding the application must be of continuous residence.
  - British Overseas Citizen
  - British Subject
  - British Protected Person
  - British Dependent Territory Citizen

UNITED KINGDOM (cont.)

- **BY NATURALIZATION**: British citizenship may be granted upon fulfillment of the following conditions:
  - Person has been a resident of the United Kingdom for five years.
  - Persons married to British citizens are required to reside in the United Kingdom for the three years preceding application, with certain restrictions on periods spent outside the United Kingdom.
  - Person is of good character and has sufficient knowledge of English, Welsh, or Scottish Gaelic.
  - Person intends on remaining in the United Kingdom or entering Crown service.

DUAL CITIZENSHIP: RECOGNIZED.

LOSS OF CITIZENSHIP: Unless it is required for other reasons, British citizens need not renounce their citizenship upon obtaining a foreign citizenship. Those who have voluntarily renounced British citizenship are entitled to reacquire it once. Otherwise, the resumption of British citizenship is at the discretion of the Secretary of State.

- **VOLUNTARY**: A completed application for renunciation, together with documentary evidence of citizenship, plus fee, should be submitted to the British Embassy. Application will be sent to England to be processed for approval. In approximately two months the person will receive the processed application as acceptance of the renunciation.

- **INVOLUNTARY**: *No information was provided.*

ANY QUESTIONS concerning citizenship, or requests for renunciation of citizenship, should be directed to the address below:

Embassy of the United Kingdom
Consular Section
3100 Massachusetts Avenue
Washington, DC 20008

Embassy Telephone: 202-587-6500
Consular Telephone: 202-588-7800**
Fax: 202-588-7850

**The Consular number reaches a voice mail answering system. Choose the number that corresponds with the "Citizen/Naturalization" category. Due to a heavy workload, the Consulate prefers that all questions be mailed or faxed.

British Nationality Law Information: **www.britian-info.org/bis/consular/bnatlaw.stm**

COMMONWEALTH OF NATIONS: The Commonwealth is a free association of sovereign, independent states, numbering 53 at the end of 1999. Most of the membership consists of former colonies and territories of the United Kingdom. There is no charter, treaty, or constitution; the Commonwealth association is expressed in cooperation, consultation, and mutual assistance for which the Commonwealth Secretariat is the central coordinating body.

ASSOCIATED STATES:
Antigua and Barbuda, Australia, Bahamas, Bangladesh, Barbados, Belize, Botswana, Brunei, Canada, Cameroon, Cyprus, Dominica, The Gambia, Ghana, Grenada, Guyana, India, Jamaica, Kenya, Kiribati, Lesotho, Malawi, Malaysia, Maldives, Malta, Mauritius, Mozambique, Namibia, Nauru, New Zealand, Pakistan, Papua New Guinea, Seychelles, Sierra Leone, Singapore, Solomon Islands, Sri Lanka, St. Kitts and Nevis, St. Lucia, St. Vincent and The Grenadines, Swaziland, Tanzania, Tonga, Trinidad and Tobago, Tuvalu, Uganda, United Kingdom, Vanuatu, Samoa, Zambia, Zimbabwe.

URUGUAY

CITIZENSHIP: Citizenship laws are based upon the Constitution of the Oriental Republic of Uruguay.

- **BY BIRTH**: Child born within the Republic of Uruguay, regardless of the nationality of the parents. Uruguayan law refers to this as "natural" citizenship.

- **BY DESCENT**: Child born abroad, one of whose parents is a citizen of Uruguay, provided the child is registered in the Civic Register for Vital Records. This is also considered natural citizenship.

- **BY NATURALIZATION**: Uruguayan citizenship may be applied for by persons who are at least 18 years old and fall into one of the categories listed below. Persons gaining citizenship through naturalization are considered "legal" citizens.
  - Person whose family has been settled in Uruguay for at least three years, and who practices any art, science, or industry in Uruguay.
  - Person who does not have family in Uruguay, but who has lived in the country for at least five years and practices any art, science, or industry in Uruguay.

DUAL CITIZENSHIP: RECOGNIZED. (Only for natural citizens; legal citizens are not allowed to obtain a second citizenship.)

LOSS OF CITIZENSHIP:

- **VOLUNTARY**: Permitted under Uruguayan law, but not required. Contact nearest Uruguayan Embassy or Consulate for necessary requirements.

- **INVOLUNTARY**: The following are grounds for involuntary loss of legal Uruguayan citizenship:
  - Legal citizen voluntarily obtains another citizenship.
  - Person is being prosecuted for certain criminal acts which could result in imprisonment, or receives a judicial verdict that imposes penalty of exile, prison, or loss of political rights.
  - Person participates in social or political organization activities that promote violence against the Republic of Uruguay.
  - Person fails to comply with the good behavior requirements for naturalized citizens.

ANY QUESTIONS concerning citizenship, or requests for renunciation of citizenship, should be directed to the address below:

Consulate of Uruguay
2715 M Street, 3rd Floor
Washington, DC 20007

Embassy Telephone: 202-331-1313/14/15/16
Consular Telephone: 202-331-4219
Fax: 202-331-8142

consuluy@erols.com
www.embassy.org/uruguary

UZBEKISTAN

CITIZENSHIP: Laws are based upon the Citizenship Law of the Republic of Uzbekistan. Citizens of the Kara-Kalpak Republic are also citizens of Uzbekistan.

- **BY BIRTH**: Birth within the Republic of Uzbekistan does not automatically confer citizenship. The only exceptions are abandoned children.

- **BY DESCENT**:
  - Child, both of whose parents are citizens of Uzbekistan, is considered a citizen of Uzbekistan regardless of the child's country of birth.
  - Child, one of whose parents is a citizen of Uzbekistan, and the other parent is stateless, is considered a citizen of Uzbekistan regardless of the child's country of birth.
  - Child, one of whose parents is a citizen of Uzbekistan, is granted citizenship based on the following situations:
    - Child born in Uzbekistan is a citizen.
    - Child born outside of Uzbekistan, at least one of whose parents has residency in the country, is a citizen.
    - Child, born outside of Uzbekistan and neither parent lives in the country, is granted citizenship upon the written request and consent of the parents.

- **BY NATURALIZATION**: Uzbek citizenship may be acquired upon fulfillment of the following conditions: Person has renounced former citizenship, has resided in Uzbekistan for at least five years, and has gainful employment.

DUAL CITIZENSHIP: NOT RECOGNIZED.

LOSS OF CITIZENSHIP: Permitted unless the person has unfulfilled obligations or debts to the state, or is under criminal sentencing.

- **VOLUNTARY**: *No information was provided.*

- **INVOLUNTARY**: The following are grounds for involuntary loss of Uzbek citizenship:
  - Person voluntarily acquires foreign citizenship.
  - Person gains employment with an institution of a foreign power.
  - Person, permanently residing abroad, has not registered with the consulate for five years.
  - Person acquired Uzbek citizenship under false pretenses.

ANY QUESTIONS concerning citizenship, or requests for renunciation of citizenship, should be directed to the address below:

Embassy of the Republic of Uzbekistan
Consular Section
1746 Massachusetts Avenue, NW
Washington, DC 20036

Embassy Telephone: 202-887-5300
Fax: 202-293-6804

emb@uzbekistan.org
www.gov.uz

VANUATU

CITIZENSHIP: Citizenship is based upon Section 10 of the Constitution, dated July 30, 1983. (UKC-Commonwealth Nation)

- **BY BIRTH**: Child born in Vanuatu, of two foreign nationals living in Vanuatu, may apply for Vanuatuan citizenship upon reaching the age of 18.

- **BY DESCENT**:
  - Child, both of whose parents are citizens of Vanuatu, regardless of the child's country of birth.
  - Child of a Vanuatuan father and a foreign mother, regardless of the child's country of birth
  - Child of a Vanuatuan mother and a foreign father obtains the citizenship of the father. However, the child can apply for Vanuatuan citizenship upon reaching age 18.

- **MARRIAGE**:
  - A foreign woman who marries a citizen of Vanuatu may automatically apply for citizenship
  - A foreign man who marries a citizen of Vanuatu may apply for citizenship after 10 years residency.

- **BY NATURALIZATION**: Vanuatuan citizenship may be acquired upon fulfillment of the following condition: Person has legally resided in the country for at least 10 years.

DUAL CITIZENSHIP: NOT RECOGNIZED.
Exception: Vanuatuan child born abroad, who obtains the citizenship of the country of birth, is allowed to retain dual citizenship until the age of 18. Then the person must renounce the foreign citizenship or Vanuatuan citizenship will be revoked.

LOSS OF CITIZENSHIP:

- **VOLUNTARY**: Voluntary renunciation of Vanuatuan citizenship is permitted by law. The renunciation must be done in Vanuatu. Contact the Mission for details and required paperwork.

- **INVOLUNTARY**: The following is grounds for involuntary loss of Vanuatuan citizenship: Person voluntarily acquires a foreign citizenship.

ANY QUESTIONS concerning citizenship, or requests for renunciation of citizenship, should be directed to the address below:

Permanent Mission to the UN - Vanuatu
416 Convent Ave.
New York, NY 10031

Mission Telephone: 212-926-3311
Fax: 212-926-4131

VENEZUELA

CITIZENSHIP: Citizenship Laws are based upon the Constitution of Venezuela.

- **BY BIRTH**: Child born within the territory of the Republic of Venezuela regardless of the nationality of the parents.

- **BY DESCENT**: Child born abroad, one of whose parents is a citizen of Venezuela, is granted citizenship under the following conditions:
    - Before child reaches the age of 18, the parents must establish residence in Venezuela.
    - Before reaching the age of 25, the person must declare an intention to accept Venezuelan nationality.

- **BY NATURALIZATION**: Venezuelan citizenship may be acquired upon fulfillment of the following condition: Person has lived continuously in the country for at least five years. Citizens of Spain and Latin America need less (*unspecified*) than five years.

- The following are Venezuelans by naturalization whenever they declare their intentions:
    - A foreign woman who marries a Venezuelan national.
    - A foreign minor child (natural or adopted) of a recently naturalized Venezuelan, provided the child resides in the country and makes a declaration of intent before reaching the age of 25.

DUAL CITIZENSHIP: NOT RECOGNIZED.
Exception: Dual citizenship is recognized until the age of 25, at which time Venezuelan citizenship ceases if the foreign nationality is maintained.

LOSS OF CITIZENSHIP: Venezuelan woman who marries a foreigner retains her nationality unless she declares her intention to the contrary or, according to the laws of her husband's country, acquires his nationality.

Venezuelan nationality by birth is recovered whenever the person who lost it returns to live in Venezuela and declares an intention to recover citizenship. Citizenship may also be recovered by residing in Venezuela for a period of not less than two years.

- **VOLUNTARY**: Letter of renunciation and passport should be sent to the nearest Venezuelan Embassy.

- **INVOLUNTARY**: The following is grounds for involuntary loss of Venezuelan citizenship: Person voluntarily obtains new citizenship.

ANY QUESTIONS concerning citizenship, or requests for renunciation of citizenship, should be directed to the address below:

Embassy of the Republic of Venezuela
Consular Section
1099 30th ST., NW
Washington, DC 20007

Embassy/Consular Telephone: 202-342-2214
Fax: 202-342-6820
www.embassy.org/embassies/ve.html

VIETNAM

CITIZENSHIP: Based upon the Law of Vietnamese Nationality, which was last revised on July 15, 1988. New citizenship laws were passed in 1999 but have not yet been implemented.

The U.S. State Department, which provided English translation of Vietnamese Law, is the best available source of information. Information from Vietnamese government sources was not readily available or provided.

- When the nationality of parents changes, all of their children 18 and under are automatically included in any change.
- The adoption or loss of Vietnamese nationality by one of the spouses does not change the nationality of the other.

- **BY BIRTH**: Birth within the Republic of Vietnam does not automatically confer citizenship. **Exceptions**: A child born in Vietnam to parents who are stateless and have permanent residence in Vietnam; a child found abandoned within the territory of Vietnam.

- **BY DESCENT**:
    - Child, both of whose parents are citizens of Vietnam, regardless of the child's country of birth.
    - Child, one of whose parents is a citizen of Vietnam and the other is stateless, regardless of the child's country of birth.
    - Child, one of whose parents is a citizen of Vietnam and the other is a foreign national, if the child was born in Vietnam or the parents had permanent residence in Vietnam at the time of birth.

- **BY NATURALIZATION**: Vietnamese citizenship may be obtained upon fulfillment of the following conditions: Person is at least 18 years of age, knows the Vietnamese language, and has lived in Vietnam at least five years.

DUAL CITIZENSHIP: NOT RECOGNIZED.

LOSS OF CITIZENSHIP: Renunciation of Vietnamese citizenship is not allowed if it affects the national security.

- **VOLUNTARY**: Voluntary renunciation for legitimate reasons is permitted under Vietnamese law. Renunciations must be made in the country. *Procedures for voluntary renunciation were not provided.* Persons falling into certain categories are not permitted to renounce citizenship. Those people are:
    - Persons in the service of the military.
    - Persons with unpaid taxes or other unpaid obligations.
    - Persons under prosecution or serving a sentence.

- **INVOLUNTARY**: The following is grounds for involuntary loss of Vietnamese citizenship: Persons living abroad who are involved in acts seriously damaging the interests of Vietnam. *Other data were not provided.*

ANY QUESTIONS concerning citizenship should be directed to the address below:

Embassy of Vietnam
1233 20th Street, NW, Suite 400
Washington DC 20036

Telephone: 202-861-2293
Fax: 202-861-0917
vietnamembassy@msn.com
www.batin.com.vn

WESTERN SAHARA

The Western Sahara, formerly Spanish Sahara, bounded by Morocco, Algeria, Mauritania, and the Atlantic Ocean, is disputed territory. The inhabitants of this area travel under a variety of national documents, but the territory itself is neither an internationally recognized state nor a recognized part of another nation.

After Spain withdrew its protectorate, Morocco and Mauritania annexed portions of the territory, but guerrilla forces proclaimed the region independent. Mauritania has signed a peace treaty with the guerrillas, Morocco controls the main urban areas, and the guerrilla forces move freely in the sparsely populated deserts. A UN-sponsored self-determination vote has been repeatedly delayed.

Any questions on the citizenship status of people claiming citizenship of this territory should be directed to the following address:

CA/OCS/CCS/NEA
U.S. Department of State
West Africa Bureau, Room 3250
Washington, DC 20520

Telephone: 202-647-3407
Fax: 202-647-4855

YEMEN

CITIZENSHIP: Citizenship is based upon Citizenship Law #2, dated 1975. The formerly divided nations of North Yemen and South Yemen were officially united on May 22, 1990.

- **BY BIRTH**: Birth within the territory of Yemen does not automatically confer citizenship. The exception is a child born to unknown parents.

- **BY DESCENT**:
  - Child born of an Yemeni father regardless of the child's country of birth.
  - Child born in Yemen of an Yemeni mother and an unknown father. However, if the child is born abroad, special permission must be obtained for the child to be declared a citizen.

- **MARRIAGE**: A foreign woman who marries a citizen of Yemen may obtain Yemeni citizenship after having resided in the country for two years, having formally requested citizenship, and having renounced previous citizenship.

- **BY NATURALIZATION**: Yemeni citizenship may be acquired upon fulfillment of the following conditions:
  - Moslems with special skills needed by the country must reside in Yemen for at least 10 years, have a viable means of support, be healthy, have behaved properly, and know the language.
  - Foreigners who have special talents needed by the country must fulfill the same requirements, but reside in Yemen for 5 years.

DUAL CITIZENSHIP: NOT RECOGNIZED.

LOSS OF CITIZENSHIP:

- **VOLUNTARY**: Voluntary renunciation of Yemeni citizenship is permitted by law. Contact the Yemeni Embassy for details and required paperwork.

- **INVOLUNTARY**: The following are grounds for involuntary loss of Yemeni citizenship:
  - Person has acquired new citizenship.
  - Naturalized citizen has committed a criminal act.
  - Naturalized citizen has lived overseas for more than two years without government permission.

ANY QUESTIONS concerning citizenship, or requests for renunciation of citizenship, should be directed to the address below:

Embassy of the Republic of Yemen
Consular Section
2600 Virginia Ave., NW STE 705
Washington, DC 20037

Embassy/Consular Telephone: 202-965-4760/61
Fax: 202-337-2017

www.nusacc.org/yeman

YUGOSLAVIA, FORMER YUGOSLAV REPUBLICS

CITIZENSHIP: The Federal Republic of Yugoslavia was proclaimed on April 17, 1992 as the union of the republics of Serbia and Montenegro. *Yugoslavia has been suspended from the United Nations and does not have a diplomatic mission in the United States. No information was provided.*

ANY QUESTIONS concerning citizenship, or requests for renunciation of citizenship, should be directed to the address below:

U.S. Department of State
2201 C St., NW
Washington, DC 20520-4818

Consular Telephone: 202-647-3445
Desk Officer: 202-647-7480

ZAMBIA

CITIZENSHIP: Citizenship law is set by the Constitution. (UKC-Commonwealth Nation)

- **BY BIRTH**: Child born within the territory of Zambia shall be considered a citizen of Zambia. However, upon reaching the age of 21, the person must apply to the Citizenship Board for the confirmation of citizenship.

- **BY DESCENT**: Child, one parent being Zambian, regardless of the child's country of birth.

- **REGISTRATION**: The following may apply to the Citizenship Board to be registered as citizens of Zambia: Any person who has been residing in Zambia for a continuous period of not less than 10 years preceding application and who has attained the age of 21.

- **BY NATURALIZATION**: Parliament may grant citizenship to individuals who are not eligible to become citizens under registration guidelines.

DUAL CITIZENSHIP: NOT RECOGNIZED.
Exceptions:
- Child born abroad to Zambian parents, who obtains citizenship of country of birth. Dual citizenship is recognized until the age of 22. Upon reaching the age of maturity, the person must choose one nationality or lose Zambian citizenship.

- Child of foreign parents, who is born in Zambia, acquires parental and Zambian citizenships. This dual citizenship is recognized until age 21 when person must register with Citizenship Board if the person chooses to become a Zambian citizen. Upon confirmation of Zambian citizenship, person has three months to renounce the second citizenship (of parents). Dual citizenship will continue to be recognized until age 22.

- Zambian spouse, who acquires a foreign citizenship through marriage, is allowed dual nationality for 3 months. Within the 3-month period, they should have renounced their foreign citizenship, taken an oath of allegiance, and registered their intention concerning residence.

- Person seeking Zambian citizenship, who is not able to renounce their previous citizenship, need not make such a renunciation and can hold two nationalities. However, the person may be required to make a declaration concerning their previous citizenship and Zambian loyalty.

LOSS OF CITIZENSHIP: Zambia's Constitution provides that no person shall be deprived of their citizenship if it would leave them stateless.

- **VOLUNTARY**: To voluntarily renounce citizenship, a letter should be sent to the consular office of the nearest Zambian embassy. The embassy will forward the renunciation to the Minister of Home Affairs where the renunciation will be registered and published in the Gazette. Once published, citizenship is lost.

- **INVOLUNTARY**: The following is grounds for involuntary loss of Zambian citizenship: Person voluntarily acquires foreign citizenship, other than through marriage.

ANY QUESTIONS concerning citizenship, or requests for renunciation of citizenship, should be directed to the address below:

Embassy of the Republic of Zambia
Consular Section
2419 Massachusetts Ave., NW
Washington, DC 20008

Telephone: 202-265-9717/9718/ 9719
Fax: 202-332-0826
zambia@tmn.com or **embzambia@aol.com**
www.zamnet.zm

ZIMBABWE

CITIZENSHIP: Citizenship laws are based upon the Constitution of Zimbabwe. (UKC-Commonwealth Nation)

- **BY BIRTH**: Birth within the Republic of Zimbabwe does not automatically confer citizenship.

- **BY DESCENT**:
  - Child whose father is a citizen of Zimbabwe, regardless of the child's country of birth.
  - Child, born out of wedlock, whose mother is a citizen of Zimbabwe, regardless of the child's country of birth.

- **REGISTRATION**:
  - Child adopted by citizens of Zimbabwe may be granted citizenship by registration.
  - Citizen children born abroad must be registered at an Embassy or consulate for their citizenship to be recognized.

- **MARRIAGE**: Person who marries a citizen of Zimbabwe must apply for Zimbabwean citizenship.

- **BY NATURALIZATION**: Generally, only three categories of people will be considered for naturalization and residence in Zimbabwe:
  - Persons possessing skills required but not available in the country.
  - Aged parents and close dependents or relatives of resident citizens.
  - Persons willing to invest capital in Zimbabwe.

- Zimbabwean citizenship may be acquired upon fulfillment of the following condition: Person must have dwelled in the country for at least five years before requesting naturalization.

DUAL CITIZENSHIP: NOT RECOGNIZED. Prohibited to anyone 18 years old and of sound mind

LOSS OF CITIZENSHIP:

- **VOLUNTARY**: Voluntary renunciation of citizenship may be initiated through the nearest Zimbabwean Embassy. Person should contact the Embassy for the proper paperwork.

- **INVOLUNTARY**: The following are grounds for involuntary loss of Zimbabwean citizenship:
  - Person voluntarily acquires foreign citizenship.
  - A citizen of Zimbabwe by registration loses citizenship if absent from Zimbabwe for a continuous period of seven years.

ANY QUESTIONS concerning citizenship should be directed to the address below:

Embassy of the Republic of Zimbabwe
Consular Section
1608 New Hampshire Ave., NW
Washington, DC 20009

Embassy/Consular Telephone: 202-332-7100
Fax: 202-483-9326
zimemb@erols.com

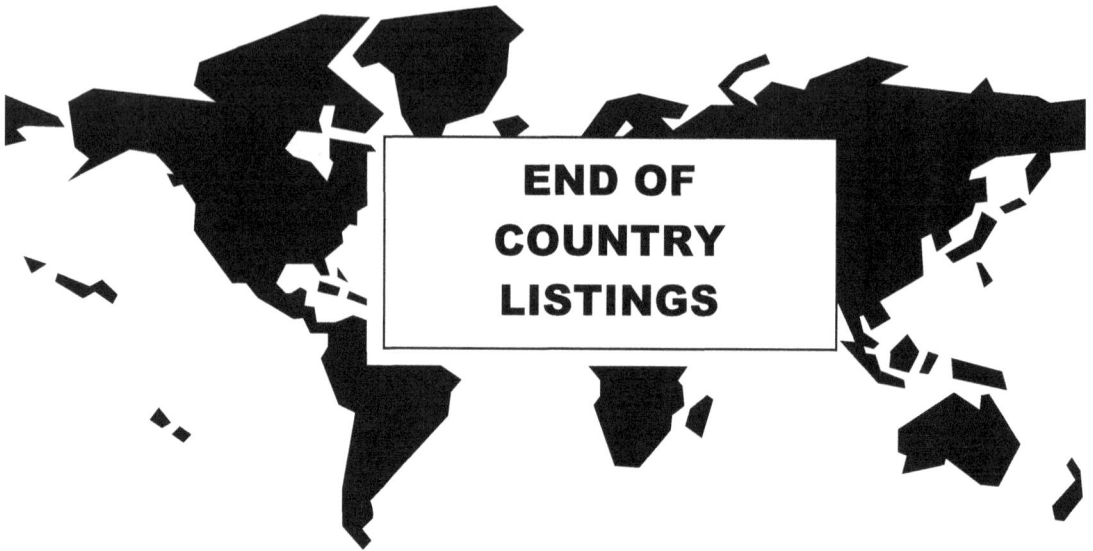

END OF
COUNTRY
LISTINGS

DEPARTMENT OF STATE
AND
LIBRARY OF CONGRESS

The U.S. Department of State does not serve as a repository of foreign law but may be able to address some issues. There are two units within the Department that have a familiarity with the laws and practices of other nations:

THE OFFICE OF CITIZEN CONSULAR SERVICES:

The Office of Citizen Consular Services in the Bureau of Consular Affairs is familiar with the citizenship laws and practices of more populous countries.

DESK OFFICERS:

The Desk Officers can be of help when questions concern a country's political, social, or cultural factors. They do not deal with other nations' citizenship laws.

The Library of Congress, International Law Division, maintains a staff of lawyers that provides research for the U.S. Congress and other government agencies about foreign legal systems - including citizenship laws. This staff represents a wide range of linguistic capabilities and has amassed a considerable archive of foreign laws and constitutions. This Division best addresses questions of legal concerns.

DEPARTMENT OF STATE CONSULAR AND DESK OFFICER REFERENCE TELEPHONE NUMBERS ARE PRESENTED BY GEOGRAPHIC REGION ON THE FOLLOWING PAGES.

AFRICAN REGION

ALL COUNTRIES BELOW: CONSULAR NUMBER: 202-647-3149

COUNTRY	DESK OFFICER NUMBER
ANGOLA	202-647-8434
BENIN	202-647-3066
BOTSWANA	202-647-9836
BURKINA FASO	202-647-2791
BURUNDI	202-647-3139
CAMEROON	202-647-1707
CAPE VERDE	202-647-1596
CENTRAL AFRICAN REPUBLIC	202-647-1707
CHAD	202-647-1707
COMOROS	202-647-6473
CONGO	202-647-3139
CONGO, DEMOCRATIC REPUBLIC	202-647-1707
COTE D'IVOIRE	202-647-1540
DJIBOUTI	202-647-5684
EQUATORIAL GUINEA	202-647-1707
ERITREA	202-647-6485
ETHIOPIA	202-647-9742
GABON	202-647-3139
GAMBIA, THE	202-647-3469
GHANA	202-647-1569
GUINEA	202-647-2865
GUINEA-BISSAU	202-647-1596
KENYA	202-647-6479
LESOTHO	202-647-8432
LIBERIA	202-647-4572
MADAGASCAR	202-647-6473
MALAWI	202-647-8434
MALI	202-647-2791
MAURITANIA	202-647-2865
MAURITIUS	202-647-6473
MOZAMBIQUE	202-647-8434
NAMIBIA	202-647-8434
NIGER	202-647-2791
NIGERIA	202-647-1597
RWANDA	202-647-3139
SAO TOME	202-647-3139
SENEGAL	202-647-2865
SEYCHELLES	202-647-6473
SIERRA LEONE	202-647-4567
SOUTH AFRICA	202-647-8432
SUDAN	202-647-4679
SWAZILAND	202-647-8434
TANZANIA	202-647-8852
TOGO	202-647-1540
UGANDA	202-647-6479
ZAMBIA	202-647-8432
ZIMBABWE	202-647-9836

CENTRAL and SOUTH AMERICAN REGIONS

ALL COUNTRIES BELOW: CONSULAR NUMBER: 202-647-3712

COUNTRY	DESK OFFICER NUMBER
ANTIGUA/BARBUDA	202-647-2621
ARGENTINA	202-647-2401
BAHAMAS	202-647-2621
BARBADOS	202-647-2130
BELIZE	202-647-3381
BOLIVIA	202-647-3076
BRAZIL	202-647-9407
CHILE	202-647-2401
COLOMBIA	202-647-3023
COSTA RICA	202-647-3518
CUBA	202-647-9272
DOMINICAN REPUBLIC	202-647-2620
ECUADOR	202-647-3338
EL SALVADOR	202-647-3681
GRENADA	202-647-2621
GUATEMALA	202-647-1145
GUYANA	202-647-2621
HAITI	202-736-4707
HONDURAS	202-647-0087
JAMAICA	202-647-2620
MEXICO	202-647-9894
NICARAGUA	202-647-1570
PANAMA	202-647-4986
PARAGUAY	202-647-2296
PERU	202-647-3360
ST. KITTS	202-647-2130
ST. LUCIA	202-647-2130
ST. VINCENT AND THE GRENADINES	202-647-2130
SURINAME	202-647-2620
TRINIDAD AND TOBAGO	202-647-2621
URUGUAY	202-647-2296
VENEZUELA	202-647-3023

We also recommend this related book:

Passport to Tax-Free International Living
by Adam Starchild
ISBN: 1893713113

If you are like most people, you undoubtedly feel that you have paid enough taxes during your career to last several lifetimes, and you certainly don't relish the idea of paying taxes once you are retired. You may not have to. There are places around the world offering outstanding lifestyles that you can enjoy during your retirement (or even semi-retirement) where you may considerably reduce the taxes you would expect to pay in your home country. In some places you may be able to eliminate income taxes entirely. The opportunities exist; they are even promoted by some jurisdictions.

These places may be thought of as *retirement havens*, which is the subject of this book. Simply put, a retirement haven is a country, jurisdiction, or city that offers special tax incentives for their residents. While such places may be attractive to various individuals, they are especially so for retirees who wish to maintain their assets in the safest and most efficient manner possible. Unquestionably, one of the most effective methods for maintaining assets during the retirement years is to reduce your tax burden.

The author does not endorse any retirement haven over another. Included in the book are places around the world that may prove suitable for individuals who are retired, or are about to retire, and who wish to significantly reduce their tax burden in a land that is pleasant, safe, and where they can enjoy a superior style of life. The golden years can truly be golden with proper planning and wise decision-making.

You may find that you wish not to move to another part of the world during your retirement, or that you don't wish to live in any particular place. Perhaps you wish to travel the world perpetually. There is a term for this — Perpetual Traveler. Indeed there are people who have retired and bought yachts that they use as an "ocean-going mobile home." They visit ports and magnificent cities throughout the world, remaining for the length of time the country allows (which may be several months), and then sailing to the next destination. By not being a "resident" of a country, you are not liable for taxes. The sophistication of personal computers and Internet data links can keep you in touch with the world and informed about your investments.

No two retirement havens are alike. Each has unique characteristics that individuals must evaluate according to their own likes, dislikes, and expectations. What this book does is summarize the MANY countries that offer a significant escape from taxes.

Retirement need not be a mundane affair in which you watch your hard-earned savings and investments dwindle away due to a high cost of living and burdensome taxes. With the proper planning it can be a time of new opportunities and enjoyment, as well as a time in which you keep more of your assets by reducing your cost of living and taxes.

Over the past 25 years, Adam Starchild has been the author of over two dozen books, and hundreds of magazine articles, primarily on business and finance. His articles have appeared in a wide range of publications around the world — including Business Credit, Euromoney, Finance, The Financial Planner, International Living, Offshore Financial Review, Reason, Tax Planning International, The Bull & Bear, Trust & Estates, and many more. Now semi-retired, he has lived in a number of countries. His personal website is at http://www.adamstarchild.com/

www.ingramcontent.com/pod-product-compliance
Lightning Source LLC
Chambersburg PA
CBHW051211200326

41519CB00025B/7070